THE Lost CITY

Also by Alan Ehrenhalt

The United States of Ambition:
Politicians, Power, and the Pursuit of Office

THE *Lost* CITY

DISCOVERING THE FORGOTTEN VIRTUES OF COMMUNITY IN THE CHICAGO OF THE 1950s

Alan Ehrenhalt

BasicBooks
A Division of HarperCollins*Publishers*

Designed by Elliott Beard

Library of Congress Cataloging-in-Publication Data
Ehrenhalt, Alan, 1947–
    The lost city: discovering the forgotten virtues of community in the
Chicago of the 1950s / Alan Ehrenhalt.
        p.   cm.
    Includes bibliographical references and index.
    ISBN 0–465–04192–2
    1. Chicago (Ill.)—Social life and customs. 2. Chicago (Ill.)—Social
conditions. 3. City and town life—Illinois—Chicago—History—20th
century. I. Title.
F548.52.E37 1995
977.3'11043—dc20   95–14160
                                                    CIP

95 96 97 98 ♦/RRD 9 8 7 6 5 4 3 2 1

**To the memory
of
William Ehrenhalt**

Born, Chicago, Illinois, January 14, 1898

Died, Chicago, Illinois, March 12, 1986

Flourished 1950–1960

CONTENTS

THE Lost CITY

Most of us in America believe a few simple propositions that seem so clear and self-evident they scarcely need to be said.

Choice is a good thing in life, and the more of it we have, the happier we are. Authority is inherently suspect; nobody should have the right to tell others what to think or how to behave. Sin isn't personal, it's social; individual human beings are creatures of the society they live in.

Those ideas could stand as the manifesto of an entire generation in America, the generation born in the baby-boom years and now in its thirties and forties. They are powerful ideas. They all have the ring of truth. But in the past quarter-century, taken to excess, they have caused a great deal of trouble.

The worship of choice has brought us a world of restless dissatisfaction, in which nothing we choose seems good enough to be permanent and we are unable to resist the endless pursuit of new selections—in work, in marriage, in front of the television set. The suspicion of authority has meant the erosion of standards of conduct and civility, visible most clearly in schools where teachers who dare to discipline pupils risk a profane response. The repudiation of sin has given us a collection of wrongdoers who insist that they are not responsible for their actions because they have been dealt bad cards in life. When we declare that there are no sinners, we are a step away from deciding that there is no such thing as right and wrong.

We have grown fond of saying that there is no free lunch, but we forget that it applies in moral as well as economic terms. Stable relationships, civil classrooms, safe streets—the ingredients of what we call community—all come at a price. The price is limits on the choices we can make as individuals, rules and authorities who can enforce them, and a willingness to accept the fact that there are bad people in the world and that sin exists in even the best of us. The price is not low, but the life it makes possible is no small achievement.

A generation ago in America, we understood the implicit bargain, and most of us were willing to pay the price. What was it really like to live under the terms of that bargain? Would we ever want to do that again?

Let us see if we can find out.

PART I

A DIFFERENT WORLD

CHAPTER I

The Limited Life

n 1975, after a long but singularly uneventful career in Illinois politics, a round-faced Chicago tavern owner named John G. Fary was rewarded with a promotion to Congress. On the night of his election, at age sixty-four, he announced his agenda for everyone to hear. "I will go to Washington to help represent Mayor Daley," he declared. "For twenty-one years, I represented the mayor in the legislature, and he was always right."

Richard J. Daley died the next year, but Fary soon discovered the same qualities of infallibility in Tip O'Neill, the U.S. House Speaker under whom he served. Over four congressional terms, he never cast a single vote against the Speaker's position on any issue of significance. From the leadership's point of view, he was an automatic yes.

And that, in a sense, was his undoing. Faced with a difficult primary challenge from an aggressive Chicago alderman, Fary had little to talk about other than his legendary willingness to do whatever he was told. The Chicago newspapers made sport of him. "Fary's lackluster record," one of them said, "forfeits his claim to a House seat." He was beaten badly and sent home to his tavern on the Southwest Side to ponder the troubling changes in modern political life.

It was not an easy thing for him to understand. The one principle John Fary had represented for more than thirty years in politics—obedience—had come into obvious disrepute. The legislator who simply followed the rules as they came down to him invited open ridicule as a mindless hack.

No quality is less attractive in American politics these days than obedience—not foolishness or deceit or even blatant corruption. There is no one we are more scornful of than the officeholder who refuses to make choices for himself. There are bumper stickers all over Washington that say, in big block capital letters, QUESTION AUTHORITY. There are none that say, LISTEN TO THE BOSS.

John Fary made a career out of listening to the boss. Of course, he didn't have much alternative. In the Chicago politics of the

1950s, you could either be part of the machine, and entertain a realistic hope of holding office, or be against it, and have virtually no hope at all. Fary actually began as something of an upstart. In 1951, he ran in the Twelfth Ward as a challenger to the Swinarski family, which more or less dominated ward politics in alliance with other machine lieutenants. After that unsuccessful experience, however, Fary made his accommodations to the system; he had no other choice.

If Fary ever chafed at the rules of his constricted political world, he never did so in public. He seemed content voting with the leadership, gratified to be part of an ordered political system, content working behind the bar at his tavern when he was not practicing politics in Springfield or Washington. He didn't appear to give much thought to the possibilities of doing it any other way. When he achieved passage of the one notable legislative initiative of his long career, a state law legalizing bingo, he celebrated by inventing a new drink called "Bingo Bourbon" and serving it to his customers on the house.

In the years when John Fary was building a political career out of loyalty on the South Side of Chicago, Ernie Banks was making his baseball career on the North Side. From the day he joined the Chicago Cubs in the fall of 1953, Banks was special: skinny and not very powerful-looking, he swung with his wrists and propelled line drives out of Wrigley Field with a speed that sometimes seemed hard to believe.

The 1950s were a time of glory for Ernie Banks—forty home runs year after year, two Most Valuable Player awards in a row, gushing praise on the sports page—and yet in other ways, his rewards were meager. He played on a string of terrible Cubs teams, so he never came close to appearing in a World Series, and because the fans didn't buy many tickets, the Cubs weren't very generous about salaries. Compared to mediocre ballplayers today, Banks was woefully underpaid, even in the real-dollar terms of his time. In 1959, the year he recorded his second straight MVP season, the Cubs paid him $45,000.

But Banks never considered leaving the Cubs and going to another team. He couldn't, because he was not a free agent. The Cubs owned him, and according to the baseball rules of the 1950s, his only options were to accept the contract they offered him or leave baseball altogether. Like John Fary, he really didn't have any choice.

If Banks spent any time worrying about his limited choices, it didn't show. The Cubs were his team; they had lifted him out of the weedy fields of the Negro leagues, and he belonged with them. After a few years in Chicago, he became famous not only for his home runs but for his loyalty and enthusiasm. He loved to tell reporters about the "friendly confines" of Wrigley Field. Warming up before a doubleheader on a bright summer day, he would say two games weren't enough. "Let's play three!" Banks would exult.

What John Fary was to the present-day politician, Ernie Banks was to the present-day ballplayer. You can compare him, for example, to Rickey Henderson, who in the last fifteen years has stolen more bases than anyone in the history of the game. Henderson will be in the Hall of Fame some day, as Ernie Banks already is. Unlike Banks, however, he has been paid fabulous salaries, and the free agency system has allowed him to jump from team to team in search of money and World Series appearances. And yet he has never seemed content with his situation. Everywhere he has played, he has expressed his frustrations at his contract, at the team management, at the fans, and even, sometimes, at his own play. The market has made Rickey Henderson free, and it has made him rich. It just has not made him happy.

The differences between Ernie Banks and Rickey Henderson are, of course, partly a matter of temperament. Some people are content by nature, and some are restless. In another sense, though, they are a metaphor for the changes in American life over the past forty years. Today we live in a time of profuse choice, with all the opportunity and disillusionment that it brings. Ernie Banks and John Fary lived in a world where choice was much more limited— where those in authority made decisions that the free market now throws open to endless individual reexamination.

This observation applies not only to baseball and politics but to all of the important personal relationships in life. In an average year in the 1950s, the number of divorces in the United States was about ten per one thousand marriages—barely a third of what it was to become by 1980. This was not because divorce was impossible to obtain—although it was difficult in a few states—or because it made anyone an outcast in the community. It was because divorce was simply not on the menu of options for most people, no matter how difficult or stressful life might become. The couples of the 1950s got married on the assumption that it was their job to make things work the best way they could. Like Ernie Banks and John Fary, they played the hand they were dealt, and refrained from agonizing over what might have been.

People just stayed married in the 1950s, to their spouses, to their political machines, to their baseball teams. Corporations also stayed married—to the communities they grew up with. Any one of a thousand examples could illustrate that point, but one will do: the story of the Lennox Corporation and its hometown, Marshalltown, Iowa.

In 1895, David Lennox invented a new kind of steel furnace and set up a business in Marshalltown. As the years went by, his company prospered as a manufacturer of boilers and, later, air conditioners. The Lennox Coporation became a solid source of respectable factory jobs that enabled generations of blue-collar families to enjoy the comforts of middle-class life. Its managers helped with countless local fairs, fund drives, and school building campaigns.

Lennox probably could have improved its profit margins in the 1950s by moving to a place where labor was cheaper, but its loyalty was to Marshalltown. Eventually, though, company officials did

investigate other locations. In the late 1970s Lennox moved its corporate headquarters to Dallas, arguing that a small town in central
Iowa was inconvenient for the air travel needs of its executives. The
factory stayed where it was.

In 1993, Lennox grew even more restless and announced that it
might have to close the Marshalltown plant altogether, not because
the company was losing money, or facing any sort of crisis, but just
because the time had come to seek out the best opportunities. The
fact that Marshalltown's very survival might depend on Lennox
was of no consequence. "Strictly a business decision," the company
vice president said.

In the end, Marshalltown managed to keep Lennox—with what
amounted to a bribe of $20 million in subsidies paid out by a local
government that badly needed the money, to a profitable corporation that really didn't. But the lesson is clear: long-standing relationships don't keep a factory open anymore. "In terms of the
morality of the situation," the mayor of Marshalltown said, "it's just
a fact of life."

There are, of course, technological reasons why companies have
gotten wanderlust in the last couple of decades. Computers and
telecommunications have made it possible to assemble products
almost anywhere in the world. But threatening to move a profitable
company out of its historic home wasn't done in the 1950s mostly
because it wasn't thinkable, in the same way that it wasn't thinkable
to cancel employees' vacations or fire them at age fifty or fifty-five
when their productivity began to slow down. Those actions also
would have helped the bottom line. But they were gross infringe-
ments on the enduring relationship between worker and manager
that factory employment was supposed to represent. Breaking up
that arrangement was not on the menu of options.

If it is true to say of 1950s America that it was a world of limited
choices, it is also fair to call it a world of lasting relationships. This
was as true of commerce as it was of sports and politics, and it was

nearly as true of the smallest commercial transactions as it was of the big ones.

When John Fary was not busy at politics, he was the proprietor of the 3600 Club, at the corner of Thirty-sixth Street and South Damen Avenue, in the Back of the Yards neighborhood of Chicago, where his father had run a tavern before him. Fary lived in an apartment above the bar, and operated the place himself most of the time.

There was a saloon like Fary's on virtually every block of his neighborhood during most of the years of his life. Each saloon was a sort of community center, a place where stockyards workers, factory workers, cops, and city patronage employees repaired at the end of the day to rest and to recycle their earnings back through the neighborhood.

When it came to picking a saloon to patronize, these people actually had quite a bit of choice. Just within walking distance there were a dozen possibilities. Fary's own brother operated a similar establishment a couple of blocks away. But once a customer chose his bar, because he liked the smell of it or liked the people he found there, it was his. The market was not a factor. He didn't switch to another tavern because he heard that Hamm's was available on tap for five cents less. The residents of this neighborhood weren't hard-nosed consumers in the current sense. They had a different view of what was important in life.

It takes only the briefest of excursions back into the daily routine of an imaginary family in John Fary's neighborhood, circa 1957, to demonstrate that theirs was indeed a different sort of life altogether.

From the meal that started off the morning, in which the selection of cereals was tiny and the bread was always white, to the recreation in the evening, provided by a TV set that received four stations, most of them carrying a western or a quiz show at any given moment, this family lived in a world where choice was highly limited and authority meant something it does not mean anymore. It was a world for which Wonder Bread and black-and-white TV are appropriate symbols. It was not necessary to make room for Pop-Tarts or toaster strudel, the Nashville Network or CNN.

If the breadwinner in this family drove to work in the morning, he almost certainly did it without the benefit of radio traffic commentators advising him on the best way to get there. One of the Chicago radio stations actually did institute a traffic alert feature in 1957, with a police officer hovering above the city in a helicopter, but most of the people who heard it were bewildered about what to do with the information. Wherever they were going, they had very few routes to choose from: the option of selecting the least congested freeway did not exist for most of them because the freeways themselves did not exist yet. They chose a city street and stayed on it until they reached their destination. If it was slow, it was slow.

Nor did this breadwinner have many choices, whether he worked in a factory or an office, about when to start the workday, when to take a break, or when to go to lunch. Those decisions, too, were out of the realm of choice for most employees in 1957, determined instead by the dictate of management or by the equally forceful strictures of habit. How to arrange the hours on the job was one of the many questions that the ordinary workers of the 1950s, white-collar and blue-collar alike, did not spend much time agonizing over.

The wife of this breadwinner, if she did not have a job herself, was likely to devote a substantial portion of her day to shopping, banking, and the other routines of household economic management. Like her husband, she faced relatively few personal decisions about where and how to do her daily activities. The chances are she took care of her finances at a place in the neighborhood, where she could deposit money, cash checks, and, at the end of the quarter, enjoy the satisfaction of recording a regular savings dividend. She knew the teller personally—the teller had been with the bank as long as she had, if not longer. But it was also likely that she knew the manager, and perhaps the owner. Once she opened an account, there was no need to reexamine the issue, no reason to check on what the competing bank further down Archer Avenue was offering for her money. They all offered about the same thing anyway.

Shopping, in the same way, was based on associations that were, if not permanent, then at least stable for long periods of time. The grocer was a man with whom the family had a relationship; even if his store was a small "supermarket," shoppers tended to personalize it: "I'm going down to Sam's for a minute," women told their children when they left in the afternoon to pick up a cartful of groceries. Because of fair trade laws and other economic regulations, the neighborhood grocery of 1957 was in fact reasonably competitive in price with the new mega-groceries in the suburbs, but price was not the important issue. Day-to-day commerce was based on relationships—on habit, not on choice.

If this Chicagoan had young children, there is a good chance she also spent part of her day on some school-related activity, volunteering around the building or attending a meeting of the PTA. When it came to schools, her family likely faced one important decision: public or Catholic. Once that decision was made, there were few others remaining. The idea of selecting the best possible school environment for one's children would have seemed foreign to these people; one lived within the boundaries of a district or a parish, and that determined where the children went to school. If St. Cecilia's or Thomas Edison wasn't quite as good as its counterpart a mile away (fairly improbable, given the uniformity of the product)—well, that was life.

It should not be necessary to belabor the question of how all these rituals have changed in the decades since then. Our daily lives today are monuments to selection, and to making for ourselves decisions that someone above us used to make in our behalf. We breakfast on choice (sometimes on products literally named for it);

take any of several alternative but equally frustrating routes to work; shop in stores whose clerks do not know us; bank in banks where we need to show identification after twenty years, because the teller has been there two weeks; come home to a television set offering so many choices that the newspaper can't devise a grid to show them all.

In the past generation, we have moved whole areas of life, large and small, out of the realm of permanence and authority and into the realm of change and choice. We have gained the psychological freedom to ask ourselves at any moment not only whether we are eating the right cereal but whether we are in the right neighborhood, the right job, the right relationship.

This is, of course, in large measure a function of technology. Birth-control pills created new social and sexual options for women; instantaneous communication by computer made possible all the global options of the footloose corporation. And it is in part a function of simple affluence. Choices multiply in tandem with the dollars we have to invest in them.

But our love affair with choice has not been driven solely by machines, and it has not been driven solely by money. The Baby Boom generation was seduced by the idea of choice in and of itself.

Most of us continue to celebrate the explosion of choice and personal freedom in our time. There are few among us who are willing to say it is a bad bargain, or who mourn for the rigidities and constrictions of American life in the 1950s.

A remarkable number of us, however, do seem to mourn for something about that time. We talk nostalgically of the loyalties and lasting relationships that characterized those days: of the old neighborhoods with mom-and-pop storekeepers who knew us by name; of not having to lock the house at night because no one would think of entering it; of knowing that there would be a neighbor home, whatever the time of day or night, to help us out or take us in if we happened to be in trouble.

There is a longing, among millions of Americans now reaching middle age, for a sense of community that they believe existed during their childhoods and does not exist now. That is why there is a modern movement called communitarianism that has attracted many adherents and much attention. "I want to live in a place again where I can walk down any street without being afraid," Hillary Rodham Clinton said shortly after becoming first lady. "I want to be able to take my daughter to a park at any time of day or night in the summer and remember what I used to be able to do when I was a little kid." Those sorts of feelings, and a nostalgia for the benefits of old-fashioned community life at the neighborhood level, are only growing stronger as the century draws to a close.

The very word *community* has found a place, however fuzzy and imprecise, all over the ideological spectrum of the present decade. On the far left it is a code word for a more egalitarian society in which the oppressed of all colors are included and made the beneficiaries of a more generous social welfare system that commits far more than the current amount to education, public health, and the eradication of poverty. On the far right it signifies an emphasis on individual self-discipline that would replace the welfare state with a private rebirth of personal responsibility. In the middle it seems to reflect a much simpler yearning for safety, stability, and a network of reliable relationships. Despite these differing perceptions, though, the general idea of community has been all over the pages of popular journalism and political discourse in the first half of the 1990s.

Authority is something else again. It evokes no similar feelings of nostalgia. Few would dispute that it has eroded over the last generation. Walk into a large public high school in a typical middle-class suburb today, and you will see a principal who must spend huge portions of his or her day having to cajole recalcitrant students, teachers, and staff into accepting direction that, a generation ago, they would have accepted unquestioningly just because the principal was the principal and they were subordinates.

Or consider the mainstream Protestant church. We haven't yet reached the point where parishioners curse their minister in the same way high school students curse their teachers, but if it is even a faintly liberal congregation, there is a good chance that the minister has lost his title: he is no longer "Dr." but "Jim," or "Bob," or whatever his friends like to call him. Putting the minister on a level with his parishioners is one small step in the larger unraveling of authority.

Authority and community have in fact unraveled together, but few mourn the passing of authority. To most Americans in the baby-boom generation, it will always be a word with sinister connotations, calling forth a rush of uncomfortable memories about the schools, churches, and families in which they grew up. Rebellion against those memories constituted the defining event of their generational lives. Wherever on the political spectrum this generation has landed, it has brought its suspicion of authority with it. "Authority," says P. J. O'Rourke, speaking for his baby-boom cohort loud and clear, "has always attracted the lowest elements in the human race."

The suspicion of authority and the enshrinement of personal choice are everywhere in the American society of the 1990s. They extend beyond the routines of our individual lives into the debates we conduct on topics as diverse as school reform and corporate management.

Of all the millions of words devoted in the past decade to the subject of educational change, hardly any have suggested improving the schools by putting the rod back in the teacher's hand, or returning to a curriculum of required memorization and classroom drill. The center of the discussion is the concept of school choice: the right of families to decide for themselves which schools their children will attend. Many things may be said for and against the concept of school choice, but one point is clear enough—in education, as in virtually every other social enterprise, individual choice is the antithesis of authority. It is a replacement for it.

Similarly, one can comb the shelves of a bookstore crowded with volumes on corporate management without coming across one that defends the old-fashioned pyramid in which orders come down from the chief executive, military-style, and descend intact to the lower reaches of the organization. There are corporations that still operate that way, but they are regarded as dinosaurs. Corporate hierarchies are out of fashion. The literature is all about constructing management out of webs rather than pyramids, about decentralizing the decision process, empowering people at all levels of the organization. The phrase "command and control" is the obscenity of present-day management writing.

Five years ago, few Americans were familiar with the term *command economy*. Now, virtually all of us know what it means. It is the definition of a society that fails because it attempts to make economic decisions by hierarchy rather than by the free choice of its individual citizens. It is the most broadly agreed-upon reason for the abject failure of communism around the world. The communist implosion both reinforced and seemed to validate baby boomers' generational suspicions about hierarchy and authority in all their manifestations, foreign and domestic, the American CEOs and school principals of the 1950s almost as much as the dictators who made life miserable in authoritarian countries around the world.

Not surprisingly, what has happened in education and economics has also happened in the precincts of political thought. There has in fact been a discussion about authority among political philosophers in the past two decades, and its tone tells us something. It has been a debate in which scholars who profess to find at least some value in the concept have struggled to defend themselves against libertarian critics who question whether there is any such thing as legitimate authority at all, even for duly constituted democratic governments. "All authority is equally illegitimate," the philosopher Robert Paul Wolff wrote in a landmark 1970 book, *In Defense of Anarchy*. "The primary obligation of man," Wolff argued, "is autonomy, the refusal to be ruled." It is only a slight exaggeration to say that the record of debate on this subject since 1970 has consisted largely of responses to Wolff, most of them rather tentative and halfhearted.

Meanwhile, the revolt against the authority figures of the prior generation has spilled out all over American popular culture, into books and movies and television programs. A prime example (one of many) is *Dead Poets Society,* the 1987 film in which Robin Williams stars as an idealistic young prep school teacher of the 1950s who unwittingly brings on tragedy by challenging two monstrously evil authority figures: the school's headmaster and the father of its most talented drama student. The student commits suicide after the father orders him to give up acting and prepare for a medical career; the headmaster fires Williams not only for leading the boy astray but for organizing a secret coterie of students who love art and literature and seek to study them outside the deadening rigidities of the school's official curriculum. The message is powerful: True community is a rare and fragile thing, and authority is its enemy. The one way to achieve true community is to question authority—to break the rules.

The message of *Dead Poets Society* cuts across the normal ideological barriers of left and right, uniting the student left of the 1960s and the Reagan conservatives of the 1980s. At its heart is a mortal fear of arbitrary rules and commands, of tyrannical fathers, headmasters, and bosses. E. J. Dionne made this clear in his 1991 book, *Why Americans Hate Politics,* quoting the 1971 lyrics of Crosby, Stills and Nash: "Rules and regulations, who needs 'em. Throw 'em out the door." That song was in fact a tirade against Richard J. Daley. But whether it was left or right hardly mattered. It was a song against authority.

The words of such songs may have long since been forgotten by most of those who listened to them, but the tune is still in their heads, even as they have grown into affluence, respectability, and middle age. It expresses itself in the generational worship of personal choice—in speech, in sexual matters, in human relationships of every sort.

If there were an intellectual movement of authoritarians to match the communitarians, they would be the modern equivalent of a subversive group. The elites of the country, left and right alike, would regard them as highly dangerous. The America of the 1990s may be a welter of confused values, but on one point we speak with unmistakable clarity: we have become emancipated from social authority as we used to know it.

We don't want the 1950s back. What we want is to edit them. We want to keep the safe streets, the friendly grocers, and the milk and cookies, while blotting out the political bosses, the tyrannical headmasters, the inflexible rules, and the lectures on 100 percent Americanism and the sinfulness of dissent. But there is no easy way to have an orderly world without somebody making the rules by which order is preserved. Every dream we have about re-creating community in the absence of authority will turn out to be a pipe dream in the end.

This is a lesson that people who call themselves conservatives sometimes seem determined not to learn. There are many on the right who, while devoting themselves unquestioningly to the ideology of the free market, individual rights, and personal choice, manage to betray their longing for old-fashioned community and a world of lasting relationships. In the 1980s, Ronald Reagan was one of them. His 1984 reelection campaign, built around a series of "Morning in America" television commercials featuring stage-set small-town Main Streets of the sort Reagan strolled down in his youth and in Hollywood movies, was a small token of communitarian rhetoric in the midst of a decade of unraveling economic and moral standards. But when people tell us markets and unlimited choice are good for communities and traditional values, the burden of proof is on them, not on us.

It is the disruptiveness of the market that has taken away the neighborhood savings and loan, with its familiar veteran tellers, and set down in its place a branch of Citibank where no one has worked a month and where the oldest depositor has to slide his driver's license under the window. It is market power that has replaced the locally owned newspaper, in most of the cities in America, with a paper whose owner is a corporate executive far away and whose publisher is a middle manager stopping in town for a couple of years on his way to a higher position at headquarters. Once the pressures of the global market persuaded the Lennox Corporation that it had the moral freedom of choice to make air conditioners wherever in the world it wanted to, the bonds that had tied it to a small town in Iowa for nearly a century were breakable.

In its defense, one can say that the global market onslaught of the last two decades was technologically inevitable, or more positively, that it is the best guarantor of individual freedom, and that individual freedom is the most important value for us to preserve. Or one can say that the market puts more dollars in the ordinary citizen's pocket, and that after all, the bottom line should be the bottom line. But in the end there is no escaping the reality that the market is a force for disruption of existing relationships. To argue that markets are the true friend of community is an inversion of common sense. And to idealize markets and call oneself a conservative is to distort reality.

What is true of market worship is true in a larger sense of personal choice, the even more precious emblem of the baby-boom generation. While we, like the authors of *Dead Poets Society,* may wish to place community and unrestricted choice on the same side of the social ledger, the fact is that they do not belong together.

A Wal-Mart store offers a bonanza of choice: acre upon acre of clothing and hardware, dishes and stationery, detergent and Christmas ornaments, the option of choosing from among dozens of models and manufacturers, a cornucopia that no Main Street merchant can compete with even if he could somehow compete on price. His business was built not on choice but on custom, on the familiarity and the continuing relationship that buyer and seller created over a long period of time. The Main Street cafe owed its existence to the irrelevance of choice—to the fact that it was the one place in town to go in the morning. Perhaps that meant that the price of eggs or the incentive to cook them perfectly wasn't what it might have been under a more competitive arrangement. But its sheer staying power provided people with something intangible that many of them now realize was important.

To worship choice and community together is to misunderstand what community is all about. Community means not subjecting every action in life to the burden of choice, but rather accepting the familiar and reaping the psychological benefits of having one less calculation to make in the course of the day. It is about being Ernie Banks and playing for the Chicago Cubs for twenty years; or being John Fary and sticking with the Daley machine for life; or being one of John Fary's customers and sticking with his tavern at Thirty-sixth and South Damen year in and year out. It is being the Lennox Corporation and knowing that Marshalltown, Iowa, will always be your home.

It would be a pleasure to be a baseball fan today and not have to read every fall about a player who won the World Series for his team and is now jumping to another team that has dangled a juicier contract in front of him. It would be nice to have some of the old loyalty back—to be able to root for Ernie Banks, instead of Rickey Henderson. But the stability of Ernie Banks's world depended precisely upon its limits. Restoration of a stable baseball world awaits the restoration of some form of authority over it— not, one hopes, the rigid wage slavery of the reserve clause, but some form of authority nevertheless. In baseball, as in much of the rest of life, that is the price of stability. The price is not low, but the benefit is not small.

It would similarly be a pleasure to allow one's children to watch television or listen to the radio without having to worry that they will be seeing or hearing obscenity, but here, too, the market has assumed a role that used to be occupied by authority.

Consider television in the 1950s. No doubt there would have been considerable viewer demand for a pornographic version of

Some Like It Hot, or perhaps a version of *20,000 Leagues Under the Sea* in which Kirk Douglas was eaten alive in CinemaScope by the giant squid. Those things were absent from television in the 1950s not because no one would have watched them, but because there were sanctions against their being shown. There was someone in a position of authority—in this case, a censor—who stepped in to overrule the market and declare that some things are too lurid, too violent, or too profane for a mass audience to see.

It is in the absence of such authority that five-year-olds can conveniently watch MTV or listen to Howard Stern, and twelve-year-olds can buy rap albums that glorify gangsterism, murder, and rape. It is a matter of free choice. Obscenity and violence sell, and we do not feel comfortable ordering anyone, even children, not to choose them. We are unwilling as yet to pay the price that decency in public entertainment will require. But if children are not to gorge themselves on violent entertainment, then it is an inconvenient fact that someone besides the children themselves must occupy a position of authority.

Some readers will no doubt object that I am portraying the 1950s as a pre-modern, pre-capitalist Eden. I am not that naïve. Nobody who spends any time studying the period—nobody who lived through it—can entertain for long the notion that it was a time in which people were insulated from market forces. The 1950s were the decade of tail fins, mass-produced suburban subdivisions, and the corruption of television quiz shows by greedy sponsors. The market was immensely powerful; it was the enemy that an entire generation of postwar social critics took aim against.

In the 1950s, however, a whole array of social institutions still stood outside the grip of the market and provided ordinary people with a cushion against it. In the last generation, as Alan Wolfe and others have eloquently pointed out, that cushion has disappeared. The difference between the 1950s and the 1990s is to a large extent the difference between a society in which market forces challenged traditional values and a society in which they have triumphed over them.

And the decisiveness of that triumph is written in the values that the baby-boom generation has carried with it from youth on into middle age: the belief in individual choice and the suspicion of any authority that might interfere with it.

Of course, there will be quite a few people to whom none of this makes any sense, people who believe that individual choice is the most important standard, period; that no society can ever get enough of it; that the problem in the last generation is not that we have abandoned authority but that there are still a few vestiges of it yet to be eradicated. Many of these people call themselves libertarians, and arguing with them is complicated by the fact that they are nearly always intelligent, interesting, and personally decent.

Libertarian ideas are seductive and would be nearly impossible to challenge if one thing were true—if we lived in a world full of P. J. O'Rourkes, all of us bright and articulate and individualistic, and wanting nothing more than the freedom to try all the choices and experiments that life has to offer, to express our individuality in an endless series of new and creative ways.

But this belief is the libertarian fallacy: the idea that the world is full of repressed libertarians, waiting to be freed from the bondage of rules and authority. Perhaps, if this were true, life would be more interesting. But what the libertarians failed to notice, as they squirmed awkwardly through childhood in what seemed to them the straitjacket of school and family and church, is that most people are not like them. Most people want a chart to follow and are not happy when they don't have one, or when they learned one as children and later see people all around them ignoring it. While the legitimacy of any particular set of rules is a subject that philosophers will always debate, it nonetheless remains true, and in the end more important, that the uncharted life, the life of unrestricted choice and eroded authority, is one most ordinary people do not enjoy leading.

There is no point in pretending that the 1950s were a happy time for everyone in America. For many, the price of the limited life was impossibly high. To have been an independent-minded alderman in the Daley machine, a professional baseball player treated unfairly by his team, a suburban housewife who yearned for a professional career, a black high school student dreaming of possibilities that were closed to him, a gay man or woman forced to conduct a charade in public—to have been any of these things in the 1950s was to live a life that was difficult at best, and tragic at worst. That is why so many of us still respond to the memory of those indignities by saying that nothing in the world could justify them.

It is a powerful indictment, but it is also a selective one. While it is often said that history is written by the winners, the truth is that the cultural images that come down to us as history are written, in large part, by the dissenters—by those whose strong feelings against life in a particular generation motivate them to become the novelists, playwrights, and social critics of the next, drawing inspiration from the injustices and hypocrisies of the time in which they grew up. We have learned much of what we know about family life in America in the 1950s from women who chafed under its restrictions, either as young, college-educated housewives who found it unfulfilling or as teenage girls secretly appalled by the prom-and-cheerleader social milieu. Much of the image of American Catholic life in those years comes from the work of former Catholics who considered the church they grew up in not only authoritarian but destructive of their free choices and creative instincts. The social critics of the past two decades have forced on our attention the inconsistencies and absurdities of life a generation ago: the pious skirt-chasing husbands, the martini-sneaking ministers, the sadistic gym teachers.

I am not arguing with the accuracy of any of those individual memories. But our collective indignation makes little room for the millions of people who took the rules seriously and tried to live up to them, within the profound limits of human weakness. They are still around, the true believers of the 1950s, in small towns and suburbs and big-city neighborhoods all over the country, reading the papers, watching television, and wondering in old age what has happened to America in the last thirty years. If you visit middle-class American suburbs today, and talk to the elderly women who have lived out their adult years in these places, they do not tell you how constricted and demeaning their lives in the 1950s were. They tell you those were the best years they can remember. And if you visit a working-class Catholic parish in a big city, and ask the older parishioners what they think of the church in the days before Vatican II, they don't tell you that it was tyrannical or that it destroyed their individuality. They tell you they wish they could have it back. For them, the erosion of both community *and* authority in the last generation is not a matter of intellectual debate. It is something they can feel in their bones, and the feeling makes them shiver.

In the course of this book, we will be paying extended visits to three communities as they existed during the 1950s in and around one large American city.

That the city happens to be Chicago is not a result of random selection, or merely a consequence of the fact that I was growing up there at the time. Chicago was, for all its millions of people and its international reputation for gangster wars, a reassuringly ordinary place. Unlike southern California, it was not a place where people went to pursue choice and break the shackles of tradition; unlike the rural Deep South, it was not a place where tradition and community still prevailed in a rigid and reflexive way. Nor was it, like New York, burdened by a civic culture of cosmopolitan cynicism. More than most cities, it believed in its mottoes: "I Will," and increasingly, under Richard J. Daley, "The City That Works."

Like nearly every American metropolis, Chicago also proclaimed itself, and felt itself to be, a city of neighborhoods. More

than most of them, it genuinely was. "Tightly knit neighborhoods,"
Mike Royko called them, "as small townish as any village in the
wheat field." Perhaps he exaggerates, as people nearly always do
when they talk about the streets of their youth from the vantage
point of middle age. There is no disputing, however, that he cap-
tures Chicago's image of itself, and a great deal of the sense of community that makes Chicago an appropriate model for the lost city
we are trying to remember.

Our first visit is to St. Nicholas of Tolentine parish, an enclave of
white working-class Catholics toward the southwestern edge of
the city. The second is the place everybody knew as Bronzeville,
the narrow strip of land on Chicago's South Side where black people of all classes and incomes were essentially forced to live by the
dictates of segregation. The third is the suburb of Elmhurst, ten
miles beyond the city border, where families went to escape the
iniquities of Chicago and to live in a place that was green rather
than gray.

These worlds of bungalow, tenement, and ranch house, different
as they were, nonetheless had something important in common.
They were clear geographical communities, and their inhabitants
identified with them on that basis. In the 1990s, when many middle-class people are more likely to identify with a job, or a set of
leisure interests, or with no entity at all larger than their own families, when courts have decided that geographical community is
not a necessary component even of a political constituency, it is
easy to forget that a neighborhood nearly everywhere in the 1950s
was a tangible thing, a piece of ground, a physical marker in life.

St. Nick's parish was a square mile of the Southwest Side, and all
those inside were part of it, whether they chose to be or not. The
newly constructed tracts of Elmhurst were pieces of territory that
somehow defined people as residents—usually proud residents—of
one particular subdivision or another. Bronzeville, squalid as it was,
constituted a piece of turf that even had a precisely definable center: the corner of Forty-seventh Street and South Park Way. "On a

spring or summer day," wrote Horace Cayton and St. Clair Drake, the authors of *Black Metropolis,* "47th and South Park is the urban equivalent of a village square."

A Chicago neighborhood, as late as the 1950s, was a place in which people lived their lives more or less in public, in full view of their neighbors. If one marker that sets off America today from America a generation ago is our attitude toward choice, then another is our attitude toward physical space.

To be a young homeowner in a suburb like Elmhurst in the 1950s was to participate in a communal enterprise that only the most determined loner could escape: barbecues, coffee klatches, volleyball games, baby-sitting co-ops and constant bartering of household goods, child rearing by the nearest parents who happened to be around, neighbors wandering through the door at any hour without knocking—all these were the devices by which young adults who had been set down in a wilderness of tract homes made a community. It was a life lived in public.

To live in a bungalow in St. Nick's parish was to live in a place where the walls of one's house did not constitute boundaries, where social life was conducted on the front stoop and in the alley, and where, even inside the house, four or five children in a three-bedroom home made privacy a rare commodity. Television was coming to such neighborhoods in the 1950s, but air-conditioning had not yet arrived, and summer evenings were one long community festival, involving just about everybody on the block and brought to an end only by darkness and the need to go to sleep.

And in the kitchenette and small-apartment world of Bronzeville, privacy was little more than a mirage. Sharing kitchens and bathrooms, sleeping on fire escapes to avoid the heat, residents performed on a public stage that recalls the swirling slum confusion of eighteenth-century London or Paris. To live in a kitchenette at Forty-third and Indiana in the 1950s was to do everything in public—to dance, drink, and even make love with somebody watching. It was an unrelentingly public world. As

Cayton and Drake wrote in *Black Metropolis:* "In the black ghetto, privacy is one of the rarest of the good things of life."

The people who lived in these communities, moreover, went out of their way to make their lives more public still by joining clubs and organizations of every sort. The ranch-house suburb was a jumble of bridge clubs, book clubs, square-dancing societies— groups that men as well as women joined willingly, if sometimes grumpily, and to which they devoted large chunks of whatever free time they had. The parishioners of St. Nick's lived their lives not only through the church but through its subsidiary organizations, the Holy Name Society, the Altar and Rosary—engines of mass neighborhood participation that brought five hundred or more residents of a single neighborhood to pancake breakfasts at seven o'clock on a weekday morning. The more ambitious black residents of the South Side, many of them trapped in substandard housing and menial service jobs, compensated by creating a wealth of social clubs that held suppers and formal dances, generated endless coverage in the local black newspaper, and added dignity to neighborhood life that was not achievable any other way. They were joiners par excellence.

In the intervening years, the balance between public and private has changed in American life. Television and air-conditioning brought people inside, off the porches. The two-income family of today has little time for clubs or organized social activity. The departure of the black middle class from the South Side has obliterated the respectable social world that existed there in the 1950s; it has left behind a world in which privacy is still difficult to come by, but in which the only semblance of organized social life revolves around the pathology of drugs, gangs, and violence.

One should not go too far in romanticizing this more public urban life of the 1950s. It was hard at all levels on those who did not want to belong—who wanted to retreat inside the home at the end of the day, to skip the bridge club or the church social affair, who had more than enough fellowship in the course of the working routine. It was a world that offered few places to hide, in a very literal sense. Community was achieved, for many people, at a cost of intrusion and lack of privacy that nearly all of us would instantly regard as too high today.

In many ways, the hyperindividualism that characterizes the baby-boom generation is a reaction to the close quarters in which its members grew up during the 1950s. In the schools, hordes of children gridlocked the corridors and the infamous one-way staircases. The average elementary school class size in America in the 1950s was thirty-three, well above the "ideal" size of twenty-five to thirty. The number did not drop until the 1960s were well along.

Life at home produced the same sorts of memories, whether it was a matter of five children sleeping in two tiny bungalow bedrooms or of living in an open-plan suburban house in which walls hardly seemed to exist. Wherever they grew up, the children of the 1950s usually did so without a great deal of privacy. "The crowding," Paul Light wrote in his book *Baby Boomers,* "created a lifelong commitment to individualism . . . the baby boomers could not be handled as individuals; the generation was too big."

It is easy to trace the reaction to the crowded 1950s in the slang expressions of the decades since then, from "do your own thing" and "it's my bag" in the late 1960s to the "personal space" of the 1980s. The baby boomers have never stopped looking for a little more room, or stopped believing that more space is somehow a good in itself.

The worship of privacy is, like the worship of choice and the fear of authority, rooted so deeply in our end-of-century value system that it has been virtually immune to serious debate, let alone reconsideration. But it is time to reconsider it nonetheless, and to confront the possibility that all of these self-evident contemporary "truths" are doing far more harm than good as they persist in the closing years of the century.

The best way I can think of to begin their reexamination is to re-visit the decade that was their crucible. One of the first things we will learn is just how different the adults of the 1950s really were—not only on the outside but in their perceptions of the world and in their deepest personal values. This wasn't just a time when people dressed differently and drove cars with tail fins and watched situation comedies in black and white. This was a moral culture much further removed from our own than we have ever stopped to realize.

In the Chicago of 1957, most people believed, as many of us have ceased to believe, there were natural limits to life. They understood, whether they lived in bungalow, tenement, or suburb, that choice and privacy were restricted commodities, and that authority existed, in large part, to manage the job of restricting them. Most people were prepared to live with this bargain most of the time. And they believed in one other important idea that has been lost in the decades since: they believed in the existence of sin. The Chicago of the 1950s was a time and place in which ordinary people lived with good and evil, right and wrong, sins and sinners, in a way that is almost incomprehensible to most of us on the other side of the 1960s moral deluge.

CHAPTER 2

The Uses of Sin

On the first day of April 1957, police opened the trunk of a car on the South Side of Chicago and found the body of Leon Marcus, a prominent local businessman and former president of the Southmoor National Bank.

The story was worth a banner headline in the afternoon papers. Then, over the course of the next few days, some interesting details leaked out. Marcus, it seems, had lent $150,000 to Sam Giancana, chief of the crime syndicate in Chicago. A receipt for the loan was found in his pocket. His bank had also been trustee for two Mafia gambling joints in the suburbs. He had a girlfriend who hung around with the girlfriends of several notorious gangsters.

That was as much as Chicagoans would ever know about the Marcus murder. And yet, as far as most of them were concerned, the mystery had been solved. Leon Marcus, as respectable as he may have seemed, was mixed up with the forces of evil. At the appropriate moment, they emerged from the shadows and punished him.

Crimes like this were not an everyday occurrence in the Chicago of the 1950s, but they were not exactly rare either. Every few weeks, it was routine to read about someone in the city who ventured too close to the vortex of evil and was sucked in.

Not all of the evils that hovered over Chicago were as big as the one that caused Leon Marcus's death. Most of them were facts of everyday life. During that same April, Louis Weintraub, a deputy bailiff at City Hall and precinct captain in the local Democratic organization, was caught extorting $50 a week from Saturnino Pena, a Puerto Rican city street cleaner he claimed to be responsible for hiring. Weintraub turned out to be an old con man with a police record dating back twenty years. A few weeks later, two policemen were arrested for planting narcotics on a pharmacist, then letting him go after he gave them $400.

No one in the community, no matter how virtuous, could fully escape contact with the forces of evil. Just having one's car towed, for example, was more often than not a harrowing adventure. A handful of shady companies monopolized the towing under contract with the city council. Cars were towed away for minor parking violations and often returned without all the driver's possessions inside. The president of one firm, Avalon Park Rebuilders, had served time for burglary. "It is common knowledge among garage owners," an operator said, "that one way a motorist involved in a wreck can get a more friendly police report is to send his car to the police-authorized towing garage."

It would be foolish to say that Chicagoans of the 1950s somehow enjoyed living in a city of petty corruption and unexplained gangland violence. But it would be fair to say that many of them took a sort of perverse pride in it. Chicago was a tough, boisterous, slightly seedy, inevitably sinful place. It had always been that way. It was an annoyance to have to slip a patrolman $10 to avoid a court appearance on a minor traffic infraction. To some, it was an outrage. But it was part of the rules. One could denounce the rules or accept them, but nearly everyone understood them. They were a civic tradition. "The contemplation of municipal corruption is always gratifying to Chicagoans," A. J. Liebling had written a few years earlier, not entirely in jest. "They are helpless to do anything about it, but they like to know it is on a big scale."

The evil that was weighing most heavily on the minds of Chicagoans that spring of 1957, however, was a much more frightening one. The city was in the midst of a string of monstrous crimes—the unsolved murders of several teenagers going back more than a year. Early in January, the Grimes sisters had been abducted on their way home from an Elvis Presley movie; their bodies were found later in a forest preserve. A few months later the remains of another teenager, Judith Mae Anderson, were found floating in an oil drum off Belmont Harbor.

These killings, gruesome as they might be, were not part of any wave of violent crime sweeping the city. Most of Chicago's neighborhoods were safe places, by night as well as by day, and the residents went about their business at all hours without a great deal of concern. The obsession with the Grimes and Anderson murder cases—the screaming headlines day after day—did not reflect fears for personal safety so much as it did the tangible presence of evil loose in the community, a fiend in the midst of good and hard-working citizens. Did "one maniac" kill all those teenagers? "The idea is on the tongues of tens of thousands of Chicagoans," the *Daily News* reported.

The nature of this obsession with evil gives us a clue to what made life in a big city of the 1950s an entirely different moral experience from urban life today. The citizens of Chicago viewed sin as a very real commodity; the task facing ordinary people was to live their lives around it and not become enmeshed.

The sins of the 1950s were, for the most part, one-on-one instances of the deadly seven: avarice, lust, and pride; envy, gluttony, anger, and sloth. The sinners were gangsters who stuffed business-men's bodies in trunks of cars; con men who extorted money from immigrant street cleaners; police who planted illegal drugs on innocent pharmacists. Corruption may have been an institutional phenomenon, but it always expressed itself in human terms, brought to life by real people who walked the city streets.

The sins of today, by comparison, are far away: pollution, racism, indifference to poverty and generalized human suffering of various kinds. In the 1990s, children grow up without having to worry that these distant and hazy offenses are linked to their own personal conduct in any tangible way.

Whether they live in an affluent suburb or an inner-city hous-ing project, children today regularly watch all the unspeakable hor-rors of the world portrayed in front of them on television: serial murder, child abuse, random shootings, ethnic cleansing. But they lack any clear moral rules for explaining them. The baby-boom generation has taken pains to provide its children with complex societal explanations for virtually all forms of human misfortune. The notion that evil acts take place because evil people commit them—"mean guys," as the average five-year-old likes to say—is one that most conscientious middle-class parents work hard to expunge from their children's minds.

A generation ago, most of us in America, grown-ups as well as children, believed in the existence of "mean guys." Today, that concept nearly always disappears in the first few years of school, replaced by a vague discomfort with the broader social evils of the modern civilized world: sexist language, racial inequalities, inattention to the global environment and its needs.

Any child who struggles to retain an active belief in the presence of evil ultimately runs up against the ingenuity of the wrongdoers themselves in finding social explanations for their own conduct, and the willingness of the adult world to accept that line of thought. When killers, rapists, and child abusers manage to persuade therapists, talk show hosts, and juries that their offenses are the product of circumstance, rather than sin, it is asking too much to expect children to grow up believing anything different.

In Chicago in the 1950s, there were no complex societal explanations of bad behavior, no histories of child abuse or substance abuse or low self-esteem, no failure on the part of insensitive parents or authorities. The explanation was that these were bad people—sinners. If you were smart, you kept your distance.

This simple idea was buttressed by mainstream religion, which took as its primary subject personal sin and its consequences. Billy Graham wrote an article for *Parade* magazine on how to spot the influence of the devil at moments of frustration in everyday life. Any theologian who wrote such an article today would be immediately branded a cult extremist with hallucinations. In the 1950s, this was standard operating procedure for the nation's most successful evangelist, one with a large following among the middle class.

It was not only conservative theologians who brought the concepts of personal sin and evil into ordinary religious debate. While Billy Graham was accusing the devil of complicity in the minor mishaps of life, Reinhold Niebuhr, the nation's most respected liberal theologian and moralist, was writing books about nuclear deterrence and social responsibility that rested ultimately on the inescapable human reality of original sin. "There is no final guarantee against the spiritual pride of man," Niebuhr wrote in *The Nature and Destiny of Man,* published in 1949. "Guilt is the objective consequence of sin." Niebuhr applied good and evil to ordinary human transactions no less than to the complexities of world affairs. Taking him seriously in the 1950s meant thinking about good and bad actions and good and bad people in the context of an otherwise comfortable midcentury American life. Among those who took Niebuhr very seriously, and never lost sight of the reality of personal sin as the wellspring of human misfortune, was the young Baptist minister from Atlanta, Martin Luther King, Jr.

King, Niebuhr, and Graham were Protestants. Chicago was a heavily Catholic city, home to the nation's single largest archdiocese and parochial school system, and in the Chicago Catholic schools, nearly 300,000 pupils received an education that dealt largely with the topic of sin: its myriad disguises, the distinctions between its mortal and venal varieties, the ways to avoid being lured into it, and the need to confess it at regular intervals. Much of the educational process consisted of implanting guilt in quantities sufficient to provide a bulwark against sin's most attractive opportunities.

Survival as an ordinary adult in 1950s Chicago meant threading your way through or around the sin that lurked everywhere. If you were a housewife living in a middle-class suburb, it may have largely meant reading about it in the papers each afternoon and congratulating yourself for having escaped its urban precincts. If you were a male living in a working-class neighborhood within the city, it was more likely to mean dabbling a little without being drawn in too deeply: putting a bet down on a horse, paying off a cop to escape paying a speeding ticket, perhaps walking into a B-girl joint now and then. A little contact with sin didn't necessarily kill you. But that there was such a thing as sin, and that it applied to individual people in their everyday lives, was a core belief that the Chicagoans and Americans of the 1950s largely held, and that we have largely lost.

The ability to live decently in such a world, to resist the dangers of self-indulgence and the moral shortcuts that doomed people like Leon Marcus, was summed up by many in a single word: *character*. People with character not only kept their word to others but possessed the discipline to choose long-term good over short-term gratification, no matter how seductive the pleasures of the moment might be. Character was something nearly everyone understood; only in the following generation did it become an obsolete idea.

By the 1980s, describing someone that you knew as "having character"—or lacking it, for that matter—somehow sounded pompous and archaic. The 1986 edition of *Webster's Third International Dictionary* placed the definition of character as "moral excellence" third from the bottom in a page-long list of meanings for the word, just above "the crimp of wool fiber" and the deportment of a dog. "Anyone who explains high rates of drug abuse, criminality or family dissolution by some defect in character," James Q. Wilson observed a few years ago, "is immediately taken to be a reactionary." In the Chicago of 1957, such explanations were simple household truths.

Morally, this was a city of black and white. Physically, it was a monochromatic gray. Residents and newcomers alike made conversation in the 1950s about Chicago's overpowering drabness. "A gray sub-civilization, surrounded by green suburbs," Nelson Algren called it. Isaac Rosenfeld, the literary critic, who grew up four miles west of Lake Michigan, said anyone who wandered into his neighborhood could not help but view "earth to be the source of all creation, the peculiar, cracked, ashy, mineral-gray Chicago earth with its derivative dust, grit and grime that rise swirling when the wind blows."

It was a city still heated largely by coal, and the weekly coal deliveries, dumped in front of the apartment entrances for the janitor to shovel into the basement furnace, kicked up a swirl of coal dust that stayed in the air almost until the truck came again the following week. The sky seemed to turn dark gray with the first frost in the fall, never to brighten for months on end. "An October sort of city even in the spring," Algren wrote, "with somebody's washing always whipping in smoky October colors off the third floor rear by that same wind that drives the yellowing comic strips down all the gutters that lead away from home."

Chicago was an incomprehensibly vast expanse of bungalows and apartments, small machine shops and grimy shopping corridors, stretching west for so many miles that the people who lived toward the far edge hardly knew there was a Lake Michigan, let alone went there. An "endless succession of factory town main streets," Liebling had called them in 1938, and they had not changed a great deal in the ensuing twenty years.

But if the streets of Chicago were gray and monotonous to an outsider like Liebling, they were endlessly fascinating to Richard J. Daley, who had lived on them for more than fifty years, and who found them reassuringly familiar. "When I walk down the street where I live," he had said in his 1955 campaign, "I see every street in the city of Chicago." He promised that with his election, "the sun will rise over all Chicago neighborhoods."

Most weekday mornings in his first mayoral term, after attending mass, Daley had his chauffeur stop the limousine in front of the Art Institute, a mile or so from City Hall, and he walked the rest of the way down Michigan Avenue and across on Madison or Washington to La Salle. This was not so much to make a show of visibility—Daley was never a compulsive campaigner—but to marvel at the variety and grandeur of the city whose slippery political ladder he had somehow managed to ascend.

Loving the Loop, in its state of relative physical stagnation in the mid-1950s, actually required a feat of imagination in itself. But Daley felt the same way about the rest of the town as well, the grimier and more monotonous places that Liebling had derided. Eugene Kennedy, the most sympathetic of Daley's biographers, says that the mayor saw Chicago as "our lady of the lake . . . she was always pure, and he would never stop building shrines and lighting candles for her."

Describing Richard J. Daley as a moony idealist at any point in his career may seem like a laughable proposition. But it was not so ridiculous in the mid-1950s. The truth, obscured now by generations of "Boss Daley" legends and vituperation, is that Daley was a sort of political reformer in his first mayoral term—a lifelong ward politician who, as an undeniably capable administrator, an adviser to Adlai Stevenson, a man trained in the details of municipal finance, was somehow going to make machine politics efficient and safe for democracy. "The old bosses were not interested in what was good for the public welfare," Daley once told *Time* magazine. "They were interested only in what was good for themselves. . . . We're the first of the new bosses."

Not everyone believed this, even at first. Prior to the 1955 campaign, the *Chicago Tribune* warned that "the grafters and fixers, the policy racketeers and others who can't do business with Mayor Kennelly and his department heads are yearning for a city administration they can do business with. Mr. Daley is no hoodlum, but if he runs he will be the candidate of the hoodlum element."

Daley responded with wounded simplicity. "I would not unleash the forces of evil," he replied. "It's a lie. I will follow the training my good Irish mother gave me." His response was revealing. Daley did not claim to be unaware that evil was loose in Chicago, or that he had no contact with it. He merely promised to keep it on a leash.

Sometimes Daley kept the leash so short as to surprise and please his most demanding critics.

Early in Daley's first term, for example, the fifty aldermen on Chicago's city council were forced out of their most lucrative and inexcusable form of graft: the business of selling driveway permits to homeowners for whatever sum of money the homeowner was willing to provide under the table. This practice had been going on for decades in Chicago. "They used to think that I was something of a queer or a boy scout," Republican Alderman John Hoellen recalled years later, "when I wouldn't take $8,000 for a driveway." Daley put the permit process in the hands of a brand-new division in the city department of streets, whose administrator was told to play it straight. The cost of a residential driveway permit was fixed at $2.75, where it stayed for years.

When the local papers caught the new administration lapsing into evil old machine ways, Daley could be forced to change his mind. Early in 1957, when the legislature passed a judicial reform bill that called for appointed rather than elected judges, the mayor asked that Chicago municipal judges be exempted. The *Daily News* called it "a shameless confession that the Daley machine's main interest in the court is as a big trough of jobs, patronage and political influence." Daley backed down. Later in the year, when the mayor's law partner, William Lynch, negotiated sweetheart contracts for billboard companies to put up lucrative neon signs along the new Northwest Expressway, the *News* went on the warpath again, charging "City Hall politics at its shadiest." Daley had the permits revoked.

None of this was sufficient to erase the aura of graft and corruption that continued to surround the machine and local politics. But it was enough to impress much of the local establishment that had seen Daley as little more than an ordinary hack when he had run the first time. By 1959, when he came up for a second term, Daley would be able to run reasonably credibly as a tough administrator, attracting the support of an elite coalition ranging from the State Street department stores and La Salle Street banks to the chancellor of the University of Chicago. He had managed to convince all of them that he was not the sort of machine mayor they needed to be embarrassed about knowing.

For the business community, what mattered was not just Daley's unexpected interest in presentable government but his active sponsorship of the downtown building boom: highways, new high-rises on the drawing boards all over the Loop, parking garages, all financed without any undue increase in the tax assessments for downtown properties. Daley's floor leader and closest ally on the city council, Thomas Keane, ate lunch with the financial establishment every day at the Bismarck Hotel, around the corner from City Hall. Sometimes the mayor came as well.

Over the years, it had been pointed out, Chicago had essentially had two kinds of mayors: saints, like Martin Kennelly, Daley's predecessor, who accomplished very little, and sinners, like William Hale Thompson in the 1920s and Edward Kelly in the 1930s, who got things built. Thompson had helped spur the city's original North Side building boom by sponsoring the construction of the Outer Drive; Kelly had presided over the building of the State Street subway. No one had yet demonstrated how to be a builder without being a crook. Daley wished to be the first.

He also realized, as a matter of political pragmatism, that an administration that took in its money legally from business in the form of campaign contributions did not need to run a wide open city the way Kelly had done, taking payoffs in broad daylight from gamblers, pimps, and shady characters of all sorts. The leader who kept an appropriate distance from the city's most sinful elements did not have to lie awake at night worrying about what they might do to embarrass him. But the modern requirements of urban sin management did not preclude Daley from being an old-fashioned authoritarian when it came to party politics.

On the night of Daley's election, in April 1955, Alderman Paddy Bauler, one of the last of Chicago's famous saloon-keeper politicians, made his much-quoted remark that "Chicago ain't ready for reform." But Bauler actually said something more prescient that night. He said that the power-brokers on the city council were about to lose virtually all the influence they had grown accustomed to. "They're gonna run nothin'," Bauler predicted. "They ain't found it out yet, but Daley's the dog with the big nuts." Unlike Bauler's remark about reform, this one, perhaps for obvious reasons, failed to become famous. But it was the most succinct possible statement about political authority in Chicago for the rest of the decade and beyond.

And it brings us very close to the question of why Richard J. Daley stands, all these years later, as a symbol of everything that makes the baby-boom generation fearful of the 1950s not only in Chicago but everywhere in America. It is his status as an icon of raw, unchecked authority.

If Daley was a new form of leader, eager to avoid the embarrassments of his predecessors, he also had a feudal mentality, a sense that loyalty was more important than anything else in politics and in government. Jacob Arvey, one of his city council mentors, had preached this during his most influential years—"Let me put it in a crude way," he once said: "Put people under obligation to you"—and Daley believed it with more intensity than Arvey.

To Daley's critics, and to the critics of the machine in general, it was the belief in slavish loyalty and obedience that was most offensive about the system, more offensive even than the petty corruption it continued to tolerate. Lynn Williams, a North Shore suburbanite who fought Daley within the Democratic Party for decades, summed up this disgust about the machine toward the end of his career. "It makes robots," Williams said. "Gears, cogs, out of the people who become workers in it. They don't do any thinking. They surrender their minds to the control of somebody else as surely as a horse surrenders his body. . . . Daley expected the kind of loyalty that a dog gives to his master who feeds him."

What Daley expected was the unquestioning obedience that politicians such as John Fary gave him for decades, in the legislature and as a member of Congress. Shortly after Daley became mayor, he seized control of the microphone at council meetings, so that a dissident alderman could find his sound shut off in midsen-

tence. Even in the 1950s in Chicago, there were significant numbers of people, educated people, for whom authority in that fashion was simply distasteful. These critics were the advance guard of
a later generation of rebels against authority in politics and beyond.
In the early Daley years in Chicago, however, it was possible for
him to demand absolute loyalty and do it successfully.

The governments of Chicago and Cook County, then as now, were
housed in the same building downtown, with the mayor and city
council in one half, fronting on La Salle Street, and the county
commissioners and county offices on the other side, toward the
Clark Street entrance. Through the halls of this building prowled a
cast of characters who were Chicago's answer to Damon Runyon:
patronage workers, favor-seekers, political kibitzers, judges, gangsters. Some would stride through purposefully en route to appoint-
ments; others loitered most of the day. It was not easy to tell them
apart except for the greetings that rang out when someone truly
important came through: "Hello, Alderman," "Hello, Judge." It
certainly wasn't easy to distinguish them by the way they looked.
As Daley biographer Bill Gleason described better than anyone
else, there was a City Hall uniform in the 1950s. At the top, it
consisted of a wide-brimmed fedora, brown or pearl gray, brim
upturned, never removed during the day for any purpose. Below it
was a shirt with no tie, buttoned at the collar, and a loose-fitting
jacket. Even Daley dressed this way before he moved into the fifth-
floor mayoral suite and switched to custom-tailored suits.

It was impossible, walking through City Hall in 1957, to know
whether the man you passed was a ward committeeman, a bailiff,
an employee in the office of the Recorder of Deeds, a police
detective, or a personal injury lawyer with connections to the mob.
Thus did politics, government, law enforcement, and crime come
together more or less effortlessly. A stroll through those halls was
always, for the innocent, an excursion to at least the outskirts of sin.
It was this unholy coterie of hangers-on that the reformers of the

era most despised—the ultimate slavish loyalists of a local political system in which obedience was taken for granted and individual political choice, anywhere but at the very highest reaches of the system, could scarcely be said to exist.

There were perhaps 60,000 patronage employees of the city and county in 1957, and there were 3,500 Chicago precincts, most of which were "captained" by city or county employees. During the day these people were bailiffs and revenue clerks and sanitation workers, but their most important responsibility was to perform favors and turn out the vote for machine candidates. If Daley won election in 1955 in part because he came across as a potentially respectable mayor, he won in larger part because the organization simply turned out the vote for him in the eleven wards it essentially controlled. In some of those wards, you had to take a precinct in order to have a job. "The organization," Lynn Williams once explained, "does not want precinct workers who are not employees of the city, because they cannot be controlled."

The precinct captains provided trash cans and helped with building permits, sent flowers to funerals, and found legal advice for neighborhood residents who needed it. In all of these duties they reported to the Democratic ward committeeman, the crucial party operative at the neighborhood level. It was the committeeman who was ultimately responsible for the ward's showing at election time, and who in return was allowed to control about five hundred jobs and was guaranteed a place on the slate-making committee that chose the candidates for aldermen and other important city and county offices. If the committeeman did not sit on the city council himself, he usually got to determine who would represent the ward there. In return for these honors he was expected to work as many as sixty to seventy hours a week at a job that carried no salary. Therefore, a ward committeeman needed to find other sources of income.

Usually this was not too difficult. Some were themselves elected officials or city patronage employees. Others made a good living as lawyers or insurance agents doing business with the city. In the

Twenty-seventh Ward on the West Side, for example, Committee-man John Touhy and Alderman Harry Sain prospered for decades by writing insurance policies on the Skid Row flophouses that lined West Madison Street, inside the ward boundaries. "To be a success in the insurance field," Mike Royko wrote later, "a ward boss needs only two things: his own office with his name on it, and somebody in the office who knows how to write policies." Mayor Daley is supposed to have put it more succinctly to an aspiring young politician: "Don't take a nickel—just show them your business card." This was where he drew the line between the decent officeholder and the crook.

Daley used to pride himself on the efficiency of service delivery in Chicago, on the cleanliness of the streets and parks, the garbage pickup, the water department. These were integral to his boastfulness about "the city that works." That these services were even passably efficient in the 1950s seems in itself a minor miracle given the larding of the offices that managed them with ward patronage employees.

The Chicago Park District, a nominally independent agency with a historic reputation for excellence, was in 1957 a sagging warehouse of ward heelers, 4,742 employees strong. One of its commissioners for much of the decade was Jacob Arvey, the Democratic Party leader in the previous era, who had lost his role as a king-maker by the Daley years but who had been given his position in the park system as a sort of retirement job. It was generally conceded that Chicago had an impressive and reasonably well-run park system in those years, but it was also inescapable that some of its nicest benefits were for sale in an extra-legal fashion. The way to get a choice boat mooring in Belmont Harbor was to find the right person at the Park District and slip him the requisite amount of money.

Given all the multifarious evils loose in the city during the 1950s, the idea of the wealthy redistributing money to the city for recreational favors did not strike many people as particularly heinous. It was a sort of underground amusement tax. But some of the underground taxes the city collected in the 1950s were morally troublesome, to say the least. Chicago was still full of illegal businesses at that time: dice games in respectable restaurants, B-girls (prostitutes) in sleazy taverns, bookies operating all over town. All of these operators had to pay under the table to remain in business. Most of the time, payment was made to a police officer, who passed it along to the district police commander, who turned it over to the ward committeeman. In most wards, the committeeman had a veto over the appointment of the commander. Each middleman siphoned off his share of the money before passing the rest along. The ward committeeman, at his discretion, returned some of his takings in the form of extra services for the ward, perhaps additional garbage cans or a children's party. The ward committeeman who allowed gambling could also demand extra patronage jobs for bartenders, bouncers, cashiers, and others who labored in the underground entertainment world.

Even here one can make the argument that no great sin was involved. These were taxes on victimless but illegal entrepreneurs who could always switch to something legal if they got tired of making the payments. What was truly unsettling was the graft that was paid simply for the privilege of doing things that were legal. If this form of corruption was not universal, it was certainly far from rare.

Even after Daley put an end to the driveway racket, almost all lifelong Chicagoans seemed to know a story about a building inspector who could invoke dozens of obscure regulations to frustrate the legitimate construction plans of a homeowner or small storekeeper who refused to make a payment under the table.

"Essentially," two machine critics wrote, "the city building department and the police levied a tax on human effort to change the walls, floors, ceilings, wires, pipes, roofs, windows, doors and cellars in Chicago. With luck, you got to pay the tax into outstretched hands and went about your business, molested no more.

But things got tough when you tried to meet code, when, because you had angered the gods or were out of your head, you had to meet every stinking little regulation. That's when you had to grunt."

In the 1930s, those who insisted on being politically uncooperative in a given ward had run the risk of not getting their garbage picked up. By the 1950s, this form of discrimination was more subtle, involving a delay in fixing a pothole or installing a traffic light in a neighborhood that had a habit of voting "wrong." Still, *injustice* was the word for it.

Then there was the matter of conducting elections. It seems clear that the machine never stole votes on the scale or with the definitiveness its critics often imagined: if it had, it would never have lost as many critical elections as it did. Nothing could have been worse for Daley than the election of a Republican as Cook County state's attorney in 1956, but he was powerless to prevent it, even if he wanted to try. Nevertheless, it seems equally certain that in a close election, especially a low-turnout election for an important but less-than-visible city office, the returns from the dozen or so machine wards could be manipulated to affect the result.

That the electoral system was not quite honest was a universal perception in Chicago in the 1950s, reinforced by the personal experiences of even the most ordinary citizens. A zealous precinct captain concerned about making a good showing on election day would sometimes walk right into the booth with the voter, or produce absentee ballots based on false affidavits of illness that he had drawn up himself.

A Chicago resident who made a visit to a county courtroom in those days frequently saw campaign posters bearing the name and likeness of the judge who was presiding there. Bailiffs handed out campaign literature to the families of defendants. It was accepted that judges simply represented one more element of the political system. They were at the highest rungs of the ladder, but they were on it nevertheless. They were slated for office as a reward for years of loyalty and faithful machine service, and unlike Supreme Court justices at the national level, they rarely disappointed the political leaders who chose them. They behaved.

It is in the courts and the electoral system that even the most sympathetic student of the Daley years, four decades later, has to stop and say that something was really wrong. This was allowing evil too close to home. B-girl operations, payoffs from bookie joints—those were one thing, the grease that kept the machine working, and the city functioning in a world where people happened to be sinners. Incentives had to exist; money had to change hands. "If he put a stop to it," the political scientist Edward Banfield said of Daley, "he would weaken both his personal political position and the whole structure of governmental power."

The corruption of the electoral and judicial processes, however, were a whole order of magnitude more frightening. A judge who had to be bought, or a cooked vote count in a West Side ward, struck too close to the irreducible core of a democratic society. They were one cost of authority and stability in Richard J. Daley's world that was simply too much for decent citizens to pay. Could Daley have run a clean political system and an orderly government too? Certainly he would have said no. But there isn't much doubt that sleaze at the polls and sleaze in the courts contributed disproportionately to public cynicism about the Daley regime in later years, even among those who otherwise found much to admire.

There was, however, a still more powerful scent of sin about Chicago public life in the 1950s, a scent that had been in the air since the 1920s and had never really dissipated. It came from the Mafia.

It was universally agreed that the crime syndicate was not what it had been in the 1920s, when Al Capone controlled bootlegging citywide and had his business rivals machine-gunned to death, or even in the 1930s, when Mayor Kelly not only gave the crime syndicate free reign to run gambling parlors but split the take with the

Mafia bosses. Still, this control was the backdrop to conversations among even the most law-abiding citizens. Seemingly respectable retail establishments were said to be Mob fronts; prominent and free-spending businessmen, like Leon Marcus, were said to have made their money on Mob enterprises. The Mob was the massive, mysterious evil that always seemed to be lurking nearby, no matter where you lived or how comfortable your circumstances. For the middle-class child in Chicago, it provided the first realization that bad guys weren't just characters in cartoons or fiends described in newspaper headlines. They were men in gray suits and fedora hats who haunted your very own neighborhood streets.

What all Chicagoans knew, even if they could not exactly explain it, was that there were complex networks of relationships among one-time Capone associates, labor union leaders, machine politicians, lawyers, and police. In 1953, a notebook belonging to Police Captain Redmond P. Gibbons had been left accidentally on the street and was found to contain telephone numbers of known gangsters, along with lists of taverns that featured gambling, and dollar amounts written in the margins next to the name of each tavern. The story was a sensation, but Gibbons was never found guilty of anything.

All the evidence pointed to an efficiently managed criminal conglomerate run for years by Tony Accardo, an early Capone intimate who lived in a mansion in the suburb of River Forest, wintered in Palm Springs, never spent a day in jail in his life, and died peacefully at home in 1992, at the age of eighty-eight. In 1956, it was said, Accardo had surrendered some of his authority to the younger Sam Giancana, in a ceremony at Tam O'Shanter Country Club.

It may sound absurd to describe the climate of organized crime in Chicago in the 1950s as a dramatic improvement over previous decades, but that was in fact the consensus of respectable opinion. The Mob had managed to make itself considerably less obtrusive. The lavish betting parlors of the 1930s had been closed down in one of the few conspicuous successes of the Kennelly reform years; the open houses of prostitution and slot machines in lounges at country clubs had been replaced by more discreet back-room dice games and B–girls in dives where respectable people were not supposed to go. For the forces of enlightenment, this climate represented a significant step in the right direction. "Gambling was wide open in Chicago seventeen years ago," the columnist Jack Mabley wrote in the *Chicago Daily News* in 1957. "Today it is confined to sneak joints. The Capone syndicate was an open, defiant, going concern. Today it is underground and weakened, although more sinister in some respects because hoodlum money has gone into legitimate business."

It was the move into legitimate business, fueled by the profits from gambling and prostitution, that gave the Mob its greatest aura of mystery in the 1950s. Which businesses were they? Without inside information, nobody could tell for sure. People said the Mob was into auto repair and catering, that it was responsible for the new string of nightclubs opening up west of the city limits, on Mannheim Road, that the way to tell a Mob front was by the inexplicably low prices it charged, too low for the quality of service it rendered. But it was virtually all a matter of rumor.

If the Mafia's move into straight business was a matter largely of speculation, however, its move into legitimate politics was easier to document. The heavily Italian neighborhoods of the near West Side continually elected people to the city council and the Illinois legislature whose connections with Capone or those close to him were a matter of record. "They vote Capone," the *Tribune* flatly said of these people, years after Capone's death. "They belong to the Mob."

One of the leaders of the West Side bloc in the legislature was Roland Libonati, best known to many Chicagoans for a photograph of himself, Al Capone, and Machine Gun Jack McGurn in the 1930s at a Cubs baseball game at Wrigley Field. Late in 1957, Libonati was slated by the Daley organization to fill a vacancy in a safe Democratic seat in Congress. "Down in the precincts," the *Daily News* complained, "it's the same old machine—unreformed, unrepentant and unashamed." Libonati had a different view. "Guilt by association don't go in my area," he said. On New Year's Eve, 1957, Libonati was elected to Congress.

One has to presume that Daley did not consider slating Libonati to be a violation of his earlier promise "not to unleash the forces of evil" upon Chicago. Perhaps the election of a man like him to Congress failed to meet the test of evil, in Daley's view, or adding him to the existing delegation was an event whose consequences were too trivial to oppose. Or perhaps the mayor felt he was improving the moral climate of his own city by shipping Libonati off to Washington.

What is indisputable is that Daley was a man who thought about good and evil, who absorbed strict standards of right and wrong from his religious upbringing and applied them to the people he dealt with in personal life. He was not a teetotaler, but he did not like drunkenness, and he did not like profanity. Two of his three rules of public speaking were "Never speak with liquor on your breath" and "Don't tell dirty jokes." (The third was "Sit down after five minutes.") But what bothered Daley more than anything was adultery. "If one of his aides or hand-picked office-holders is shacking up with a woman, he will know it," Mike Royko wrote of Daley. "And if that man is married and a Catholic, his career will wither and die."

Nearly everyone who has written about Daley has been struck by the fundamental incongruity of a moralistic man who was sincerely troubled by the language, drinking habits, and marital infidelities of those around him—and yet, for all his efforts to create a "modern" and "respectable" political machine, still permitted massive corruption to persist.

It was not simply a matter of tolerating gangsters and their associates, or cops who shook down motorists, or the bookies who operated in the shadows of Daley's personal world. Most damning of all were the politicians close to the mayor who were on the take. The roster of Daley intimates from the 1950s who were eventually nailed on corruption charges is remarkable: Alderman Thomas Keane, the chairman of the city council finance committee, was using inside information to buy and sell thousands of parcels of land at huge profits; Press Secretary Earl Bush was using his advertising firm to solicit bribes from companies holding contracts for the construction of O'Hare Airport; Matthew Danaher, Daley's South Side neighbor and protégé, the man who was in charge of patronage and sat in an office right outside Daley's on the fifth floor of City Hall, was taking payoffs from real estate developers.

Decades later, it should be safe to venture the final judgment that Daley himself was not doing any of these things. Millions of dollars and years of effort were spent by both press and prosecutors to investigate the possibility that Daley was corrupt, and not a shred of evidence was ever produced. But Daley could not have failed to notice what his friends were up to. "If it was true that he had no connection with any of these enterprises," Eugene Kennedy wrote, "it was also fair speculation that he knew about them, because everything in Chicago finally had to be cleared with him."

Richard J. Daley was a manager of sin, a decision maker who accepted the reality of sinful citizens and constant temptation, tolerated them up to a point, even took advantage of their presence to keep an organization functioning, but did his best to control the level of misdeeds and to prevent them from taking over and breeding chaos. It was his task neither to condone corruption nor to wipe it out but to manage it in accordance with the limitations of human weakness, which Daley had been told of in parochial school and in which he profoundly believed.

A community that understands sin tends also to know faith, and so it should come as no surprise that Chicago in the 1950s was a place whose residents possessed a reassuring, if ultimately naive, faith in several things: in technology and progress in general and in the future of Chicago in particular. These were people who believed in the concept of posterity, in a sense that is all but incomprehensible to us a generation later.

Throughout the decade, the city's business leaders loved to make speeches predicting astonishing achievements yet to come. "All that you can see ahead for the Chicago area is progress and success," Thomas Coulter, the head of the Chicago Association of Business and Industry, told a luncheon during the summer of 1957. "Chicago will become the greatest city the world has ever known—perhaps in twenty-five years."

Chicago was practiced in the routine use of superlatives. North Michigan Avenue was the "Magnificent Mile." State and Madison was "the world's busiest corner." Midway was "the world's busiest airport." Merchandise Mart was "the world's largest office building." The *Tribune* was, by self-proclamation, "the world's greatest newspaper." Columnist Jack Mabley boasted that "you ride the length of Chicago's magnificent shore line and think that other cities, corruption or no, should have been able to produce something as beautiful." Everyone talked this way. Lake Michigan had the status of a civic achievement. And so much was happening in those first Daley years that seemed to point the city in a new direction, toward progress and prosperity and even a newly respectable image.

After more than twenty years of physical stagnation, new office buildings were going up all over the Loop. "To the Chicagoan," Bill Furlong had written in the *New York Times* magazine in May 1957, "the opening last year of the forty-two-story Prudential building was a feat rivaling the Manhattan project." Just a few years earlier, real estate men in Chicago used to joke about turning the Loop back to the Indians. No one was talking that way anymore. Early in 1957, Cook County voters had passed a brand-new $113-million construction bond issue. "The people have given their decision," Mayor Daley said, "in favor of our plans to make Chicago the world's greatest city . . . to lay the groundwork for everything material that is needed for civic greatness."

And yet there was an insecure quality to this optimism. Carl Sandburg and Frank Lloyd Wright—perhaps the two greatest living symbols of Chicago achievement—demonstrated it quite clearly in the fall of 1957 when they appeared together as part of a seven-day festival of local pride sponsored by U.S. Steel and officially dedicated to "the sound building and far-sighted planning of the World's Most Dynamic City."

It had been sixty years since Sandburg had first glimpsed Chicago at the turn of the century and seventy years since Wright had arrived and started drawing architectural plans. Sandburg was now seventy-nine years old and living in North Carolina; Wright was eighty-eight and living in Arizona. But they both came back and played their parts. Wright talked about his idea of a mile-high Chicago skyscraper, while Sandburg put on a hard hat, toured a downtown construction site, and proclaimed that "I can see a resurgent spirit in this town" similar to the one he remembered in the years after the 1893 World's Fair.

One evening the two giants gathered for an informal discussion that was televised on Channel 11, Chicago's brand-new educational television station. For thirty minutes Wright and Sandburg reminisced and talked about technology and the bright days ahead. Then, after the moderator had signed off, Wright turned to Sandburg and said something he didn't realize the entire viewing audience could hear: "We'd better get out of here, Carl, before somebody starts telling the truth."

To accuse Wright of hypocrisy is too much. He was reflecting the Chicago psychology in an eerily appropriate way. It was the worst of places, and it was the best of places, too. Chicago was full of corruption and sin and it was full of innocent optimism. And most important, one could see those qualities simultaneously and not be confused.

That same summer of 1957, Chicagoans could watch Kim Novak at the State-Lake Theater in the movie *Jeanne Eagels*. The advertising for the film was a torrent of seemingly contradictory adjectives. "Sinful, Stormy, Shocking, Profane," one ad said as it marched down the left-hand column of the newspaper page. "Virtuous, Sacred, Serene, and Inspiring," the same ad answered back from the other side of the page. Not only did readers understand an ad like that, but they bought tickets for the movie expecting to see every one of those qualities in front of them at some point during the two hours.

Today we laugh at such advertising, in part because it is hyperbolic, but also because the words no longer mean much of anything to us. A "sinful" woman? A "profane" script? What on earth would make a movie "virtuous" or "sacred"? We have a hard time even trying to answer the question.

The reason we cannot answer it is because of the blurring of moral judgment that remains the legacy of the 1960s. We know that racism is wrong, sexual harassment is wrong, thoughtless degradation of the environment is wrong, gratuitous violence against innocent people on the streets of a big city is wrong. Further than that we find it difficult to go. We are never quite sure where, if anywhere, the notion of personal responsibility applies.

Is Chicago a sinful city? By the standards of the 1950s, the level of sin has declined substantially. The Democratic machine, if it can still be said to exist, is no longer free to stuff ballot boxes; nobody has to bribe an alderman to get a driveway built in front of his house; respectable businessmen do not get stuffed in the trunks of cars because they made the mistake of associating with the Mob. That sort of evil has all but disappeared. But are the schools better, the streets safer, the local government more responsive to the day-to-day concerns of the residents? Virtually everybody realizes that the answer to these questions is no. Is there a feeling of community that fosters attachment and commands the loyalty of forty years ago? The answer to that question is equally clear.

If we are serious about the idea of restoring a sense of community in America, we must do more than simply offer up platitudes in its behalf. We must ask hard questions about where community flourishes and where it dries up. It is for that purpose that I want to pay a return visit to the Chicago of forty years ago, and to the different moral and social universe its residents inhabited. I do not choose this particular place because I think it was the embodiment of some communitarian ideal, or because I expect naively that the lost city of the 1950s will one day be restored intact. My interest is in the future. I think it is time for us to begin gathering up those belongings from a past world that we will wish to find a place for somewhere in the next.

Let us start by giving ourselves an aerial view of the larger territory.

CHAPTER 3

Midsummer in America

It is the end of June and in much of America it is hotter than anyone can remember this early in the summer. The Good Humor company is swamped: every truck it can find has been sent on the road yet still it cannot keep up with the demand. It is a good time for a cookout, but only if you already have a grill. Most hardware stores have run out and are waiting for the next shipment. More Tartan sun lotion has been sold in the first six months of 1957 than in the whole summer of 1956.

In Chicago, where the temperature has already edged close to 100 degrees several times, the health commissioner has used his authority to issue a dispensation. He says men should stop worrying about wearing ties to work and women shouldn't feel they have to wear girdles. In New York, Billy Graham wonders if the devil didn't send a heat wave to lower the attendance at his six-week Madison Square Garden crusade.

In the more affluent precincts of suburbia, it is swimming pool season, and more pools are being built than anybody ever thought possible. A year ago there were fifty-seven thousand of them in private American homes, and by the end of the coming summer, there will be more than eighty thousand. Chester Slawy, the president of Suburban Pools Inc., can't get over it. "One pool in a virgin neighborhood," he boasts, "will sire five more." In Atlanta, developer Kirby Smith doesn't mind making a prediction: "The swimming pool will be just as commonplace as the bathtub ten years from now."

One reason for Smith's optimism is that, for most people in the middle class, the air conditioner is almost as much of a luxury as the swimming pool. Fewer than 10 percent of all homes have one. Suburbanites still go to public places to cool off: theaters, restaurants, bowling alleys. Inside the home, in a devilish June like this one, it is too hot to be comfortable.

But it is not too hot to be complacent, and that is what thousands of college seniors seem to be this month as they defy the unseasonable climate in cap and gown. Dr. Philip Jacob of the

University of Pennsylvania has just finished surveying fifty campuses all over the country, and his conclusion is unequivocal: young Americans are happy. "Students are gloriously contented," he concludes, "both in regard to their present day-to-day activity and their outlook for the future. Few of them are worried."

You might expect that Dr. Jacob would therefore be happy himself, but what he has found disturbs him. "The great majority," he complains, "appear unabashedly self-centered." Their interest in the problems of the larger world is curiously absent. They are "politically irresponsible and often politically illiterate as well."

One might hope for a little more charity. These 1957 graduates were born in the depths of the Great Depression, lived most of their early years in wartime, and became teenagers amid the shortages and uncertainties of immediate postwar America. The affluence of the moment is something neither their parents nor their childhoods conditioned them to expect. Is a little generational irresponsibility such a terrible thing?

The answer, to Dr. Jacob and to many of the luminaries invited to address the graduates this June, is yes. It is about time, they say, for the cream of American youth to learn a little social responsibility. More than that: a little individuality. The Class of 1957 is showing every sign of turning into a generation of contented sheep. To hear their critics tell it, they are giving the very notion of community a bad name.

"We hope for non-conformists among you," theologian Paul Tillich tells one audience of graduates, "for your sake, for the sake of the nation, and for the sake of humanity." But what he sees is the opposite: "an intense desire for security both internal and external, the will to be accepted by the group at any price, an unwillingness to show individual traits, acceptance of a limited happiness without serious risks."

A. Whitney Griswold, the president of Yale, sees something even worse: "a nightmare picture of a whole nation of yes-men, of hitch-hikers, eavesdroppers and peeping Toms, tiptoeing backward

offstage with their fingers to their lips." Abram L. Sachar, the president of Brandeis, uses the ceremonies at the University of
Massachusetts as an occasion for ridicule. "There are many young
people today," he says, "who would not sign a petition for pink
raspberry ice cream in the dining hall commons for fear that someday they may have to explain their color predilections to zealous
congressional committees." Sachar remembers all too vividly how
timid academics were in confronting the tyranny of McCarthyism
only a few years ago. He is afraid the rising generation may turn
out to be more timid still.

Rene McColl is feeling equally pessimistic this June as he flies
home to England. Two years ago, when he arrived in the United
States as correspondent for the London *Express,* he was exultant
about postwar American culture. "America today," he wrote, "is
calmer, more moderate—and more quietly self-confident. The
giant has lost his jitters."

McColl is in a different mood this summer. Like the commencement speakers, he is troubled by all the complacency he sees around
him. "I am hopping away," he writes now, "from this great, swarming ant-heap of a country, away from the jumbo swirl of riches and
plenty, and dragon-huge, Taj-Mahal conspicuous motorcars. Away
from a roaring torrent of informality."

Billy Graham, who is in a Manhattan hotel getting ready for the
biggest and most important crusade of his career, is not troubled by
any of those things. In the view of his critics, he is part of them. In
the last days before the start of the crusade, *Christian Century* magazine has launched a blast at everything the thirty-nine-year-old
evangelist represents. Graham is, the magazine complains, the "new
juncture of Madison Avenue and the Bible Belt. Radio and TV will
be carrying the voice and image of bland sincerity into homes
being conditioned to recognize packaged virtue."

But if Graham had any inclination to worry about those complaints, he is probably too busy to do so. By invading New York

City, he has taken on a mammoth task. He is walking into the capital of American iniquity and asking that its citizens repent their sins. He is not expecting it to be easy or pleasant. "I'm prepared," he vows, "to go to New York to be crucified if necessary. If I knew what I had to go through there, I would probably flee with terror. But if the city can be reached, God will do it." He has hired three thousand crusade counselors to help the people who come to Madison Square Garden make what he calls "decisions for Christ." Each counselor has undergone a course of nine training sessions.

The year 1957 has been, by almost any tangible standard, a very good one for religion, not just for Billy Graham's evangelism but for the mainstream Protestant denominations, Judaism, and the Catholic Church as well. There are now 103 million members of 308,000 American churches and synagogues, an increase of more than 3 percent in the past year alone. More than 62 percent of American adults tell survey researchers that they are enrolled church members. Religion seems to be finding a comfortable niche in the office and on campus.

The State Mutual Life Insurance Company has just completed a new headquarters building in Worcester, Massachusetts, and has taken pains to include a "Meditation Room," complete with stained-glass windows. The company wants its executives to pray before they attempt to make crucial business decisions.

Yale has introduced religion this year as a new undergraduate major. Two thousand students attended sunrise Easter services at Stanford. In Oakland, California, at Mills College for women, Professor George Hedley is astonished. "The more heavily theological my sermons are," he says, "the more interest the girls show."

And yet some wonder aloud whether this enthusiasm for religion is the right kind. For every theologian pleased to hear about all those people going to church, there seems to be at least one who is worried because they are there for the wrong reason.

While Billy Graham prepares his crusade, the Reverend James

Pike, pastor of the Cathedral of St. John the Divine, a huge
Episcopal church in upper Manhattan, is preparing an article for
the September issue of *Coronet* magazine. "For many," he will say,
"God is something to be used. If it is a sense of peace and tran-
quility one lacks, 'God' is perceived as quite as good as—or better
than—a sleeping tablet or a tranquilizer." Worse, Pike believes, the
clergy themselves have bought into all the comfortable material
traps of 1950s America. "Our highest praise these days for one of
the cloth," he says, "is not that he is a holy man, but that he is
efficient. We talk eagerly of statistics, modern conveniences, debts
paid off, development funds, but rarely do we hear a comment
about growth in things of the spirit."

Most people, of course, are not thinking about religion one way or
the other. They are thinking about summer, and about family vacations. Many of them are already on the road. *Time* magazine draws
their portrait and it is a reassuring one. *Time* looks out across the
country and sees "mothers navigating from well-folded road maps,
and children racing the heat to finish their ice cream, with the head
of the family snaking along the parkways and turnpikes, spiraling
down cloverleafs that weren't there last year, digging deep for tolls,
for souvenir pillows and plaques."

Not only are the highways new and still a little bit unfamiliar but
the cars are as well. This is the second year of the styling revolution
that converted the big boxy sedans of the early 1950s into long,
low, sleek cruisers, and for many people, there is still something different and special about them. Detroit is selling that difference for
all it is worth. "The most striking thing about these cars," Chrysler
says, "is their exhilarating newness." They symbolize the fast pace
and constant change that are said to be facts of present-day life.

They are, in effect, being sold as jet planes. Witness the ads
for the 1957 "swept-wing" Dodge: "It unleashes a hurricane of
power. It breaks thru the vibration barrier. It is swept-wing mas-

tery of motion." To drive one, Dodge insists, is to "step into the wonderful world of auto dynamics."

But these cars are not just dynamic—they are luxurious too. They represent a luxury and affluence that few in the postwar middle class envisioned even four or five years ago, a popular luxury that reduces the difference between a Chevrolet and a Cadillac, a Ford and a Lincoln, to a question of degree, and not very many degrees at that. A Lincoln is just a frilly Ford, and at some level of consciousness practically everybody knows it, even the people who buy Lincolns. "You can live like a king," one Ford ad says, "in a king-size cruiser—without paying a princely price." Chrysler tells you the same thing: "Never before has it been possible to own so much glamour and prestige for so little."

And even as families take their first vacations in these machines of modern affluence, the marketing of the 1958 models has begun. General Motors has already bought the air time on a Sunday evening in October for its two-hour television special celebrating the company's fiftieth anniversary. It will be called "The Pursuit of Happiness."

Ford is doing something far more dramatic: it is bringing out a brand-new car. Nobody has seen it yet, but George Walker, the Ford engineer who created it, is more than happy to talk about the Edsel concept. "Beauty," he says, "is what sells the American car. And the person we are designing it for is the American woman. A woman is naturally style conscious from birth . . . she wants beauty on wheels. We've spent millions to make the floor covering like the carpet in the living room."

That means making it soft, thick, and light brown. For some reason this is the year of the beige in home floor covering. Designers are reaching for their dictionaries to come up with new variations on basic beige: nutria, sandalwood, pecan. Gray has gone out of favor after a run of several popular years.

More than likely, the new beige living room carpet is surrounded on all four sides by pastel walls of one shade or another. Pastels are the answer to many of this year's decorating questions: pea green, ocean blue, muted yellow, and pink. Blue has not been popular as a wall paint color for twenty-five years, but this spring it made a comeback, the bold new leader in the pastel revolution. All over America, walls are suddenly being painted light blue, not only in living rooms but in the family rooms of the year's best-selling split-level suburban homes.

It seems as if everything in the home is going pastel. All sorts of things that used to come only in white are becoming part of the pastel color scheme. Refrigerators are turning pink and turquoise. Light bulbs are pink, pale blue, and pale green. The plumbing industry reports that the use of pink fixtures is up 14 percent in 1957; yellow is up 8 percent. For a nominal cost, millions of families are even acquiring pastel pets—birds in blue, green, and yellow that occasionally make a recognizable sound.

Maybe pastel living rooms are, as some of the ads insist, more relaxing for the tired commuter at the end of a long day. Certainly they carry a hint of the informality and casual living that the split-level house of 1957 is supposed to engender.

In fact, *informality* is a popular word this year in fashion as well as in home furnishings. Men's sport shirts are outselling dress shirts two-to-one; a decade ago the ratio was exactly the opposite. Women's dresses have become softer and looser. The latest hit this spring was the chemise, known officially as the "relaxed silhouette" and unofficially to male critics as the sack. *Vogue* calls the whole combination of trends the "second decade look"—looser fashions to replace the tight fits of earlier 1950s clothes. There is a lot of color in this year's female fashion: orange, yellow, brilliant blue, and emerald green.

More than just informality is painting chemise dresses orange and family room walls pastel blue; the desire exists to do something faintly exotic. The 1957 family likes a few hints of the exotic mixed into a conventional suburban life in a conventional suburban house. You find basement family rooms with the wet bar made entirely of bamboo and an eight-foot-wide Hawaiian mural stretched out behind it. In the living rooms of perfectly conventional middle-class people, you see sculpture from Africa and the South Pacific. It is as if, anchored in the limited happiness of suburban life, middle-class Americans wish to contemplate a different sort of good life somewhere far away, perhaps on a beach in the tropics, watching the sunset, drink in hand, the high-pressure, anxiety-generating life of the 1950s nowhere in sight.

Or perhaps in Spain. This past winter, the Barcelona Hotel opened in Miami Beach, offering an exotic escape to the urbanites of the cold American north. "Just for you," it promised them, "castles in Spain brought to reality." The Barcelona has the Flamenco nightclub, the Granada Room restaurant, the Don Quixote coffee shop, and the Bravo Bar. The rate is $16 a night.

What its promoters did not realize, however, was how much business they would be doing this summer, when it is even more uncomfortable in Miami Beach than in Philadelphia or New York. There were 110,000 visitors to Miami Beach last winter; it now looks as if the summer total may reach 90,000.

It is a different crowd. The average age of the winter vacationer in Miami Beach is fifty-eight; the average age so far this summer is twenty-six, and the majority of those checking in are single women, traveling in pairs or groups. They are taking advantage of a summer package deal: $104 buys airfare, seven nights in the hotel, three meals a day, and a free bottle of suntan lotion.

To do any of these things—drive a swept-wing Dodge, live in a house with thick beige carpeting, check in for a week at the Barcelona—is to live in luxury that is still a kind of fairy tale to the young American adult. It is to participate in a miracle of modern capitalism. Some go further and say that the ordinary middle-class American of 1957 is a capitalist himself.

Keith Funston says that all the time. He is president of the New York Stock Exchange and the nation's foremost exponent of "people's capitalism"—the theory that the clerk or factory worker who uses his savings to buy a few shares of blue-chip stock is not only helping the securities industry but strengthening America against the threat of hostile economic doctrines that infect societies abroad.

This year, many of the major American corporations are echoing Funston's views. "In a people's capitalism," General Electric explains, "everyone benefits from profits. Profits which benefit the many are at the very heart of America's competitive economic system. Millions of people from all walks of life—not just a wealthy handful—own America's businesses." The Northwestern Mutual Insurance Company has an even simpler definition. "Anyone who owns a life insurance policy," the company proclaims, "now is a capitalist." America is one wide-based capitalist community.

It is a miracle indeed. But can it last? It is not just the middle-class mortgage payer who is asking this question. The titans of people's capitalism are asking it too. They didn't expect the boom of the mid-1950s any more than the ordinary citizen did. And they have the same tendency to pinch themselves in the night and wonder if they might be dreaming.

They received a jolt earlier this year when George Humphrey, the Cleveland manufacturer then serving as President Eisenhower's secretary of the Treasury, frightened most of the country by warning that if inflation and deficit spending were not controlled, the result could be "a depression that will curl your hair." Humphrey retired this month, delivering a valedictory that did its best to reassure those he had scared just a few months ago. He told the nation that he saw a "prospering America with . . . more and better jobs, more homes, more cars, more leisure."

But it is hard not to see the warning signs even in the midst of all the consumer luxury. Personal consumption might be setting new records, but the expansion of 1955 and 1956 is clearly slowing down. Corporate profits are not what they were a year ago, the stock market is sluggish, tight money is affecting the home construction industry, and—most worrisome of all—inflation is running at a consistent rate of nearly 4 percent.

The Scripps-Howard newspapers see fit to warn their millions of readers about the potential catastrophe hidden in the rapid growth of installment buying. American consumers, Scripps-Howard editorializes, "apparently haven't the judgment to see the possible disaster lurking in the nothing-down and a dollar forever debt." President Eisenhower himself is worried enough about the same problem to issue some words of advice to the middle-class consumer who might not realize how fragile the economic miracle happens to be. "Buy selectively and carefully," he urges. "We should not be spending recklessly and adding fuel to this flame."

And yet even the president knows that to accuse American consumers of spending money recklessly on baubles and trinkets is to stretch the truth. Attracted as they may be to thick carpets and sleek new cars, the Americans of 1957 are also investors. They believe in the future, even the distant future, and they like to spend their money on it.

There is no better example than life insurance. Some 115 million Americans own life insurance policies this year, 11 percent more than even a year ago. A full 57 percent of American families have every member insured; 86 percent have the breadwinner insured. This year, for the first time, the major companies are offering purchasers the opportunity to put the entire family on a single policy.

The insurance industry exists to sell the future and it does that very well. But so do all sorts of corporations. "It is always our duty to act for the long run," says Frederick R. Kappel, the president of AT&T. "In all our undertakings, the long view is essential."

Perhaps that is only rhetoric. But it is rhetoric that the American people respond to. All across the spectrum, businesses are reaching the consumers by arguing that there is something more important than the bottom line. Chase Manhattan Bank has been running a series of ads that feature a Norman Rockwell–style portrait of a Chase banker strolling to a café on Main Street in a small upstate New York town, chatting with a group of flannel-shirted regular fellows, a homespun symbol of community and authority at the same time. "A banker has to know a community inside out before he can give it financial guidance," the ad says. "So bankers live and work in the communities they serve. They share the ups and downs of home-grown economies. And they willingly accept the civic leadership placed in their hands by neighbors." This may be a world of turmoil and change, Chase Manhattan wants to tell us, but bankers, like other businessmen in American society, are reliable anchors against that change.

The argument for farsighted capitalism extends into corners of the economy where one would never expect to see it. Even a liquor company—classic purveyor of momentary pleasure—can jump on the bandwagon. "We make fine bourbon," says Stitzel-Weller, the manufacturer of Old Fitzgerald. "At a profit if we can. At a loss if we must. But always fine bourbon."

Anybody reading the ads that fill up America's newspapers and magazines and airwaves has to agree that this consumer economy is built on the long view—on solid things, products with a future. Products as solid as the steel in a brand-new Buick or Chrysler. Car models may come and go, but the steel industry behind them is selling stability.

Republic Steel believes in stability with a passion. "Steel is basic," the company tells us, "now and in the foreseeable future. Steel-making is a good life with more than three thousand different kinds of jobs. New and exciting methods are on the horizon. New chemistries of steel are being developed. New processes are being explored. All this activity means the creation of new jobs for ambitious men."

And steel means something else: an American economy with something reliable and permanent holding it up. "The low price of steel and steel products," Republic says, "is the foundation for every bargain we enjoy today—from pleasures such as canned music to daily necessities."

America's economic future is, for all the reassurances of Madison Avenue, a legitimate worry. For many people, it is a pressing concern even at a moment when there is so much bounty to enjoy and be thankful for. Of course, the economy is not the only problem they name. Some remain preoccupied with the Cold War and the mysterious intentions of the men in the Kremlin. Some worry about juvenile delinquency.

But if you take a close look at the anxieties of middle-class America in this early summer of a very good year, you find something else, something remarkable. Ordinary Americans worry most about worrying too much. They fear that they are neurotic. They complain that something about the pace of modern life is preventing them from reaping the pleasures that ought to be theirs.

If they don't notice it on their own, experts with the most impeccable credentials are on hand to tell them. This past spring, *Life* magazine ran a five-part series on modern psychology and its lessons for living. The author, Dr. Ernst Havemann, was in no mood to spare his readers the truth. "About a third of all adults are neurotic," Havemann declared, pronouncing this a conservative estimate. "Every expert knows that there are fewer completely happy people than there seem to be. . . . Some of the experts think civilization itself is the villain—that the human brain is simply unable to cope with the noise, speed and complexity of modern life."

While that series was running, Dr. Albert Ellis, the noted psychotherapist, was promoting his new book, *How to Live with a Neurotic: At Work and at Home.* Ellis offered statistics roughly comparable to Havemann's. "Almost everyone is neurotic to some extent," he concluded. "Three out of ten are so neurotic that they can sometimes be 'impossible to live with.'"

It is a vicious cycle. We begin to worry, we become preoccupied with worrying, and before long we are full-fledged neurotics, incapable of appreciating the sweetness of life and carriers of further neurosis to those we love.

Dr. Peter Steincrohn writes about this problem all the time in his syndicated newspaper column. His focus, he says, is on "apparently normal, loveable people who go about their business, minding their own affairs, providing shelter and food for their wife and children. Yet they get sick. Why? Because they have allowed themselves to become embroiled in the hurry, worry and scurry of modern life." Dr. Steincrohn believes that "tension puts an awesome strain on the pituitary and adrenal glands."

Other experts go so far as to proclaim that tension can kill us. The past year has seen a number of remarkable breakthroughs in the study of psychosomatic illnesses—physical maladies that neurosis ultimately brings about. Some specialists are now beginning to say that most physical ailments are psychosomatic at their source.

Among the most prominent exponents of this view is Dr. Hans Selye, the Viennese-born psychiatrist who is director of experimental medicine and surgery at the University of Montreal. Selye's conclusions are shocking. "Stress," he reported this year, is "the ultimate cause of the average person's death." If it were not for the stress of modern life, Selye has found, the average life span could be thirty years longer.

For middle-aged Americans just reaching the pinnacle of success, those are frightening words indeed. They call to mind all the stories one knows, all the recent obituaries one has read, of high-powered executives, men in their forties and early fifties, seemingly as healthy as ever, slumping over their desks with coronary thrombosis. It is enough to make one desperate, especially when combined with the documented fact that the average executive workweek is now fifty-three hours, far more than any psychiatric specialist believes is healthy.

Even if the busy executive manages to put aside fears of early heart disease, however, he is almost certain to spend some of his time thinking about ulcers. They are a topic of constant conversation this year at the cocktail parties of the upper middle class, a symbol of the price affluent America is being asked to pay for the postwar comforts it did not expect.

In some large cities, overworked executives can join ulcer clubs to commiserate with each other and soothe their stress-ridden stomachs. The club in Chicago meets every two months, under the direction of Dr. Heinrich Necheles, head of the Gastrointestinal Research Laboratory at Michael Reese Hospital. Dr. Necheles is no firebrand. He is a man of reassurance and practical wisdom. His advice is simple and easy to follow: "If your ulcer can't stand a cocktail," he says, "take a half-hour nap before you dine." Above all, he tells the businessmen, try to achieve some perspective. "Don't take yourselves so seriously. You are just motes in the eternity of the world."

But preprandial naps and perspectives on the cosmos are insufficient treatment for many anxiety sufferers in this oddly anxious year. The most conspicuous and most talked-about source of relief is a pill. Its rise to prominence has been startling.

It was only five years ago, in 1952, that the first tranquilizer was used on patients in mental hospitals. It was only in 1954 that the first two varieties, Thorazine and Serpasil, were made available to private physicians for prescribing at their discretion. But in 1956 alone, 35 million tranquilizers were prescribed in America—Thorazine, Serpasil, Equanil, and especially Miltown, the capsule that seems to be on the verge of reaching a status as the universal antidote to the tensions of present-day life.

Some of the nation's leading psychiatrists argue that people should begin using these pills before the stress becomes unbearable.

"Their most definitive use is as preventives," explains Dr. Anthony Sainz of the University of Iowa. "Severe mental disturbance usually begins when a behavior problem develops into a neurosis. If people would seek help early, one of the tranquilizers could do away with the symptoms, relieving the anxiety and irritability and keeping the neurosis from developing."

Tranquilizers are more than just a medication; they are part of the culture. This year, Warner-Chilcut began test-marketing Paxital, a tranquilizer for the family pet. "It could even save him from ulcers," the company boasted.

But there exists on the market a far more important tranquilizer than any being prescribed by doctors, a tranquilizer so familiar that many of us simply regard it as a necessity of life. It is, of course, alcohol.

It isn't the volume of our drinking; it's the curious way in which so many of us are growing obsessed with it, with the martini after work and the highball after dinner. We love to talk about our drinking, to make jokes about it, to tease each other.

Not long ago, a woman with seventeen children attracted national attention when, after being jailed for drunkenness, she emerged exulting that she hadn't had such a good night's sleep in years. Don Sherwood, a popular San Francisco disc jockey, likes to talk about his personal fantasy of "floating to Hawaii on a tide of martinis." As people pack up their cars for vacation this summer, a remarkable number of them are loading portable martini coolers in the trunk.

This preoccupation with alcohol is reflected even in the advertising of soft drinks. "Canada Dry ginger ale," the company's ads assure us, "will never dominate your highball." Drinking equipment is finding a respected place on the Christmas, birthday, and Father's Day shopping lists. A few months ago, one Chicago newspaper prudently advised its readers that "silver bar stools, cocktail pitchers and shakers are gifts that any host will appreciate."

One of the more popular movies this spring was *The Joker Is Wild,* a biography of comedian Joe E. Lewis, in which drinking is seen as the source of Lewis's downfall, but the whole subject is handled so ambiguously that one reviewer jocularly referred to the movie as an "alcoholocaust." Magazine profiles nearly always contain a paragraph or two about the subject's drinking habits. James Gould Cozzens, author of the best-selling *By Love Possessed,* pretty much stokes his creative engines on gin: "an ice-cold, bone-dry martini with lemon peel. Two at lunch, several at end of day, three beers at night."

There are medical, cultural, and religious spokesmen in America who warn that we are overdoing it, who point to the health statistics, the family quarrels, the lost work productivity in which the national infatuation with alcohol seems somehow to be implicated. Cirrhosis of the liver is moving up as a cause of death; it is now the number four killer of Americans between the ages of forty-five and sixty-four. Last November, the American Medical Association for the first time recognized alcoholism as an illness and recommended that its patients be admitted for treatment in general hospitals. Even so, for most of America's leaders, alcohol is simply a part of the comfortable life of the 1950s, and a respectable part at that.

Occasionally there are public arguments over the role of liquor in our daily lives. At the turn of the year, Rabbi Louis Newman of Temple Rodeph Shalom urged New Yorkers to begin 1957 by "calling a halt to the orgy of extravagance, folly and license" that had previously marked New Year's Eve, to "take stock of their days, not of their liquor larders," to remember that "the sight of our streets filled with inebriates is unpleasant" and that "religion stands for sobriety at all times." For those pains, he was rebuked by his Manhattan colleague, Rabbi W. F. Rosenblum of nearby Temple Israel. For his part, Rosenblum said he was tired of "all those blue-nosed religionists who want to take all the frolic and all the fellowship out of New Year's Eve."

In the months since then, in most of America, Rosenblum has

gotten the better of the argument. It is still possible to find thousands of clergymen, in the South and rural Midwest, in the more conservative Protestant denominations, who are willing to inveigh against the sin of intoxication. But in the more liberal pulpits of middle-class America, it is much more common this year to come upon pastors like the Reverend Carl T. Uehling, of St. John's Evangelical Lutheran Church of Newark, New Jersey. After all, Reverend Uehling told a group of fellow pastors recently, "Jesus Christ was a drinking man."

Of course, there is another convenient, if perhaps equally addictive, medium of escape from the tensions of modern life: television. The three major networks are riding high this year despite a raft of criticism about a mediocre set of programs. If the insurance companies like to sell the future, television has become supremely effective at selling the moment—its decision makers live as prisoners of the numbers provided to them each week by the Nielsen, Trendex, and Arbitron rating services.

Nobody epitomizes the compromises of the medium better than Ed Sullivan, the Sunday-night impresario whose variety show has been ranked second in the Nielsens for most of the year. He is the ultimate conformist, a happy slave to audience opinion and public taste. "Your rating," Sullivan said a few months ago, "is the entire expression of your work."

This spring, Sullivan proved conclusively that he lives by his doctrines. He signed up the entire New York Metropolitan Opera Company for five appearances and proudly presented the first four. But when he realized that the fourth show, a performance of *Tosca,* starring Maria Callas, had cost him six Trendex points against Steve Allen on NBC, he abruptly canceled the fifth and last appearance. The Met's director, Rudolph Bing, was outraged. "I have met the worst musical illiterate in the world," he said.

Last year, of course, Sullivan did something even more dramatic. Determined to reap the rating points of Elvis Presley's national television appearance but claiming to be worried about conservative reaction, he gave a classic demonstration of his wisdom. He ordered the cameras to show Presley only from the waist up—the gyrating hips were left to the viewer's imagination. It was a Nielsen smash.

The show also survived the scrutiny of the CBS censor. All three networks employ censors to judge the appropriateness of regular programming, and these men are not afraid to exercise their authority. Earlier this season, a skit about a lecherous Santa Claus was ordered removed from a Christmas comedy special. There are some strict rules for advertisements as well: no American flags shown in commercials, no toilets in cleaning ads, no athlete's foot commercials during the dinner hour.

The NBC censor, Stanton Helffrich, whose formal title is director of continuity acceptance, is more than willing to talk about the nuances of his work. This year, for example, he is spending a great deal of his time sanitizing westerns. "Instead of all that killing," Helffrich says, "we prefer wingings and nippings in the arm and leg. There is no reason for bad grammar, and the good guy and the bad guy could just as well shoot it out in front of the post office as in the local bar."

But Helffrich's most ingenious intervention of the season involved a dance presentation of Salome and the Seven Veils. His instructions to the director were remarkably precise: "Dress her in a flesh-colored leotard. Have the camera pan on her neck. Then, once everybody knows she's wearing something under the veils, you can go to town."

For better or worse, Stanton Helffrich understands what the American mind of 1957 is all about. We do not seem to know what to think of sex. We want to be entertained by it, to be teased with it, and then to have the object of temptation removed, in a gesture of conspicuous prudishness, before any real social damage can be done.

For the first few months of the year, a controversy raged in

Hollywood over *Baby Doll,* Elia Kazan's film version of the Tennessee Williams play about a nineteen-year-old married child-woman who sucks her thumb, sleeps in a crib, torments her sexually frustrated husband, and ultimately is seduced by the husband's friend. Cardinal Spellman of New York called the movie "revolting and morally repellent" and the Catholic Legion of Decency placed it on the list of forbidden films. Joseph P. Kennedy did not allow it to be shown in any of his twenty-three theaters.

But the fact remained that *Baby Doll* was available to any adult who was interested in seeing it. Moreover, for most of the weeks that *Baby Doll* was being screened all across the country, Grace Metalious's novel *Peyton Place,* exposing lust and hypocrisy in a small New England town, was ranked first on the national bestseller lists. "I know about small towns," Metalious said at the height of the book's popularity. "A rock in a field may look firm, but turn it over and you'll find all kinds of things underneath." As the summer begins, there seems to be no letup in the national appetite for tantalizing movies. There are popular movies about drugs (*A Hatful of Rain*), sin in the suburbs (*No Down Payment*), and vicious gossip-mongering (*The Sweet Smell of Success*).

America seems to be perched uneasily this summer between prohibition and tolerance, looser than in any recent time about letting itself be teased by sex in print and on the screen, befuddled about just where the line should be drawn but determined to draw it somewhere.

One significant decision seems to have been made: the country has concluded that Elvis Presley—lip sneer, gyrations, ducktail, and all—is something less than an immediate threat to public morals. A year after his appearance on the *Ed Sullivan Show,* Elvis has worked his way into the cultural mainstream. He still attracts some intense anger—composer Sigmund Spaeth recently called his music "a reversion to savagery" that "shows the violent and illiterate age we're in"—but there are fewer comments of that sort than there used to be, and Presley's upcoming military service, apparently manipulated as a public relations maneuver by his manager, is about to further soften the singer's image. Meanwhile, Hollywood is showing or getting ready to show *Don't Knock the Rock, Rock Pretty Baby, Rockabilly Baby,* and *Jailhouse Rock.* Only the last of the four is an Elvis movie.

Of course, much of the entertainment industry would still prefer a more wholesome young star to promote, and in Pat Boone, it looks as if they have found one with some potential. Handsome, polite, religious, conservatively dressed, married and the father of three children at age twenty-two, Pat Boone is being touted as the presentable alternative to Elvis. His records are selling well, he made the cover of *Time* in June, and theaters across the country are about to show *Bernadine,* a movie in which Boone stars as a misunderstood but unmistakably decent teenage boy who fantasizes about cars and girls but never places an inappropriate hand on either one.

But for most American adults, in this spring of 1957, another young man in his twenties proved a more compelling role model, and he was not an entertainer. He was a quiz-show contestant.

For eight weeks, starting in January, a twenty-nine-year-old Columbia University English instructor strained and grimaced and shyly smiled his way through round after round of challenges, earning the unbelievable sum of $129,000 on the question-and-answer show *Twenty-One.* Charles Van Doren was the first such contestant to become a genuine national hero. Something in his quiet determination, grace, and humility made an obvious point about what young American manhood in the 1950s might be at its best. One of his opponents, Ruth Miller, called him "the teenagers' parents answer to Elvis." By March, he had received hundreds of marriage proposals in the mail. It seems like the cleanest kind of fun. Only a college classmate of Van Doren's, refusing to be identified, manages to suggest that there is something disturbing about it all, even to the hero himself. "Charles," the classmate says, "has strong opinions on the debasement of values by commercialism. But he can't condemn commercialism now. He's under a kind of Faustian pact with the devil."

The hankering after role models, whether Charles Van Doren, Pat Boone, or Elvis Presley, reveals the depth to which America is worried about its young people. Arrests of persons under eighteen in America are up 17 percent this year over 1956. No one really knows what will happen two or three years from now when the huge crop of immediate postwar babies turns adolescent. It is a frightening prospect.

Two years ago *juvenile delinquency* was a term largely reserved for use by social scientists. This year it has sprouted ominously into national attention. The subject has been all over the newspapers and the national magazines this spring and has become the focus of an increasing number of movies. It is even about to reach Broadway: As the summer begins, Leonard Bernstein is conducting rehearsals for his play *West Side Story,* a musical about teenage gang wars in Manhattan with a plot based on *Romeo and Juliet.* Countless friends urged Bernstein not to do the project, telling him it was "a show full of hatefulness and ugliness." But he has persisted, and it is on schedule, due to open in September.

The U.S. Senate now has a Subcommittee to Investigate Juvenile Delinquency and in May it issued a report. The problem, according to the subcommittee, is not a shortage of recreational facilities, or poor housing, or even low economic status. The problem is weak family life and too few psychiatrists and social workers to handle its consequences.

A few weeks after the report's release, *Newsweek* weighed in with a cover story on juvenile delinquency that sounded positively alarming. "Today's teenage gangs," the magazine said, "take killing in stride ... they join the National Guard and steal a .45 automatic;

they even have submachine guns." *Newsweek* speculates that the sanctioned violence of World War II somehow started the trend toward youth gangs and advocates a sustained national effort to put a stop to them. "If we could get the same cooperation the Salk vaccine got," says Boston Juvenile Court Judge John J. Connelly, "we'd lick the problem."

The country is full of school officials who believe the solution to delinquency is an unwavering hard line—that you can't let teenagers dress, talk, and act as they wish and expect to keep them under control. You have to exercise some old-fashioned authority. During this past school year, in Mount Vernon, New York, a twelve-year-old boy named Arthur Ebert charged his music teacher with assault after the teacher picked him up by the scruff of his neck, threw him into a corridor, and slapped him until he required hospitalization. At trial, the teacher said the boy had slouched at his desk and had been generally insubordinate. Mount Vernon City Judge John P. Griffith ruled in favor of the teacher, citing Proverbs chapter 23: "Thou shalt beat him with the rod and shalt deliver his soul from the netherworld."

But those who advocate a softer line have some conspicuous successes to point to. There are, for example, key clubs, a network of teenage organizations dedicated to fighting delinquency by enlisting the "key" members of each class in a high school to declare themselves against delinquency. In the school year just ended there were 1,443 clubs in the country, boasting 33,892 members. The number one key club goal for 1957 was to stop vandalism. "We pledge to abstain from any form of vandalism," the members in Dallas promised, "and earnestly recommend that others do the same." A full 95 percent of Dallas teenagers signed the pledge and it is said that vandalism is down considerably.

Then there are the one-man anti-delinquency crusades. In Holyoke, Massachusetts, Bill Dean, the principal of Holyoke Trade High School, fights delinquency every morning by personally cooking breakfast for the school's 275 male students. "Give a boy a full stomach before he goes to class," Dean says, "and he'll think of his work in positive terms." Dean insists that his pancake breakfasts have virtually eliminated tardiness, absence, and suspension from the school.

Coronet magazine is even more impressed. "With skillet and understanding," the magazine says, "this gentle, soft-voiced principal seems to have stemmed the tide of wise guys in black leather jackets and Hollywood haircuts who are making a shambles of many of the country's schools."

Like most magazines in America, *Coronet* is always on the lookout for success stories, for people who manage in challenging circumstances to promote the best in family and community life. In every issue, for example, it salutes a "Mother of the Month" who has demonstrated solid achievement both at home and in the broader world.

The issue about to go to press right now honors one of *Coronet's* own freelance writers, a woman who, the editors say, somehow "manages to outlast three children, ages eight, four and one, and still have energy enough to write fascinating stories such as the one on page 135 of the August issue." That particular story, "With Love We Live," is about two mental patients who fell in love while confined to an institution. Its author, and the *Coronet* mother of the month for August 1957, is Betty Friedan.

Summer is beginning peacefully in Elmhurst, ten miles west of Chicago, where thousands of freshly arrived suburbanites are finding that there is too much to do at home to allow the luxury of a vacation. For those who have bought homes in Brynhaven, the town's newest and most heavily advertised subdivision, there are basements to finish and, despite the unwanted early heat wave, there is digging to do in the front and back yards. The most common form of socializing is the barbecue, provided you can get hold of one of the new grills and learn how to use it without setting the patio on fire. As if the barbecue craze were not spreading fast enough, Soukup's Hardware on York Road is offering Elmhurst residents free barbecue lessons this month and throwing in free steaks from Otto's Meat Market, "to acquaint the public with the family fun of covered barbecue cooking."

Nothing very exciting is going on in town, and Elmhurst works hard to make a virtue of that. The council is preparing a celebration for mid-August, when it expects to mark the community's one-thousandth consecutive day without a traffic fatality inside its borders. "We've been using many gimmicks to keep death away," the public safety director says.

Elmhurst did get a rare burst of embarrassing publicity a couple of months ago, when York High School students organized an assembly performance by a black singing group from Bronzeville, on Chicago's South Side, then had to cancel it because none of the suburb's hotels or motels would allow the group to stay overnight. Elmhurst doesn't like that sort of thing; it considers itself an enlightened, progressive community.

But the incident came as neither a surprise nor a cause célèbre in Bronzeville, whose residents are used to having the indignities of segregation imposed on them amid the routines of daily life. Being denied hotel rooms is only one of those indignities, and a relatively small one at that: far more worrisome this summer are the difficulties that even affluent Bronzeville blacks confront in finding space in Chicago hospitals and public schools, which still operate on what amounts to a Jim Crow basis. This past year, nearly three-quarters of Chicago's children attended schools that were either 100 percent white or 100 percent black.

Bronzeville is celebrating some small victories this summer, however, and feeling optimistic about change. A year-long crusade by the *Chicago Defender,* Bronzeville's newspaper, has forced the products of black-owned businesses onto store shelves all over the city. Last month, A&P, Kroger, and Walgreen all began carrying Baldwin Ice Cream, whose manufacturer likes to call it "the pride of a people." And nearly everyone is looking forward to the opening of Dunbar High School, across the street from Olivet Baptist Church, in the old heart of the community. The fact that Dunbar will be all black is less important to most people than the fact that it is a state-of-the-art facility, the most impressive building the Chicago Board of Education has ever built in a black neighborhood. The newspapers make a point of referring to it as "$7-million Dunbar High School."

Meanwhile, preparations are underway for this summer's annual Bud Billiken Day, the parade and festival that is the symbol of the vitality and hope of black Chicago. More than 500,000 people will picnic and play in Washington Park from dawn to dusk on an August Saturday; there will be 30,000 marchers, 75 floats, and 50 bands. Jackie Robinson will be the guest of honor.

If it is a summer of hope for Bronzeville, however, it is also a summer marked by fears that violent confrontation may be the price of advancement. A few months ago, Jesse Booker saw his home pelted with stones after he moved from Bronzeville to Garfield Park, a neighborhood west of the dividing line that separates black and white Chicago. Even more ominous was an event that took place in March. Alvin Palmer, a black high school student who lived near Bronzeville's western border, strayed one night to the distant and all-white Southwest Side, and was challenged at a bus stop by a gang of teenage thugs. An argument followed, and Palmer, seventeen years old, was beaten to death with a hammer.

Even for a community accustomed to insults and violence, the murder of Alvin Palmer was a genuinely terrifying event. What sort of place had he ventured into, the residents of Bronzeville wanted to know. What sort of people were these?

In fact, the murder was as frightening to the inhabitants of St. Nicholas of Tolentine parish, where it occurred, as it was to those of Bronzeville. On the night of the murder, police dragged teenage boys out of bowling alleys and ice-cream parlors all over the neighborhood and demanded to know whether they knew anything that would help find the killer. Within a couple of days, they had enough information to arrest Joseph Schwarz, a drunken high-school dropout and notorious bully with whom the parish was already far too familiar. In short order, Schwarz was tried, convicted, and sentenced to fifty years in prison. If the members of the parish had been allowed to vote on his sentence, however, it is very likely they would have chosen the death penalty.

It is not that the residents of St. Nick's parish are comfortable with the idea of integration, or even with the presence of unfamiliar black faces on their neighborhood streets. But what they fear most in the world is disorder—any set of events that threatens the hard-won lower-middle-class lives that seem to them not only precious but very fragile.

PART II

PARISH

CHAPTER 4

Bungalow People

"St. Nick's parish, 6 rm brick—beautiful."

I t was possible to read an advertisement like that in the summer of 1957 and understand instantly just what was being offered and why it might legitimately qualify as a thing of beauty.

The ad was for a bungalow. St. Nick's was in the middle of the Bungalow Belt, the world of tidy little one-family homes that extended west from the edge of the black ghetto all the way to the Chicago city limits. Most of these houses were built in the 1920s, in the wave of construction that had created the Southwest Side and given the term *Chicago bungalow* a precise architectural and social significance. More than fifty thousand of them went up in Chicago between 1921 and 1929, and a whole new generation was being erected in the 1950s; the Southwest quadrant of the city was now a sea of single-story bungalows, block after block of them, small and square, with tiny but exquisitely maintained front lawns. There were hundreds of these houses in St. Nick's parish alone.

They were long and narrow, most of them really brick variations on the old "shotgun house," built on lots as much as 130 feet deep but only 24 or 25 feet wide. They were extremely close together: 6 feet usually separated the wall of one home from the wall of its neighbor, but the pitched roofs hung over as much as 24 inches, so often there was just 2 feet of sky between the tip of one family's bungalow and the tip of the next.

Nearly all these bungalows were built out of two kinds of brick: the more attractive "face brick" for the front, and the soft, coarse Chicago common brick on the sides. Besides looking cheap, common brick had the unfortunate characteristic of retaining heat in the summer. Late on a steamy August evening, you could walk down any bungalow block and see men out in their undershirts, hosing down the side of the house to make the bedroom a few degrees cooler.

But nobody thought the appearance of the side of the house to be much of a problem. The bungalows were so close together that one had to make a special effort even to notice the side of the building. Driving down the street, what you saw was one front after another, and the fronts, clean and well-laid in dark-brown brick by Swedish or Italian immigrant masons, always looked good.

There were several distinct variations on the Southwest Side bungalow, even during the brief construction heyday of the 1920s. There were bungalows with a large, open front porch, built during the first few years of the decade. There were simple square boxes, built after the open porches went out of fashion, in 1924 and 1925. And there was the octagon bungalow, with a bay window, often in stained glass, bending out gracefully toward the sidewalk and the neighborhood. You could buy one of these in 1957 for about $15,000, and one decent income from the railyards or the police department or the mixing line at Nabisco was enough to pay the mortgage. The octagon bungalow was the pride of a parish like St. Nick's. *Beautiful* is not too strong a word for it.

St. Nicholas of Tolentine wasn't one of the biggest Catholic parishes in Chicago, but it was a world unto itself. Its territory was sixty-four square blocks of urban neighborhood, from Fifty-ninth Street south to Sixty-seventh, and from Kedzie Avenue west to Pulaski Road. It had once been much larger, but the area had grown so rapidly in the postwar years that two new churches, Queen of the Universe and St. Mary Star of the Sea, had been carved out of its original boundaries.

Even at its more compact size, the territory that comprised St. Nick's parish had a population of fifteen thousand. Nearly all of those inhabitants were Catholic, and the vast majority of them attended mass at St. Nick's every Sunday and sent their children to the parish elementary school, where fewer than twenty nuns taught a thousand pupils.

St. Nick's had a reputation on the Southwest Side as an Irish parish, but it was mainly the priests who gave it that reputation; the parishioners themselves were a diverse mixture of Irish, Polish, Germans, Italians, and Lithuanians. Some of them had memories of earlier days in other parishes populated exclusively by people from their own home country, but those days were long gone by the 1950s. St. Nick's was the ultimate in white ethnic diversity.

It was a neighborhood about as wide in its job base as in its ethnicity. The Southwest Side was no one-industry town. The people of St. Nick's were policemen and firemen, pipefitters and steamfitters, workers in the Clearing railroad yards and at Midway Airport, only a mile away, the busiest single airport in the world. And they worked in the factories that had given the Southwest Side a self-image as "the candy capital of the world"—Kool-Aid, Cracker-Jack, Tootsie Roll—and Nabisco, at Seventy-third and Kedzie, where more than two thousand people turned out Oreos and Mallomars, chocolate chips and Lorna Doones. You could smell Nabisco in the morning in half the neighborhood.

For those who remembered the stockyards, it was not that bad a smell. Most of the jobs were hard physical jobs, and some of them were no more than semi-skilled, but they produced a middle-class family living. In St. Nick's parish, one could be a laborer by day and a happy bourgeois property owner at night. "Those were really clean jobs, for factories," one of the children of the Southwest Side remembers. "My mom would come home smelling like raspberry Kool-Aid. All you had in the air at Kool-Aid was sugar dust."

Most of the residents had not been in the neighborhood that long. Before World War II, they had lived in dank apartment buildings further east, Back of the Yards, or in nearby enclaves such as Pilsen or Brighton Park. St. Nick's parish was a giant step up from those places. It wasn't the suburbs, but it was home ownership, and decent space, and brick walls, ten inches thick, instead of rickety old wood. It was a comfortable front porch, instead of a front door that had to be placed one floor above the ground just to keep the entrance out of the mud.

In the old neighborhoods, many of these families had lived in "two-flats," old brick buildings with one apartment upstairs and one downstairs, and sometimes a third living space in the basement. Often these buildings had housed entire extended families, with half a dozen people putting their wages into the mortgage; sometimes, the family that bought the place rented out both upper flats, lived in the basement, and used the double rent to make the monthly payment.

The move to a Southwest Side bungalow was a move away from all that— away from uncles and cousins under the same roof, away from having to cater to renters, away from the immigrant experience in general. It was a move to a one-family house, with at most a widowed parent or in-law in residence. It was a move to a home where you didn't have to worry so much about the noise your children were making, or the noise someone else's children were making upstairs.

What it was not was an escape from the public world of urban family life. Your neighbor's children might not be pounding on the floor above your head, but they were just on the other side of the wall, a few feet away. You couldn't really avoid them; it was vital to get along.

The octagon bungalow had its share of amenities. Besides the stained-glass bay window, there was oak trim, a fireplace in the living room, and a built-in breakfront in the dining room to display the special-occasion dishes and other family keepsakes. But in the end you could not forget that it was a shotgun house: entry straight into the living room, then dining room and kitchen directly behind it, with one tiny bedroom off the dining room, and two other tiny ones back behind the kitchen.

In large families, one of these back bedrooms was simply called the "boys' room," and all the male children slept there, in bunk beds, with linoleum on the floor and in most cases a crucifix high above them on the wall. The "girls' room" normally had a throw rug in place of linoleum, flowery curtains in the windows, and a picture of the Virgin Mary on the wall. Sometimes the girls' room had bunk beds, but more often the daughters of the family just slept side-by-side in as many conventional beds as were necessary to house them. No matter how large the family was, there was only one bathroom in the house, and everyone waited turns to use it, in a sequence that could feel like forever on a winter morning or a busy Saturday night.

For many families the bungalow was made even more confining by an extreme reluctance to use the front room for anything but a special occasion, so that the little dining room and kitchen were all that was left for group activity. Most of the time, it was the kitchen table that was the real social center of the house, the place where children did their homework, where husband and wife conferred about the family accounts, where next-door neighbors were entertained over coffee in the morning or a shot of whisky at night.

It was a crowded setting for a family of two adults and three or four children, an interior space within which none of the inhabitants could ever really expect to have more than a few feet of turf to themselves for more than a few minutes at a time. For the typical homeowner, the move west to a bungalow in St. Nick's parish brought with it a whole array of satisfactions and pleasures. But personal privacy was not really one of them.

In many ways, the most important living space for these families lay just beyond the walls of the house. Almost all the bungalows built in the 1920s had an imposing array of front stoops—big stone ledges along the stairway from the porch down to the sidewalk, often as many as three levels on each side of the building. Close to a dozen people could sit in front of the house on a summer evening, conducting several conversations at once, or just watching the traffic on the street. It is hot until well past dark in Chicago from early July until Labor Day, and the Southwest Side, miles from any hint of a lake breeze, is the hottest part of the city. In the 1950s, there were no air conditioners in these bungalows to draw people indoors on the long, hot evenings. The front stoop was the place to catch whatever semblance of fresh air might be found. Everybody was out there. "You could have gone down the alley," one resident remembers, "and walked in the back door of every house and robbed people blind. Everybody was out on the front porch."

The front stoop was an entertainment center as well, a social space that, at least until the middle years of the decade, managed to hold its own against the indoor encroachment of television. For kids, in the first hour or so after dinner, it was a place to perch and wait for the ice-cream truck, whose arrival on each block signaled a mad dash from stoop to street and back again.

For kids, though, there was another extension to the house, and that was the alley in the back. All the bungalows backed up into an alley, which was functionally a trash pickup lane but also a recreation center where baseball, football, or virtually any game could be converted to a field of play not much wider than a bowling alley. At a time when dozens of school-age children lived on a single Southwest Side block, the alley could attract huge crowds of competitors, and it could attract them all summer and into the chilly autumn months, long after the adults had come in from the front stoop. The alley was a virtual Main Street of bungalow childhood.

As winter approached, playing in the alley increasingly meant playing in an environment of coal dust, because the coal that heated nearly all these bungalows lingered in the air from November until almost May. You could smell coal in the neighborhood, especially on an overcast day; in the late fall, coal dust brought darkness even earlier than it would otherwise have come.

It was a tacit assumption in the alleys and on all the streets of the neighborhood that one child's parent was every child's parent, equally responsible for the behavior of the children on the block, and equally authorized to mete out small doses of justice. Boyhood quarrels in the alley or acts of petty vandalism were handled by the parent who happened to be nearest to the scene. It didn't occur to any of the families that a particular parent down the street might have different ideas about discipline than they did; when it came to discipline, everyone on the block worked from the same assumptions. These common values were what made mutual parenting possible in an urban neighborhood in the 1950s and they form a stark contrast to parenting in the generation since then.

Not that there wasn't considerable anxiety about discipline and what might be happening to it in the relative affluence of postwar life. Most of the young parents in the neighborhood felt their authority over their children was less imposing than their own parents' authority had been over them; they worried about juvenile delinquency, even in a place where the crime rate was, by today's standards, startlingly low.

In the mid-1950s, parents on the Southwest Side were not only thinking about delinquency but asking their children to think about it as well. In 1955, the Fathers' Club at Lindblom, the nearby public high school, sponsored an essay contest entitled "Youth Combats Delinquency." First-prize winner Jeri McGovern wrote as a traditionalist: "Please do guide us," she pleaded with parents. "Don't let us go it all alone." Runner-up Arnoldene Macerak reflected the currents of change that both generations were feeling: "Even though young people have to be disciplined," she argued, "the day of the whip is over."

But if crime and delinquency were an issue, the fact remains that St. Nick's parish was a safe place in the 1950s, a place where doors could be left unlocked with no fear of consequences, where guns were extremely rare and random personal violence was all but unknown. One read terrible stories in the *Southwest News-Herald* about robberies on Sixty-third Street or family quarrels that led to shootings, but to most people in St. Nick's parish, they were just stories. They were news precisely because of their rarity. In a big city they were bound to happen here and there, but for most residents such events were not part of the currency of neighborhood life.

There was a white ethnic underclass on the Southwest Side made up mostly of drifters who dropped out of high school, joined gangs, hung out in Marquette Park, and did their best, like Joseph Schwarz, Alvin Palmer's killer, to look for trouble. But most of their fights, in an era long before the flood of firearms, were rumbles only a step or two removed from the ritualized ballet of *West Side Story*. People were hurt, but hardly anyone was killed. Modern gang violence was simply not a presence on the streets of the parish.

For one thing, those streets were being monitored during all the waking hours of the day by the informal law enforcement system of the neighborhood, the at-home mothers who devoted much of their time to keeping it glued together. Some of the women did work, more in fact in this area than in the affluent suburbs, because budgets were often tight on one working-class salary. There were office jobs for women at most of the factories, or at the counters at Midway Airport. The majority, however, were home. If they missed the blue-collar life that many of them had known as "Rosies," as replacement workers during World War II, they did not say so, and they do not say so now. Caring for the family and the neighborhood seemed to them highly meaningful work.

St. Nick's was a word-of-mouth neighborhood, and it is remarkable just how powerful a medium of communication word of mouth could be. The church didn't need a bulletin and the school didn't need a newsletter—anything that had to be known, good news or bad, could be transmitted through the entire square mile of the parish in just a couple of hours. "When they talk about networking," says Martin Barry, a Cook County judge who grew up in St. Nick's, "those women in the fifties were a tremendous network."

All these years later, we have difficulty accepting the connection between the warmth that characterized urban neighborhood life in the 1950s and the intrusiveness that went along with it. The feelings of safety and familiarity that existed for those growing up in St. Nick's parish were in part created by mothers who stayed home and knew more about what teenagers were up to than the teenagers wanted them to know. Many of those teenagers reached maturity convinced that emancipation from prying neighborhood eyes was as great a gift as adulthood could possibly bestow. That a neighborhood free of this sort of intrusiveness can be a cold and alienating sort of place is a lesson that these same baby boomers have been very slow to learn.

St. Nick's parish had two commercial centers: one on either end of Sixty-third Street, at Kedzie Avenue on the east and at Pulaski Road on the west. If most Southwest Siders identified themselves with parishes in those days, a significant number also identified themselves with street corners. Hardly anyone said, "I come from Chicago Lawn," or West Lawn, or West Elsdon. What they said was, "I grew up around Sixty-third and Kedzie," or "I come from Fifty-ninth and Pulaski."

Those particular corners were just the sorts of places A. J. Liebling was talking about when he referred to Chicago as a city of "endless factory town main streets." Sixty-third and Kedzie had the standard equipment of neighborhood commerce: a Walgreen's, a Kresge's, and a locally owned men's store facing each other on corner lots, with a shoe store, a sporting goods store, a candy store, a grocery, and a movie theater, all independent and locally owned, within a block or so. A little further down the street was Marzano's Palace of Pleasure—forty-eight lanes, three full floors of bowling, one set of alleys right on top of another.

It was hard to go more than a few days in the neighborhood without needing or wanting something at one of the two commercial corners. Commuters, schoolchildren, and housewives did their business there because it was familiar and comfortable and because it was hard for them to get any place much farther away. The Southwest Side was geographically isolated from most of Chicago in the 1950s—you had to take three buses to get downtown, for example, and except at rush hour, the bus service could be agonizingly slow. Many families in St. Nick's parish went downtown exactly once each year: to see the Christmas decorations in the State Street stores. Otherwise, they stayed close to home, grumbling occasionally about their isolation but treating it as a fact of life. The neighborhood merchants, of course, liked this situation. In the 1920s, when there had been talk of extending the Chicago El all the way west to Kedzie, they had fought it, and they had won.

Most of the people in St. Nick's owned cars, but nobody drove to the stores. Early in the afternoon on every weekday, the sidewalks of Sixty-third Street echoed the tinny song of shopping cart wheels rolling along the pavement, as women dragged them to the grocery store and back home. Later in the day, kids as young as five and six traced the same route as they trooped down to the store for a fresh loaf of bread. The mom-and-pop groceries sprinkled through the area usually gave credit when necessary. They recorded each family's debt in a black account book, one family per page, no interest charged. On paydays, at least some of the debt was expected to be paid off.

On Monday and Thursday nights, Sixty-third Street was crowded with knots of local residents who came out to window shop and make conversation, whether they intended to buy anything or not. Late shopping nights were a neighborhood social occasion, an important element of the word-of-mouth network. They were a mechanism for making contact not only with fellow shoppers but with the merchants who were neighborhood institutions themselves.

The very act of shopping was embedded in the web of long-term relationships between customer and merchant, relationships that were more important than the price of a particular item at a particular time. The sense of permanence that bound politicians to organizations, or corporations to communities, reached down to the most mundane transactions of neighborhood commercial life.

Once or twice a week, most housewives in St. Nick's parish rolled their shopping carts to Bertucci's Meat Market at Sixty-fourth and Pulaski to stock up for a few days and to trade gossip with Nick Bertucci. They weren't making much of a price sacrifice: in the summer of 1957, Bertucci was selling porterhouse steak for 99 cents a pound and pork chops for 89 cents, which was competitive with the nearest supermarkets.

Many of Bertucci's customers believed that by shopping with him, they were getting higher-quality cuts of meat. In fact, there was very little difference. Bertucci bought his roasts and chops from the same suppliers that the A&P used. But the relationships, the first-name treatment that Bertucci offered shoppers, constituted a permanent investment that the people in the neighborhood wanted to make, whether they were maximizing their short-term gain or not. This was one situation in which the consumers actually had a reasonable amount of choice. Shoppers could buy their meat at Kroger, A&P, or Jewel, or they could patronize any of three or four other small meat markets relatively close to home. But most of them preferred to make a selection and stick with it, reaping the benefits of custom and stability that today mark people as relics in a market-driven world.

The grocery stores and the meat markets were not the only establishments that based their livelihood on personal relationships. So did the big-ticket merchants: the sellers of cars, appliances, and furniture.

The retail furniture business on the Southwest Side, for example, was built on a whole web of sturdy relationships: buyer-to-store, store-to-wholesaler, even store-to-store. On Sixty-third Street east of Kedzie, at the far end of the neighborhood from Bertucci's Meat Market, Lindon Furniture sold sofas and bedroom sets to the families of St. Nick's parish. Many of its customers were newlyweds who brought in their parents to help with the decisions. Price mattered. Elick Lindon used to invite customers to browse the furniture floor at Marshall Field on the promise that he would match what Field was quoting. But in the end, trust was usually what cemented the deal. "If somebody liked you, trusted you, believed in your quality, they were pretty loyal to you," says Bill Grice, who was the store's top salesman during those years.

Beneath those transactions, stores like Lindon Furniture were built on another set of relationships, with the factory representatives who came in every two weeks to make recommendations and take orders. There were no computers to help with the buying decisions; the merchant pretty much had to trust the supplier to give sensible advice and not to stick him with expensive sofas that he couldn't sell. And there was a mutual interest in honesty: the supplier knew that a string of bad recommendations would jeopardize the relationship and cost the manufacturer dearly in the long run. "There was a big trust factor from the retailer to the factory salesman," says Grice. "You could pretty much go by what he said."

There were dozens of small- to medium-sized furniture stores on the Southwest Side in the 1950s and all the owners knew each other. They met every Friday morning at the Chicago Furniture Mart, where they went to talk to suppliers, look at new models, compare notes about advertising and promotional gimmicks, and to drink coffee and gossip. Not all of them liked each other—it was a tough, competitive business and store owners were always worrying about what the guy down the block was thinking up to outwit them. But it was a business built, for better or worse, on personal relations.

A few blocks south of the St. Nick's parish border, at Seventy-third and Kedzie, stood the Nabisco plant, a great gray battleship of a building, opened just after World War II, when Nabisco consolidated its small-scale bakery operations on the old West Side and moved into serious mass production.

By the mid-1950s, there were two-thousand people working at Nabisco on the Southwest Side, making cookies, pretzels, and crackers. The men were bakers and mixers; the women worked in the packing department. The plant ran twenty-four hours a day, three full shifts.

If you were a mixer, your job was to propel butter, sugar, salt, and baking soda in thousand-pound batches into 2,000-pound mixing bowls. If you were a baker, you fed the mixed dough into one of five ovens, each 200 feet long. Packing was a much lighter and cooler job, but it was even more tedious. It meant stuffing cookies into boxes all day or all night long, seven hours and ten minutes of work, with twenty-five minutes off for lunch, a ten-minute break toward the beginning of the shift, and a fifteen-minute break toward the end. If you were on the day shift, you showed up at 5:30 in the morning, and walked out of the front gate at 1:30 in the afternoon.

In the late 1950s, factory employees of Nabisco were all paid less than $2 an hour—a great improvement over the maximum wage of 80 cents in 1946, but no princely sum for so hard a job.

Nabisco was not exactly a neighborhood factory. Many of the people who worked there had come over from the old West Side bakeries and commuted across the city to the new plant on Kedzie. A large proportion were Italians who wanted to continue living where they had always lived. Still, as the years went by, more and more people who got jobs in the plant had a Southwest Side connection, and many of those new employees lived within the boundaries of St. Nick's parish.

Inside the plant, as in the world of retail business, life was a web of relationships. Whole families worked there, some of them the legacy of mom-and-pop bakeries Nabisco had bought out decades before. Some families had two and even three generations inside the plant. Nepotism was not only accepted but fundamental. A young employee who misbehaved would frequently be taken aside and warned that his conduct was jeopardizing the long-term employment possibilities of all his relatives.

Management had its own rules of relationship. Virtually all the foremen and production managers had come off the lines themselves; Nabisco promoted from within the plant to encourage harmonious relations. The man supervising you on the mixing line might well be a man with whom you had worked side by side a decade before. If the system led to some painful jealousies, it led to powerful loyalties as well.

Some of those loyalties were reflected in old-fashioned rules of corporate paternalism. When a worker called in sick, the Nabisco medical department called his house. After two days, they sent a nurse. Some of this routine reflected concern for employee health; some of it was undoubtedly snooping to guard against truancy. But it was a measure of the communal quality of blue-collar life even in a mammoth industrial plant with two thousand people on the payroll.

All this communalism clearly had its bad points. Corruption was the most notable among them. The Nabisco workers were members of the Bakery and Confectionery Workers, a union so close to management that it continually negotiated sweetheart contracts that failed to bring workers the wage levels they would have obtained under a less cozy arrangement.

And that was not the worst of it. Some of the top officials of the Bakery Workers International, based in Chicago, were embezzling union funds. The president, James Cross, had more than once borrowed money from a top executive of a baking company and then returned the favor by letting up on an organizing drive or contract dispute. The union was exposed publicly during hearings of the U.S. Senate rackets committee, and in 1957 the Bakery and Confectionery Workers of America were thrown out of the AFL-CIO. It was only in 1959, when a reform faction took the Nabisco local into a clean union, the rival American Bakery and Confectionery Workers, that the employees at Seventy-third and Kedzie began getting decent representation.

Even for those who fought against corruption in the union, however, the 1950s at Nabisco stand out in memory as a time of decent working conditions and genuine fellowship. "It smelled good. They gave you uniforms. It was clean," says Joe Prieto, who started the 1950s on the mixing line at the Kedzie plant and ended the decade by being elected president of the local on a reform ticket. "Everybody got along. Everybody was happy. Everybody in that plant was family."

Here the social balance sheet is fairly easy to draw up: on the one hand, steady jobs, lifetime work, opportunities for friends and relatives, camaraderie on the mixing line; on the other hand, a set of union leaders who were robbing the membership blind. These were old-fashioned family values at their most enticing and yet most treacherous. In families there is warmth, and there is also favoritism, inequality, and manipulation of the unsuspecting. At Nabisco in the 1950s, there was no shortage of authority. It was merely that the authority was crooked.

Today, at Nabisco, as in nearly all industrial plants of its sort in America, there is no Jim Cross living in luxury by skimming off workers' dues. The indignities are those of the market: low real wages and benefits, transience, amd limited personal contact among those who do the work. If you ask modern factory workers whether they would rather be victims of old-time personal labor corruption or modern market economics, they waste little time in nominating the market as the more terrifying evil by far.

Every Friday night, many of the workers at Nabisco and other nearby factories performed one of the rituals of Southwest Side life in the 1950s: they went to make their deposit at Talman Federal Savings, the financial fulcrum of their newly won middle-class lives. Talman was where they kept their savings, and it was, for nearly all of them, the holder of their mortgage. Friday night at Talman was a social occasion. It was always crowded, no matter what time they went. There were long rows of couches all over the enormous lobby, and nearly all of the seats were occupied by people who had stopped to talk.

On Fridays near the end of each quarter, the scene in the lobby was even more hectic. Talman customers by the hundreds came in to have their quarterly dividends stamped in their savings passbooks. There was no real need to do this, since the dividends were added to their accounts automatically. But few Talman savers wanted to miss the personal experience. The quarterly dividend was tangible evidence that they were accumulating wealth, however slow the process might be.

Ben Bohac, the legendary founder and chairman of Talman Federal, milked these occasions for everything they were worth. He hired Rudy Wasek to play the "Third Man Theme" and other old favorites on a zither in the lobby. Sometimes he brought in the choir from St. Gall's Catholic Church, across the street. Quarterly dividend time was a community celebration.

A generation later, with Talman merely a division in the much larger La Salle National Bank, shorn of its independence and its personality, it is difficult to convey just what this one S&L meant in Chicago in the 1950s, and the symbolic importance it had for the people in St. Nick's and the parishes around it.

In 1957, Talman was the seventh-largest savings and loan association in the United States, and the largest located outside a downtown financial center. More than 80 percent of its $200 million in assets came from first mortgages on single-family homes. The block-long building at Fifty-fifth and Kedzie, opened by Bohac in a gala ceremony in 1956, was the biggest individual S&L office anywhere in the country.

Talman's size was in part a function of Illinois law. Illinois was one of only two states that still did not allow branch banking, so the big downtown commercial banks could not open offices on the Southwest Side. Neighborhood residents who wanted a mortgage from one of these banks had to trudge down to La Salle Street, to the main banking office. Hardly any of them wanted to do that and there is no evidence that the bank officers were eager to see them. "For the average working man to walk into a bank downtown was too much," recalls Stanley Balzekas, a Southwest Side car dealer. "You can't get a guy from Harvard or Yale to talk to a guy that hadn't shined his shoes in three weeks."

Ben Bohac not only catered to the humble bungalow buyers of the Southwest Side but seemed, at times, to worship them. Bohac believed in his ethnic customers with a passion that made him a

Midwest version of A. P. Giannini, the Italian immigrant who built the Bank of America in California. On the banking floor at Talman, as long as Bohac was in charge, it was always possible to find someone to wait on you in Polish, Slovak, or Czech.

It was widely believed among Talman customers that Ben Bohac had never foreclosed on a mortgage in thirty years of doing business. That was a myth; he had foreclosed on plenty of them during the Depression. But other legends about Bohac were indeed true: that he had started his business out of the kitchen of his apartment, naming his bank after the street he lived on, and knocked on neighborhood doors to convince people to trust him with their money; that he had kept the financial records in Bohemian for the first seven years; that he used to go out in his Packard to kick the bricks of a house before agreeing to lend money on it; that he could call the leaders of the Illinois legislature and discourage them from passing any bill he thought inimical to S&L interests; that he spent each working day at a desk in the middle of the Talman banking floor, greeting borrowers by name and asking what he could do to help them.

It was not just money that Bohac was determined to lend to his customers; it was an entire outlook on life. Year after year, Talman Federal spent a fortune taking out full-page ads in the Chicago newspapers, each presenting a little moral essay or lesson in economics for the benefit of the community Bohac liked to call Talmanville. There was more sermonizing in the pages of these ads in 1957 than there was from the pulpit at St. Nick's. If, in some of the more fashionable precincts of Chicago, the 1950s were the decade of Hugh Hefner and the Playboy philosophy, there is no question that for a much larger portion of the city they were the years of Ben Bohac and the Talman philosophy.

Talman was not shy when it came to advising its depositors about how to conduct themselves. The bank prided itself on "looking beyond the houses we lend on, into the lives and circumstances of the people that live in the houses." What it told them was profoundly conservative: put the money away, avoid extravagant consumerism, and get out of debt the minute you can. "When Talman makes a loan to you on your home," the bank explained, "you and Talman become partners, for the primary purpose of clearing your home from debt as soon as possible. We want you to pay as little interest as possible until you get clear out of debt. . . . Everybody wants to get out of debt. And when you show people how to do it, they do." Bohac took personal pride in the fact that while the average Talman mortgage was written to last eighteen to twenty years, half of them were paid off within six years.

Bohac's little essays liked to joke about what he called the "Bohemian easy repayment plan"—100 percent down. "We put the Bohemian label on it," the bank explained, "because the Bohemians, notably, know how to have fun being thrifty. A Bohemian is a guy who owns a three-flat building, takes off his shoes in the house, and goes to the savings and loan every Friday night." Bohac may have been poking a little fun at his neighbors, but there is no question that he was also seeking to validate their style of life and to recommend it to others—not just to make money for Talman but as a form of lighthearted moral instruction.

The Talman philosophy was tinged with populist resentment at the downtown banks and reminders of the superior virtue of the hardworking bungalow dweller: "Ordinary, humble people, accustomed to being 'pushed around' by big financial institutions, have found at Talman a respect for their personal dignity, their intelligence, and their good sense. . . . The great mass of quiet, inconspicuous people have more means, as well as more sense, than they are usually given credit for. We know these neighbors of ours pretty well, and we are proud of them. A poor person who can save money shows extraordinary strength of character—and such people don't remain poor very long."

For the residents of the Southwest Side in 1957, Talman Federal Savings was a symbol of community, a voice of authority, and a highly successful business all at the same time. And it was an engine

that generated seemingly unlimited self-confidence and optimism.
"All things considered," the Talman sermon writers proclaimed at
year's end, "no people on earth ever had it so good as we have here
and now, in Chicago. How thankful we should be."

These sorts of comments crop up all through the public record of
the 1950s, interspersed with fears about the bomb and juvenile
delinquency and the stress-creating pace of postwar life in general.
Earlier in 1957, *House Beautiful* had proclaimed that "our era,
despite its imperfections, is the most widely and deeply enjoyed
golden age of all time." Not long before, *Life* had reported that
"millions of Americans were purring with contentment"; *Time*
declared the United States to be a country "in which fear and fret-
ting were made ridiculous by the facts of national life."

The most interesting thing about these statements is not their
excess but that nobody would dare say anything similar today: not
the editors of *House Beautiful,* not a minister from a pulpit, not a
politician seeking reelection, not even a banker seeking deposits.

What does it mean that people talked this way in the 1950s and
somehow expected to be believed? Was this society in group
denial, suppressing things it knew all too well about the dark side
of America, simply in order to participate in a middle-class con-
sumerist charade? Or could we say something more charitable—
not that the 1950s were a golden age, on the Southwest Side of
Chicago or anywhere else, but that they were a time when life as
it was seemed so much better than life as it might have been.

Imagine being thirty-two years old in 1957, having grown up in
a Chicago two-flat somewhere Back of the Yards, spending your
first dozen years watching members of your family and those
around you losing their jobs and, often, what little savings they had
managed to accumulate. Imagine, if you were a male, heading
straight from high school to boot camp in 1943, followed by a long
solemn ride to Europe or the Pacific; or, if you were a female,
going straight from high school to a defense production line, tight-

ening bolts hour after hour, separated by an ocean from the boyfriend you had hoped to marry, without any guarantee that you would see him alive again. Imagine the excitement and chaos of life in the months right after V-J Day, with unlimited dreams but shortages of everything and all the experts predicting an economic slump that would rival the Depression of the 1930s.

Then take one ten-year leap and imagine living in an octagon bungalow in St. Nick's parish, paying off a Talman mortgage in monthly installments on a single blue-collar income, driving a new 1957 Chevrolet. It is no mystery and no slur on their sensibilities that these people believed the hyperbole that Ben Bohac dished out to them. Ulcers, juvenile delinquency, the threat of nuclear war—all of these were minor themes. The major themes were stability and confidence. They are themes that the baby-boom generation, middle-aged and younger, raised in affluent expectation and now living amid stagnant reality, cannot instinctively understand.

And so we dwell on the obvious flaws, on those segments of American society that got very little out of the 1950s. If you were a member of the Smith College class of 1952, intellectually vibrant and ambitious, graduated with honors in English or art history, and you found yourself five years later pushing a stroller each afternoon along the sidewalks of Scarsdale, waiting to meet the 6:15 train; or, for that matter, if you were the young ad executive coming home on that same train, working compulsively, drinking too many martinis, worried sick about losing an account or a promotion; or, certainly, if you were a black high school student in a big city, reading about jobs in banking or law or journalism and gradually finding out that these fields were closed to you—if you were any of these things, the boosterism of Ben Bohac was bound to ring hollow.

So much of what has been written about the 1950s over the last couple of decades has been written for the express purpose of proving the good things a mirage. And that work has been done well. We have just about convinced ourselves that a majority culture that denies opportunity to a significant fraction of its people cannot be a decent one, no matter how well it serves the aspirations of everyone else. But what standard are we measuring postwar America against? Has there ever been a society that provided prosperity, opportunity, and optimism on an equal basis? Is equality of discontent somehow preferable to a stable and comforting middle-class majority culture with blind spots? Americans did pay a price for the lives they led in the 1950s, but that does not excuse us from the responsibility of measuring that price against the benefits that accrued.

In drawing up our balance sheet for 1950s America, we need to examine the holes in its assumptions of contentment. But that the contentment was real—and widespread—is a truth that needs to be remembered as well. Majorities, however unfashionable or inarticulate, have a right to be heard. It is not the place of the historian or the critic to mock the comforts of ordinary people.

CHAPTER 5

The Flock

Saint Nicholas
Room 206
1953

There are 1,100 seats in the main sanctuary at St. Nicholas of Tolentine church, and on Sunday mornings in 1957, most of them were filled every hour on the hour: at seven o'clock, when the nuns attended and Monsignor Fennessy sometimes presided; at nine, when the parish children filed in and arranged themselves next to their school classmates; at noon, when the stragglers got their final chance to avoid starting the new week on a sinful note. Among the people who lived in the parish and considered themselves Catholics, the vast majority were there at some point on Sunday.

But when it came to the mass itself, they were simply spectators. They were there to sit quietly and watch. The priest celebrated mass in Latin, facing the altar, his back to the congregation. The choir did all the singing. At the appropriate moment, the communion bell rang and parishioners were permitted to step forward, kneel on a red cushion, and receive in their mouths the wafer that was the body of Christ. An altar boy hovered next to them with a huge silver platter to catch any pieces of the wafer that happened to fall.

For the parishioner, there was no participation, no individuality, no choice. Individual empowerment was a concept even more foreign to the traditionalists in the pulpit at St. Nick's than it was to the Cook County Democratic Party or the blue-collar employers of the Southwest Side. Hierarchy existed, in religion as in other institutions, for the express purpose of removing the burden of choice from the individual. Today, we laugh at that idea, but in the late 1950s, at St. Nick's and at parishes like it all over urban America, it was simply the way things worked.

To the older parishioners at St. Nick's, the church itself was something of a miracle. All through the 1920s and the bleak Depression years, they had worshiped in a "temporary" basement sanctuary while Father Fennessy had maneuvered for the funds to build a permanent church. In 1937, improbably, he came up with the money and won the permission of the archdiocese to start construction. The work was done largely by the unemployed men in the neighborhood. On May 7, 1939, it was dedicated, a dignified and imposing red-brick building in fourteenth-century Perpendicular Gothic, one of the last traditional churches erected in Chicago before World War II halted construction and modern architecture changed all the rules of design.

Over the front entrance was chiseled the name of the saint in whose memory the church had been established. Few of the worshipers knew much about St. Nicholas of Tolentine, but he was not an inappropriate choice for a parish such as this one. He had been an urban priest, called to help the city-states of thirteenth-century Italy cope with a period of bewildering change and turmoil. "Nicholas," a church pamphlet once explained, "worked to counteract the decline of morality and religion which came with the development of city life."

He could be a symbol of something else, as well: assimilation. An Italian saint, his name translated into English, serving as the patron of a church in which Irish priests ministered to Roman Catholics of almost every conceivable European ethnicity. St. Nick's was the sort of parish that George Cardinal Mundelein, the legendary archbishop of Chicago, had dreamed about in the early years of the century as he searched for ways to break up the immigrant parochialism that had established parishes of, by, and for single nationalities. "It is of the utmost importance," the cardinal had declared in the 1920s, "that the nationalities gathered in the United States should gradually amalgamate and fuse into one homogeneous people." St. Nick's in the 1950s was about as close to that vision as American Catholicism would ever get. It was the classic "post-immigrant" parish.

It was also considered a plum assignment for any young priest. "It was a solid, rock-ribbed Catholic area," says Father Robert Dovick, who arrived there at the end of the decade. "The schools were filled, the bills were being paid. It was a good reliable parish— like Sears Roebuck. It would always be open." At St. Nick's, there were hardly any desperately poor people and no alienated rich who had fallen away and needed to be lured back into the fold. This parish was full of people who were glad to be at mass every Sunday, expressing their gratitude for the comforts that had been unexpectedly bestowed upon them.

After the mass and the gospel reading, the parishioners listened to a sermon—a relatively minor event in a church like St. Nick's, compared to what it was in most Protestant congregations at the same time. The archdiocese provided a weekly scriptural topic upon which each priest was expected to speak briefly. At a given moment on a Sunday morning, Catholics all over Chicago were listening to virtually the same sermon. In addition, however, each priest was allowed to deliver a homily, and those varied enormously according to the interest and temperament of the speaker. Sometimes they were friendly suggestions about how to improve relations with other members of one's family; sometimes they were reminders of which books and movies the Legion of Decency had declared inappropriate for Catholics during the most recent weeks; sometimes they were warnings against backsliding when it came to saying prayers or going to confession. Most of the time, though, one way or another, the homily had something to do with the subject of sin. "The push was that sin is everywhere," one parishioner remembers. "Satan is around the corner."

In the view of some of the more devout church members, Satan was around the corner in a very literal sense: at Hoffman's tavern, on the corner of Sixty-third and Hamlin, only a few hundred yards from the church door. Hoffman's opened at noon on Sunday and it was possible to be there within seconds after the sermon concluding the 11:00 mass, cleansed of the previous week's sins and ready to run a new tab. It was also possible, even more ominously, to tell a parent or a spouse that you were off to the noon service and then head for Hoffman's instead, arriving just as the doors were opening. "High Mass at Hoffman's" was what they called this particular brand of truancy.

Hoffman's was a typical corner saloon in ethnic Chicago—long, narrow, dark, and smoky, with a beckoning scent halfway between bourbon and perfume, a little intimidating to a stranger but downright cozy to a regular customer. It was a place John Fary could have walked into from his 3600 Club a few miles away and felt comfortable upon entry. It was, all but officially, the St. Nick's parish bar, the place where anybody in the neighborhood could find a card game or place a bet on a horse. Some of Hoffman's more daring regulars used to entertain themselves by doing imitations of Monsignor Fennessy, mimicking the unnerving crack in his voice. But there was nothing really anti-clerical about the place—some of the younger priests used to drop in for a drink now and then themselves.

One is tempted to say that had there not been a Hoffman's or its equivalent in every parish on the Southwest Side, the archdiocese would have had to invent them. To the children growing up in the neighborhood, to the workingmen who stopped by occasionally, to the regulars who found it hard to leave, these taverns were the everyday symbol of the temptation that lurked within the community and within themselves. In a wider culture that glamorized drinking, where entertainers joked of floating to Hawaii on a tide of martinis, alcohol in a working-class parish was, in its way, serious business. The Sixty-third Street bus stopped right in front of Hoffman's, and the neighborhood had more than its share of men who ducked in for a single quick one on the way back from the plant in the afternoon and lurched home hours later, headed for domestic trouble.

St. Nick's was a drinking man's parish; it was also a place where the priest could talk about sin from the pulpit and know he was calling up images of a particular saloon in many of the parishioners' minds.

For most of the men, however, there was a more respectable neighborhood fellowship institution: the Holy Name Society, the equivalent of a men's social club under parish sponsorship.

Holy Name, an institution that traced its origins back to Pope Gregory X in the thirteenth century, had been revived in New York and Chicago in the early 1900s as a way to keep grown men attending communion, to bring them together with other Catholic males rather than Protestants, and to help raise money for church activities. In some cities, Holy Name societies staged monster parades every year—thousands of men marching through the downtown streets to remind the Protestant establishment just how many Catholic votes there really were in the community.

For the most part, though, Holy Name societies functioned as little neighborhood fraternities. The one at St. Nick's was a typical example: a close-knit group of male church members who liked Father Joseph Lynch, the associate pastor and Holy Name spiritual director, and shared his passion for sports and cards.

To be a pillar of Holy Name was to take religious observance a little more seriously than other male parishioners. The members of the group attended mass and took communion together; at Easter time, when the Blessed Sacrament was exposed for adoration at a side altar in the church, the men of Holy Name took turns standing guard over it all night in ritualized half-hour vigils.

For most of the participants, however, Holy Name was primarily golf outings and bowling leagues, trips to White Sox games and father-daughter nights when stewardesses from Midway Airport came to discuss the attractions of an airline career. And it was the communion breakfast: the monthly mass meeting where as many as five hundred neighborhood men gathered to take communion and to listen to a talk by a Notre Dame athlete, an official in the Daley administration, or, once in a while, a touring Catholic celebrity who happened to know somebody in the parish. Jack Dempsey found his way to a Holy Name breakfast at St. Nick's in the 1950s. These were not haphazard affairs—at 5 A.M. on the morning of a Holy Name breakfast, twenty to thirty neighborhood women would be in the kitchen of the church preparing to cook bacon and eggs.

Women had their own social institution at St. Nick's—the Altar and Rosary Society—but it tended more toward work than entertainment. The Altar and Rosary women cleaned and decorated the church, took care of the vestments, and cooked funeral meals when necessary. Women who attended St. Nick's were more or less expected to contribute at least something to Altar and Rosary; the meetings filled the parish assembly hall to overflowing.

Social events were part of Altar and Rosary. Members got together in the afternoons to tour a rug-cleaning factory or listen to a luncheon speech by a downtown interior decorator. But these affairs did not play the role for parish women that the breakfasts and sports outings did for men. The chores were more important.

As, for many of them, was religious observance itself. These women of Altar and Rosary took the name of their organization and their devotional responsibilities seriously. From time to time they held a block rosary—a procession in which they carried a statue of the Virgin from one house to another, repeating the rosary at each place they visited.

St. Nicholas of Tolentine was typical of blue-collar urban parishes in that about two-thirds of the really active members—the ones who did more than go to mass on Sunday—were women. They practiced a Catholicism heavy on individualized devotion: saying the rosary, praying to the saints for guidance on a regular basis, and organizing novenas—formal weeklong prayer periods, usually focused on the Virgin.

What was sometimes called the "cult of the Virgin"—the central experience of Catholicism for millions of American women—was still going strong as the 1950s began. Indeed, 1950 had been proclaimed the official "Marian year," the year in which the pope issued a formal definition of the Virgin's ascension into heaven. All over urban America, women's groups such as Altar and Rosary celebrated the event. On the Southwest Side of Chicago, some parishes were forming rosary clubs, in which all who joined had to promise that two or more family members would say the rosary every single night.

Unknown to most of these parishioners, they were practicing a brand of Catholicism that was being called into question during those years by the rising generation of better-educated and more sophisticated clergy and laymen. The rosaries, the novenas, the unceasing pleas to the saints for help, all struck the new Catholic elite as a variety of superstition. "Immigrant Catholicism," it was called, or something worse: "ghetto Catholicism"—an obscurantist form of cult worship that stood in the way of Catholics being fully accepted in the American cultural mainstream. In Boston, in New York, in Chicago, the prosperous postwar Catholic elite now viewed the devotional practices of parishes like St. Nick's as an embarrassment.

Even more than the saints and the rosaries, however, these critics focused on the authoritarian character of the mass—the passivity imposed on whole congregations that simply took their seats and waited quietly as the priest, his back to them, droned on in a language they were not even expected to understand. What was needed, one of them wrote, was "to capture the ancient Christian sense of the mass as community." In other words, participation.

Thus, a decade and more in advance of the Second Vatican Council, the Catholic Church in every big American city was debating the question of liturgical reform, spurred on by its best-educated and most thoughtful adherents. And changes were taking place, changes that were slowly winning the sanction of the hierarchy in Rome. By 1956, the pope had issued a "decree for the renewed liturgy of Holy Week," allowing worshipers to file forward and kiss the cross instead of merely watching. On Holy Saturday, the day before Easter, all were allowed to light candles in the darkened churches. In 1958, Rome agreed to permit experiments with a dialogue mass, in which a priest would read the Gospel in Latin, but a lay "lector" would then read it back in English. The dialogue represented the first revision in centuries involving any lay participation in the mass.

■   ■   ■

By 1957, the Catholic Church was already in the midst of change, and the center of all this change and intellectual ferment was the archdiocese of Chicago.

In the mid-1950s, Chicago was to Catholicism what New York was to most other American institutions. It was the biggest American archdiocese, encompassing more than 2 million practicing Catholics, 400 parishes, 2,000 priests, 9,000 nuns, roughly 300,000 parochial school pupils. Between 1948 and 1958, the archdiocese opened an average of six new parishes every year.

As a focal point for ideas and activity, Chicago faced little competition, because the New York archdiocese in those years was under the personal domination of Francis Cardinal Spellman, who was preoccupied with anti-communism, local politics, and the suppression of obscenity. He had no interest in church reform, which he opposed in any case. In the spring of 1957, Spellman was devoting a large portion of his time to blocking the appearance of *Baby Doll* on New York movie screens, or failing that, preventing Catholics from seeing it.

In Chicago, on the other hand, Samuel Cardinal Stritch was tolerating, if not exactly endorsing, a whole series of liturgical experiments that essentially anticipated Vatican II. In 1957, while Spellman was denouncing *Baby Doll,* Father Reynold Hillenbrand of Chicago's Sacred Heart parish all but proclaimed revolution by turning the church altar around so that the priest would face the congregation. "Liturgical reform," a church historian would later write, "seemed to be spreading around the diocese like an infection."

The reformers were also instrumental in promoting the Christian Family Movement, an institution founded in Chicago that by the late 1950s had enrolled 30,000 married couples all over the United States. "Cells" of six CFM couples met once a week to discuss not only Catholicism but such issues as poverty, segregation, and the spread of nuclear weapons.

These protoreform efforts have been chronicled in detail in histories of the postconciliar church, and celebrated much like the

early civil rights protests that paved the way for Montgomery and
Martin Luther King Jr. They are presented, most of the time, as
inspirational tales offering reassurance about how even the most
hidebound institution can be led toward change.

And yet the church at the parish level in the Chicago of the
1950s was no dinosaur limping dejectedly toward its appointment
with Vatican II. It was a thriving, self-confident institution at the
peak of its influence. It was not searching for a new identity. It was
simply not very interested in change. It cared about tradition and
authority.

Father Andrew McDonagh was reminded of this lesson very
quickly when he came to St. Nicholas of Tolentine in 1955 as a
young associate pastor, author of a master's thesis on labor relations,
brimming with intellectual vitality and social liberalism. He did
not find St. Nick's receptive to his ambitions. "There was nothing
going on in the parish," he recalls. "No social action." He started a
unit of the Christian Family Movement but had to do it almost in
secret to escape the questioning of Monsignor Fennessy and Father
Lynch. He held nighttime religion classes for teenagers in the
church building and discovered that Monsignor Fennessy would
occasionally come by and turn out the lights at eight o'clock,
whether the session was finished or not.

One day in 1955, McDonagh and Fennessy traveled together to
nearby St. Gall's to attend a mildly innovative Christmas service
that featured the active participation of neighborhood children. As
they were leaving, Fennessy turned to McDonagh and observed
how pleasant it had been to see all the young people singing and
dancing. Then he squared his jaw and said what was really on his
mind. "There's one thing I want you to remember," he told his
young curate. "I loathe change."

Fennessy's opposition to change did not stem from any lack of
familiarity with it. He had been a boy in village Ireland in the
1870s, a seminarian in Baltimore in the 1890s, a young priest in

Chicago before World War I, ministering to a parish composed largely of immigrants like himself. By the 1950s he was an ancient monsignor, a dominant presence at St. Nicholas of Tolentine, where he had been pastor for thirty years, and whose impressive building he had almost single-handedly created.

To those who saw him, children and grown-ups alike, Fennessy seemed to be a creature not only of another era but another world. He spoke in a thick Irish brogue—"communion" came out more like "commoonin." He had a perpetual tear in his voice and a slight speech impediment brought on by a series of minor strokes in old age.

Fennessy did not project an image of power or control so much as a lordly spirituality. For decades he had walked the neighborhood day and night, dressed in a black cassock that reached down to his shoe tops. He greeted people on their front stoops and handed out dimes to children. On Sunday nights he would knock on parishioners' doors and stop in for conversation. "He glided around like a ghost," one child of the parish remembers. "He would appear everywhere. It was his personal fiefdom. He was in the playground, in the hallway, in class. He appeared on the playground, and the grab-ass would stop. He had that effect. He was lord of the manor, and there was no mistaking who was in charge." Fennessy represented authority of the most natural and unaffected kind, based on neither persuasion nor coercion, but simply on the identity and credibility of the person exercising it. It took generations of parish life in Europe and in America to create. It has taken only one generation to obliterate.

There was a quality of emotion about Fennessy's Catholicism, even a hint of superstition, that stood in total opposition to the ideas of the reformers at the archdiocese downtown. His intensity at prayer could frighten even the most devout altar boys. "He was mesmerized during the mass," one of them recalls. "He would go into a trance." At times, his ministry seemed to border on faith healing. He would lay his hand on the shoulder of an ailing or troubled woman and reassure her that everything would be all right. He believed in communication with the saints, although he was careful to define it properly: "We definitely do not pray to saints," he once told a local newspaper. "We merely ask them to use their special influence."

Michael J. Fennessy believed in social action, but it was social action limited to the narrowly defined world of St. Nick's parish. In the winter he bought coal for the poorest families in the neighborhood. That his priesthood might require him to do more than that, to reach out into other parts of Chicago and agitate for housing or racial justice, was an idea as foreign to him as the vernacular mass or the turning of the altar to face the people. He looked after his parishioners. If every pastor did that, then all the Catholics in Chicago would be accounted for. That seemed ministry enough.

Like Richard J. Daley, a man thirty years his junior but a product of the same "ghetto Catholic" environment, Monsignor Fennessy felt that sin was all around him, built into the fabric of individual human lives. His job was not to condemn it or to reform it away but to accept it and forgive it. This he did in the confessional with a generosity that only enhanced his reputation for saintliness. When it came time for confession, Monsignor Fennessy's booth was the one nearly everyone wanted to be in. "Don't worry," he liked to tell the parishioners when he saw them afterward. "Everything is fine."

The reason that Fennessy could exercise authority in the gentlest of ways was that someone else was there to exercise it with an intimidating bluntness. This was Father Lynch, who had been associate pastor at St. Nick's since 1938, and whom parishioners of all ages had learned not only to respect but fear.

The son of a South Side tavern owner, Joseph Lynch might have been attracted to any profession that allowed him to invoke rules and issue orders. It was easy to imagine him as a policeman or a drill sergeant. In fact, he had been a captain in the marines during the war. He volunteered for service as a chaplain after Pearl Harbor and hit the beaches of the Pacific with the troops for two years. When he returned to St. Nick's, he declined to talk about his war experience, but he seemed to have changed a great deal. His wavy pompadour had been replaced by a crew cut, he barked directions at people, and he lost his temper very quickly if they challenged him. "You could see he was a military man," recalls Chester Brzoski, who knew him at St. Nick's both before and after his marine service. "He had that air about him. It seemed that he liked the military, even war."

A fair number of Chicago parishes actually operated this way in the 1950s, with a saintly monsignor serving the spiritual needs of the congregation and a tough disciplinarian below him making the trains run on time. But St. Nick's may have been the ultimate in good cop–bad cop church management. Father Lynch remained there as associate pastor until after Fennessy's death in 1959, far beyond the time when he might have received a parish of his own. He took care of the finances, oversaw the operations of the school, and decided who the altar boys would be. Where the monsignor would smile and reassure his people, his associate would threaten them. "Father Lynch was always trying to find out who was doing right and wrong," remembers Bill Grice, who grew up at St. Nick's in the 1950s. "But he was mostly interested in wrong."

Personal privacy was not high on Father Lynch's list of values. He not only gave out the school report cards but shared the contents of them with other families, so that parents would know they could be held accountable semi-publicly for the children's poor performance. He would tell one family about the problems of another in which the husband was drinking too much. On weekend evenings in the summer, he would walk through the parish looking for teenage parties, barging in unannounced in his clerical collar and making sure there was no alcohol present. If he saw boys riding around in hot rods, he lectured them about it. There was never much of a line at his confession booth, and it was composed almost entirely of girls. The boys all knew that where Monsignor

Fennessy would merely ask, "Are you sorry for your sins, lad?" Father Lynch would demand to know all about them in detail. Sometimes he would do more than that. Once, when a boy entered the confessional to ask where the basketballs were, Lynch left the booth and thrashed him.

When he stood at the altar with his back to the congregation, Lynch seemed to have an extrasensory knowledge of what was going on behind him. When a parishioner tried to sneak out the door a few minutes early on Sunday, thinking perhaps of a quick dash to Hoffman's, Lynch liked to wheel around and humiliate him, telling him to get back in the pew where he belonged. He wanted the entire parish to hear everything he had to say: the requests for money, which Monsignor Fennessy never deigned to make, and the warnings about which books and movies the Legion of Decency was proscribing at that particular season.

If it was football season, Father Lynch didn't want anyone to leave the church before he could pressure them to attend the upcoming game. "We would like to have your attendance," he would say pointedly from the altar. The Catholic elementary schools played on Sunday afternoons in Chicago in the 1950s, and as far as Father Lynch was concerned, football was merely an extension of the religious service, and not a trivial part at that. He himself paced the sidelines at each game, arguing the referee's calls and passing around a cigar box for donations that had somehow escaped him during the morning collection.

All the Southwest Side parochial schools played football, but none took the sport more seriously than St. Nicholas of Tolentine, where the team's spiritual adviser demanded that it never lose, and where it rarely did. The trophy case in the school entrance hall was jammed with statuettes and the best players were held to a punishing standard of success. When they played badly, Father Lynch sometimes pulled them out of class for a lecture the next morning.

Virtually all the boys went out for football, even ones without a trace of athletic ability. Nearly all the eighth-grade girls were cheerleaders. The Holy Name Society bought the uniforms, which were kept in the basement of the rectory. Every winter, Holy Name held a sports banquet and showed a film such as *The Spirit of West Point,* or a similar one Father Lynch deemed appropriate. After the film, all the boys who attended were given an award. The seventh and eighth graders were given rosaries to remind them of their coming religious obligations upon graduation from the school. The younger boys all received gold footballs.

It was not always clear whether Father Lynch considered Rome a holier city than South Bend, Indiana, where the Fighting Irish won symbolic victories for their countrymen everywhere and for Catholicism. The St. Nick's team wore the Notre Dame colors, blue and gold, and the same style helmets. It was possible to board a train for South Bend at Sixty-third and Lawndale, just a block from the church, and Father Lynch led a Holy Name Society delegation to many of the home games.

In his fanaticism for football and competition, Father Lynch was not diverting himself from religious observance and faith—he was perfecting it. He was a sincere believer in the doctrine promulgated in 1924 by Father John O'Hara, then prefect of religion at Notre Dame and later archbishop of Philadelphia: "Notre Dame football is a new crusade; it kills prejudice and it stimulates faith. . . . It is a red-blooded play of men full of life, full of charity, of men who learn at the foot of the altar what it means to love one another, of men who believe that often play can be offered as a prayer in honor of the Queen of Peace."

It comes as no surprise to learn that Father Lynch had his enemies at St. Nick's parish, people whose behavior toward him was restrained only by the dignity owed his collar, and who felt emancipated when they heard, upon the death of Monsignor Fennessy in 1959, that a new pastor would be coming over from the archdiocese and Father Lynch would be forced to leave.

For all his obsessions, however, Joseph Lynch had his admirers as well. There were, of course, the men of Holy Name, the ones with whom he traded sports stories, played poker on Friday nights, and occasionally shared a drink at Hoffman's. There were the football players who swore they tried harder because they were terrified of him and who insist, forty years later, that once they developed the habit of trying harder at football, they tried harder at everything. There were the boys from huge, impoverished families who got into the best Catholic high schools because Father Lynch went to the principal's office and refused to leave until he was promised a scholarship for them.

Anybody who grew up in a Catholic parish in America in the 1950s remembers a Father Lynch, a disciplinarian with a short fuse and a streak of meanness. But in a larger sense, just about everybody who grew up in the baby boom knows him. He was the gym teacher who forced uncoordinated boys to do exercises they couldn't do; the shop foreman who took a sadistic delight in humiliating teenage summer employees in their first day on the job; the father who blew up at the dinner table at what seemed the mildest expression of dissenting opinion from the children's end.

Most of these people had one thing in common. They had been through some rough patches in life, years of Depression and years of war, and because of the war, many of them found themselves a few years behind, starting a career long after they would have been launched upon it in better times. Joseph Lynch was still an associate pastor in his late forties, under the thumb of the aged monsignor whose physical decline and inattention to detail he was perpetually having to cover for.

Few of these men seemed to regret their formative experiences, but one thing always angered them—and often turned them into tyrants. It was the easy complacency of the postwar kids who considered comfort and stability nothing less than their birthright, even in a working-class neighborhood like St. Nick's. Something embedded in the life experiences of all the Joe Lynches of the 1950s turned every smirking teenager and every daydreaming nine-year-old into an ingrate, oblivious to all the sacrifices that had gone into making the soft life possible.

We of the baby-boom generation will be having nightmares about Father Lynch—or some secular equivalent—for a lifetime. These men did a great deal to shape the attitude toward authority that blossomed in the 1960s and has defined individualism as a nonnegotiable right ever since then. The Father Lynches of the world gave authority a reputation it has yet to lose—and may not lose until all the postwar children who endured them begin to pass from the scene. The consequence is that an entire generation of Americans has found it difficult to think sensibly about the legitimate role that authority must play in any decent and civil society.

Even those in the neighborhood who felt less than comfortable with parish life, who quietly chafed at the tyranny of Father Lynch, sent their children to the St. Nick's parish elementary school. It was the equivalent of a neighborhood public school: more of the children in the parish went there than attended the real public school across the street.

Tuition at St. Nick's was virtually free. Each family paid two dollars a month and that covered as many children as the parents wanted to send. Those two dollars bought the educational services of eighteen nuns whose classrooms each contained more than fifty students. To look at a photograph of a St. Nick's classroom in those days is to confront an endless sea of faces, so many that it almost seems like trick photography. The vastness is only accentuated by the uniformity of their appearance: white blouse with red tie and Peter Pan collar for the girls, light blue long-sleeved shirt and navy blue tie for the boys. A child who showed up out of uniform was sent home for the day.

All these years later, what many of the St. Nick's students of the 1950s remember first is the waiting—waiting to recite, waiting to file into the cloakroom at the end of the day, waiting for permission to go to the bathroom after lunch. It could take an hour for fifty students to take their bathroom turns one at a time.

The philosophy of the nuns at St. Nick's, and in every Catholic elementary school in Chicago in those days, was that waiting was a form of learning. It was a way of acquiring discipline. The core idea of education in these schools was not teaching children to think independently. It was teaching them to execute—to acquire the discipline to do things in the right way. Thus, they were drilled endlessly in phonics, penmanship, and spelling, then taught how to diagram sentences. It was following directions that mattered the most.

When it was time for religion, all the students learned from the Baltimore catechism, a manual of questions and answers that called for rote memorization and Pavlovian responses when a question was asked. Who made the world? What is man? Where is God? Each called for a one-sentence answer that began and ended discussion on the subject.

Every Friday, most of the children of St. Nick's went to confession, where they admitted disobeying parents, fighting with siblings, using bad words, lying about their homework, occasionally lifting something from a store on Sixty-third Street. To atone for these sins they would be asked to recite a given number of Hail Marys or another familiar prayer. They would depart, most of them, feeling absolved, exhilarated, and ready to begin the cycle again.

And every Sunday morning, at nine o'clock, they would arrive for mass and sit together with members of their school class rather than with their families. That way, the nuns could take attendance.

Thinking about the nuns at St. Nicholas of Tolentine means confronting the issue of authority in its starkest form. They had all begun their religious vocations by taking vows of obedience, and they were required to be utterly subservient to the priests, both in everyday conduct and in following the letter of any law the priest chose to lay down.

Yet when it came to running the school, the nuns were given a virtual blank check. Priests in many parishes didn't even set foot in the school in an ordinary week. St. Nick's was a little different— Father Lynch walked over from the rectory fairly often to confer with the principal, Sister Ellen Marie, or to talk to one of the boys about a football game. He made sure that he was there to hand out report cards. Still, he observed the essence of the unwritten agreement of parish politics: as long as the nuns displayed appropriate deference on the proper occasions, they were free to run their classrooms any way they wished.

And so they did, some with a ferocity that stamped itself onto the memories of the children for life. There were nuns at St. Nick's school who treated discipline not only as a means of enforcing order but as an opportunity for their own self-expression.

One nun liked to collect a bunch of erasers, stack them on her desk, and fire them at misbehaving kids, which she did with unerring accuracy, scattering chalk dust for rows around. Children in other classrooms were sometimes asked to kneel on marbles, or eat soap, or scrape gum from the hallway stairs. One teacher liked to pull up a chair at the desk of an unsuspecting student and sit only a couple of inches away from his face.

Students could be punished by their teachers for things they did outside the classroom as well in inside. The nuns made it clear that residents of the parish were entitled, even expected, to come to the school to report any acts of suspected vandalism if they thought they knew who committed them.

Whatever the offense, however painful the punishment, there was no right of appeal to one's parents. The assumption of all St. Nick's families was that the nun was right, the punishment fair. "The nuns had almost complete control over you," says Bill Grice. "If they wanted to whack you or punch you, they could just do it.

The parents would go along with it, and if you complained, you'd be in trouble with your parents. A lot of the parents gave up their authority to the school and to the religion."

Besides, any parents who might have been tempted to side with a child in one of these disputes had a powerful incentive not to: if they showed up at the rectory to complain about one of the nuns, Father Lynch would simply throw them out. He kept to his part of the bargain.

If the nuns were obsessive about their teaching, it was understandable enough. Teaching was all they did in life; children were the only people they even saw on a regular basis. When the chapel bell rang at four every afternoon, the sisters had to be out of the school building and back in the convent for the thirty-minute evening prayer and meditation. When it was over, most of them turned to their evening task of grading papers and doing lesson plans until bedtime. The only interruption was dinner, for which the sisters arranged themselves at the table according to seniority, with the mother superior being served first and the youngest nun in the convent waiting until last.

The nuns at St. Nicholas of Tolentine were Adrian Dominicans, members of a Michigan-based order that followed the rule of St. Dominic. To the children who saw them every day, they were slightly exotic creatures, veiled visitors from another world, the aura of mystery enhanced by descriptions of them in religious handbooks as "brides of Christ" or "living saints to the community." In reality, they were working-class girls from Chicago and Detroit, most of them Irish, the children of autoworkers, pipefitters, and South Side cops. By policy of the order, the novices recruited from Detroit were sent to teach in Chicago, and vice versa, so their commitment to giving up mundane life would not be compromised by contact with old friends and family.

For the first three years after taking holy vows at age eighteen, an Adrian Dominican nun was not allowed to return home at all;

after that, she could go back once every three years, but she had to sleep in a nearby convent, not in her parents' house, and a companion had to go with her. The nuns in the St. Nick's convent could write home, but not to anyone beyond their immediate families except at Christmastime. They were not allowed to make any telephone calls.

For the teaching she did, an Adrian Dominican nun was paid a salary of less than $100 a month. This was not a serious issue. The necessities were all provided and there were very few opportunities for leisure. It was the willingness of these women to work long hours for meager wages that made the entire edifice of Catholic education possible. Yet for all the hardships, all the restrictions, at least one teenage girl a year from St. Nick's parish chose this life, cutting herself off from her neighborhood world forever.

It is impossible to isolate a single motivation behind such a choice. Some of these women, children of the Depression, had seen their mothers raising huge families on tight budgets, looking old and tired in early middle age, and even proclaiming at impossible moments, jokingly but suggestively, "I should have joined the convent." It wouldn't have been difficult for some of them to decide that anything was preferable to the home environment they remembered. To them, religious vows meant a lifetime of security, worth obtaining even at the cost of personal freedom. Other girls, in an age before birth control, saw an escape from more or less permanent pregnancy or a sexually demanding life that did not appeal to them. There was at least a modest working-class prejudice in 1950s Chicago against a woman who remained in the community and chose to be single; a nun, on the other hand, was admired for her saintliness. Parents were congratulated for having produced her.

For many girls, though, religious vows were a positive choice, a desire to emulate the sisters they saw as the most powerful role models in their early lives. Mary Ann Yanz, growing up around the corner from St. Nick's in the 1950s, used to watch the nuns at mass on Sundays and think about how lovely they looked and how happy they seemed. "There was a certain joy about the nuns," she says. In fifth grade she informed her teacher that she wanted to be a nun and was told she was too young to make such a choice. But at thirteen she went to convent school, at eighteen she had her white novice's veil, and at twenty-one she was off to Detroit, living in a convent there, teaching in an elementary school. She never knew how much she was paid; there was nothing to spend it on anyway. As for the restriction, the regimentation, the subservience to the priests, none of that really bothered her. "You just went along," she says. "That was the time, and you went along."

In the revolutionary aftermath of Vatican II, a whole literary genre grew up around memories of Catholic education at schools such as St. Nick's, a genre of angry memoirs written by graduates who felt humiliated by the rigidity of it all, scarred by the relentless determination of the nuns to enforce absolute conformity and stamp out any hint of individual expression.

"Nuns are generally sullen, suspicious cynics with a strong sense of savagery," John R. Powers wrote in his 1973 novel, *The Last Catholic in America.* "They aren't at all human. . . . We weren't a necessary part of their master plan to attain the eternal reward. We were simply annoyances strewn along the path to heaven." Powers was writing about St. Christina, a working-class Chicago parish not too distant from St. Nicholas of Tolentine, on the far South Side. The world he describes is a world of superstition and absurdity, a world where, in the view of the authorities, "even smiling was suspect."

For all the absurdity, Powers demonstrates at least a trace of affection for some of the characters and rituals. Others were more bitter. Robert Byrne, writing around the same time about a parochial school in a smaller midwestern city, shows no charity at all. "Sister Raphael," he writes, "was the opposite of friendly, with a face that was chiseled out of cold flint. To her each day was a grim fight, to the death if necessary, to impose absolute discipline on her enemies. . . . When she was slapping me I imagined her as a Nazi camp commander. That way resisting her efforts to make me cry became a high patriotic act. I saw her habit as a black military uniform and her ruler as a riding crop."

At the end of Byrne's novel, *Memories of a Non-Jewish Childhood,* the young hero's older brother returns home from military service and issues an order to the family: "Get him out of St. Procopius before he's ruined completely. That place is no good. It's like a nuthouse."

But the single most powerful piece of this genre, and by far the best known, is Christopher Durang's play, *Sister Mary Ignatius Explains It All for You,* performed all over the country during the early 1980s despite the futile protests of the Catholic Church itself. In Durang's play, four 1959 graduates return to confront Sister Mary Ignatius, their childhood tormentor. "We thought you were a bully," one of them says. "We wanted to embarrass you," says a second. "You used to take the point of your pencil and poke it up and down on my head when I didn't do my homework . . . and when I didn't know how to do long division, you slammed my head against the blackboard."

"You didn't do anything to me in particular. I just found you scary," a third alumnus tells her. "Well," says Sister Mary Ignatius, "I am scary."

No doubt some of the parochial school graduates of the 1950s who saw *Sister Mary Ignatius* had a few misgivings about it, perhaps winced at some of its viciousness, felt uncomfortable as one of the students exacted ultimate revenge by murdering the teacher. Still, it is accurate to say that the play reflects many of the feelings of the current middle-aged Catholic elite about their education in parochial schools in the postwar years. "More kids come to hate the church through its schools," the essayist Wilfrid Sheed wrote, "than through anything else that happens to them . . . kids can never remember whether something or other was fair or not, they can only remember injustices."

This literary portrait of the ordinary parish school has come down to us today—a portrait of injustice, stifling conformity, and endless clerical nagging. It is not only an indictment of the nuns and the schools—it covers the priests as well.

"Are you ready to die this very instant?" the character that Powers calls Father O'Reilly badgers his flock at "St. Bastion's" on a typical Sunday. "Were you on time for mass this morning? Have you been paying attention every moment to what has been going on up at this altar? Have you been keeping God's laws? Have you been saying your morning and evening prayers? Have you been taking care of your family? Have you been going to confession every week? Have you have you have you?" The inquisition never ends.

There is no point-by-point rebuttal to be made to this indictment of 1950s parish Catholicism. There is only the observation that history has been written, in this case, almost entirely by the discontented. Children who yearned to be different, to express their individuality, to test the limits of authority, were not very happy in the St. Nicholas of Tolentines of America in the postwar years. They were the ones who grew up to write novels and plays about their miseries.

But the majority of children who sat in those huge classes and wore the uniforms, who confessed their tiny sins to the Father Lynches of their world, did not grow up articulate enough to write any novels or plays, or angry enough to want to write them if they could. All these years later, if you bring up the question of punishment, they respond with a classroom horror story or two, and then ask how else the nuns were supposed to keep order in a class of fifty or sixty kids. Or they say it was what they themselves needed at the time. If you mention the capricious quality of parochial school justice, they are apt to say that it was reasonable enough training for an adult world where justice is in short supply.

In St. Nick's parish, it is difficult to find people who believe the changes of the 1960s rescued them from a religion that stifled their individuality. No doubt there are people who feel that way. But the common view is one of loss. If they were mere spectators at mass in the 1950s, they were spectators at an event whose very sameness and simplicity gave them a feeling of belonging not only to a parish but to a religious community worldwide. "It was more of a mysterious celebration, with the people watching rather than participating," says Father Michael Goergen, St. Nick's pastor in the early 1990s. "But it was beautiful. It was moving. They miss it."

And it is not hard to get them to say so. "There was a mystery," says Martin Barry, a St. Nick's altar boy in the 1950s and now a Cook County judge. "There was a mystery, and there was an awe. Whatever you want to call it."

St. Nicholas of Tolentine parish was a complex, enveloping institution. In exchange for membership, which was not easy for most people to avoid, it provided what Christopher Durang would call a straitjacket, but what others might describe as a moral and social anchor. It promulgated rules to live by or rules to rebel against. One could respond to the arbitrary authority of Father Lynch and Sister Ellen Marie by accepting them or by despising them; it is not clear that there was a middle way. In either case, however, one had a good chance to emerge with some sense of direction.

That is one advantage that authority, even arbitrary authority, does provide: when you reject it, you know what you are rejecting. It is an advantage that the American generation that grew up in the 1950s, for all its later confusion, made profitable use of. If, in their youthful flailing, they rarely knew quite where they were going, they nearly always understood where they were coming from. That may seem like a modest endowment, but it is one that their children will not be able to claim.

PART III

GHETTO

CHAPTER 6

Frozen in Place

I f St. Nick's parish was a world of limited choices, a far more limited world existed five miles further east, where the bulk of Chicago's black community—hundreds of thousands of people—lived together in Bronzeville, a neighborhood they were all but prohibited from escaping.

Any discussion of the city we have lost during the past generation must eventually confront the issue of Bronzeville, and the question that may be most troublesome of all: Have we lost something important that existed even in the worst place that the Chicago of the 1950s had to offer?

Anybody who did not live in a black ghetto is bound to be leery of asking the question, with its implied assumption that segregation had its good points. But the fact remains, long after Bronzeville's disappearance from the map, that a remarkable number of people who did live there find themselves asking it.

"Fifty-first and Dearborn was a bunch of shacks," Alice Blair wrote thirty years later, after she had become Chicago's deputy superintendent of education. "We didn't have hot water—and the houses were torn down for slum clearance to build Robert Taylor Homes. But in those shacks, there was something different from what is there now."

What was it, exactly? Several things. "People took a great deal of pride in just being where they were," says John Stroger, the first black president of the Cook County Board of Commissioners. "It was economically poor, but spiritually and socially rich. People had hope that things would be better." Stroger echoes what Vernon Jarrett, the longtime Chicago newspaper columnist, said rather hauntingly a few years ago. "The ghetto used to have something going for it. It had a beat, it had a certain rhythm, and it was all hope. I don't care how rough things were."

Then there is the bluntness of Timuel Black, a lifelong civil rights activist, looking back at age seventy-five on the South Side as it used to be and as it has become: "I would say," he declares at the end of a long conversation, "at this point in my life and experience, that we made a mistake leaving the ghetto."

These fragments prove nothing. To many who read them, they will suggest merely that nostalgia is not only powerful but dangerous, that late in life it can generate a fondness for times and places that should be properly remembered with nothing more than relief that they are gone. And yet something valuable did die with Bronzeville, and we can learn something about community and authority, faith and hope, by tracing their presence even in what was, by common agreement, an unjust and constricted corner of the world.

What Bronzeville had, and so many of its graduates continue to mourn, was a sense of posterity—a feeling that, however difficult the present might be, the future was worth thinking about and planning for in some detail. Most of the inhabitants of Bronzeville were farsighted people, able to focus on events and ideas whose outlines were hazy and whose arrival might still be very far away. They were looking forward to a time in which it would be possible to break free of the constrictions and indignities of the moment.

Forty years later, in a time-shortened world hooked on fax machines, microwave popcorn, and MTV, the word *posterity* carries far less meaning than it once did. Its gradual disappearance is one of the genuine losses of modern life. To find the concept so vibrant and well entrenched in a place as deprived as Bronzeville in the 1950s seems to mock the freer but far less anchored world that most of us inhabit today.

The indignities of life for a black person on the South Side in the 1950s are unlikely to come as news to very many readers of any race, but some details are worth dredging up. They reveal the triumphs and comforts of Bronzeville society to have been that much more impressive.

It was, for example, uncommonly dangerous for a black Chicagoan to get sick. Of the seventy-seven hospitals in the metropolitan area, only six would accept black patients at all, and five of those had quotas, so that once a certain small number of beds were occupied by blacks, the next black patient would be turned away, no matter how ill he or she was. It was not unusual for blacks who could perfectly well afford private hospital care to be taken to Cook County Hospital, the spartan and overcrowded charity institution on the West Side.

Most of the time, though, even in an emergency, they would be rushed to Provident, the city's only "black" hospital, sometimes speeding past one white facility after another to get to the Provident emergency room. In 1956, Provident saw an emergency patient every nineteen minutes, five times the average for the city's other hospitals. And it was, of course, the only place where a black doctor could aspire to practice; the other hospitals did their hiring on a strict Jim Crow basis.

Getting stopped for a traffic ticket on the South Side was not the same experience for blacks that it was for whites. Until 1958, all traffic tickets in Chicago mentioned the race of the driver. The police maintained a special task force, known to just about everybody as the "flying squad," which was supposed to zero in on high-crime neighborhoods but in fact spent a good deal of its time harassing black citizens, middle-class as well as poor. It was standard practice for flying squad officers to stop black motorists for traffic violations, frisk them, and search their cars before writing the ticket, often abusing them verbally and physically in the process. The abuses nearly always took place when someone was driving alone, so there were rarely any witnesses.

The force that patrolled these neighborhoods was still mostly white, and the supervisors were essentially all white. There were 1,200 black police officers in Chicago in 1957, but only one black captain, and no lieutenants. In the Englewood district, where many of the new recruits were sent, black patrolmen were nearly always given the most tedious assignments: guard duty night after night, or a motorcycle beat in the depths of winter. The two-man teams were all segregated; blacks and whites were not allowed to work together.

Meanwhile, the public schools were not only segregated but

demonstrably unequal. Most of the white elementary schools on the South Side were underused, while the black ones were jammed far beyond capacity. Some black schools in Bronzeville were handling more than 2,000 pupils a day on a double-shift basis, with one set of children in attendance from 8 A.M. to noon and another from noon to 4 P.M. At the same time, there were nearly 300 vacant classrooms elsewhere in the city and more than 1,000 classrooms being used for nonessential activities of one sort or another. But the school board did not want to adjust the district lines to permit black kids to take advantage of the space that existed beyond the racial borders.

The incidents of hospital bias, police harassment, and school inequity pointed up just how indifferent Jim Crow was to class distinctions in the 1950s: having money was simply no help in these situations. There was a fourth indignity that somehow makes this point even clearer, and it had to do with travel and vacations.

For $20 a year in 1957, a black family could join an organization called the Tourist Motor Club. What they received in return was a list of hotels and restaurants where blacks would be allowed inside the door, and a guarantee of $500 in bond money in case they found themselves being arrested for making the wrong choice. "Are you ready for any traveling emergency—even in a hostile town?" the Tourist Motor Club asked in its ads, and not unreasonably. "What would you do if you were involved in a highway accident in a hostile town—far away from home. You could lose your life savings—you could be kept in jail without adequate reason. You could lose your entire vacation fighting unjust prejudice."

Vacations were for those who could afford them. The problem that united everyone in the black community—wealthy, working class, and poor—was housing. Unlike St. Nick's or any other white community in Chicago, the ghetto was almost impossible to move out of. The rules of segregation simply made it difficult for a black family to live anywhere else, whether it could afford to or not.

By 1957, that had begun to change. Chicago's South Side black population was expanding, block by block, into what had been white working-class territory on its southern and western borders, and a new, separate black enclave had emerged a few miles west of downtown. But as a practical matter, the number of decent housing opportunities opening up for blacks was far smaller than the number needed. Thus, most of the city's black community remained where it had been since the 1920s: in a narrow strip south of Twenty-third Street, roughly eight miles long and still no more than two or three miles wide.

This ghetto had been badly overcrowded by the time of World War II, and in the years since then it had grown more crowded still. The number of black people in Chicago had increased nearly 40 percent between 1950 and 1956, while the white population was declining. And the newcomers were simply stacking up on top of one another. The Kenwood-Oakland neighborhood, centered around Forty-seventh Street, had gone from 13,000 white residents to 80,000 blacks in a matter of a few years. "A new Negro reaches this sprawling city every fifteen minutes," the young black journalist Carl Rowan wrote in 1957, seeming a little overwhelmed himself. Parts of the South Side that had once been relatively spacious and comfortable now held more people than anyone had imagined possible.

The physical world that those migrants confronted was the world of the infamous "kitchenette"—a one-room flat with an icebox, a bed, and a hotplate, typically in an ancient building that once held a few spacious apartments but had been cut up into the tiniest possible pieces to bring the landlord more money. The bathroom and stove were shared with neighbors, a dozen or more people taking turns with the same meager facilities.

This was the world that Gwendolyn Brooks, the great poet of Bronzeville life, had been writing about powerfully for years. "This sick four-story hulk," she wrote of one building in "The Lovers of the Poor,"

> *this fiber with fissures everywhere. . . .*
> *Tin can, blocked fire escape and chitterli*
> *and swaggering seeking youth and th*
> *middle passage, and urine and st*
> *And again the porridges of the underslun*
> *And children, children, children.*

At the Martinette Apartments at Twenty-third and . thousand people, nearly two hundred of them children, lived single seven-story building. For $7.80 a week, tenants got a room, a bed, part of a dresser, a stool, a radio, and a chair. Thomas Jefferson, newly arrived from Jackson, Mississippi, shared one of those rooms in 1957 with his sister, Matilda Russell, the two of them working and sleeping in shifts. Down the hall, Anita Reed was raising five children in two rooms for $14 a week, sharing kitchen and toilet with Mrs. Eddie Davies and her four children.

A few blocks south, at Thirty-fifth and Indiana, was an even worse building, each floor divided into fourteen rooms, with an average of three people in a room, doing their cooking in the hallways, where the only sinks and stoves were located. The trash was dumped into the corridors and picked up every three weeks; there was a permanent smell of gas, but it took as long as six months to get someone from the gas company to come and check it out. The rent was between $25 and $31.50 a month. "Life in a kitchenette was just basic survival," recalled Earl Goff a generation later. "A place to stay and a hot stove so you wouldn't freeze."

Nearly all of the worst shacks, in the oldest part of Bronzeville, closest to downtown, were gone by 1957, torn down to make room for Lake Meadows and Prairie Shores, two new private high-rise housing projects built by the New York Life Insurance Company. Neither of these projects did anything for the housing of poor people; they replaced three thousand dilapidated apartments with two thousand comfortable ones for the middle class,

or three times as much money. The thousands of tenants
ed by the construction were mostly dumped back into the
ning portions of the ghetto further south. But Lake Meadows
Prairie Shores did manage to rid the city of the slum territory
at tore most deeply into its conscience.

More meaningful help was being promised. In 1956, the city
council passed an ordinance outlawing the additional conversion of
apartments six rooms or smaller into two or more family units. "In
a short time," the council declared, "the so-called common kitchen
will be extinct."

That promise could be made only because of the massive public housing projects that were under construction in the heart of
Bronzeville, along South State Street in what had once been the
main commercial corridor. Stateway Gardens opened in 1957:
eight separate buildings, two of them ten stories, the other six seventeen stories high. "You can't call Stateway Gardens a ghetto," said
Alvin Rose, executive director of the Chicago Housing Authority.
"It is beautiful." Every unit had a kitchen.

Meanwhile, the land was being cleared nearby for the even
larger Robert Taylor Homes, and, in another part of Chicago, the
Cabrini-Green high-rise project. "A new mighty city of concrete
and steel," the *Chicago Daily News* called Cabrini, "pushing off the
shell of decadence."

Much has been written in the past two decades about the tragic
mistakes of public housing in Chicago and every other big American city: the ugliness and sterility of the buildings themselves, the
corrosive effects they had on the families that moved there, the
breeding grounds for crime and violence they all ultimately
became. In Chicago the whole process has been especially well
documented from the beginning. The original plan had been to
locate public housing projects at numerous sites scattered around
the city. White resistance made this politically impossible, as it
would have been anywhere, so all the projects were built in existing black neighborhoods, and that meant building them very tall—

creating the "vertical ghetto," as Stateway, Taylor, and the other Chicago projects quickly became known.

When it comes to the history of public housing, there isn't much disagreement anymore. It is universally acknowledged as a disaster. Our concern here, however, is not what the projects created; it is what they helped to destroy. The bulldozer that cleared the land for Stateway Gardens and Robert Taylor Homes brought an end to much of the Bronzeville that had existed since the 1920s, the one that Horace Cayton and St. Clair Drake had written about in their book *Black Metropolis* in 1945. A little later, the collapse of the Jim Crow system finished it off completely.

In an era of limits, when the system dictated that people everywhere in America play the hand they were dealt, Bronzeville was a caricature of the system. It was a community all but frozen in place.

But it was a community. One is tempted to say that Bronzeville flourished despite adversity, but it takes only a moment's reflection to realize that the opposite is much more nearly true: Bronzeville flourished because of adversity. Its residents became experts at community building because they felt the urge to band together against a larger and less friendly world that excluded them from any meaningful participation, no matter how respectable they might be. They cultivated a sense of the future that gave them the patience and the strength to deal with the present.

Under all of Bronzeville's challenges, a whole network of institutions grew up and faced the task of bringing hope, comfort, and meaning to ghetto life. Churches, businesses, and the Democratic political machine were all crucial to survival. And there was one institution that kept all of them in communication with each other: the black newspaper, the *Chicago Defender.*

For more than half a century after its founding in 1905 by Robert Abbott, a Georgia native who had come north for the 1893 World's Fair, the *Defender* was the indispensable voice of a community that had to have one. It can be argued with some credibility that the

Defender in the 1950s was the best newspaper in the city: not the most comprehensive or the most carefully edited but the most honest in dealing with Chicago's social realities, the realities of segregation and of life in the community it served.

"The *Defender* in the fifties was a very important force in molding public opinion," says Timuel Black. "Everyone read the *Defender*. Every copy was read four or five times. People who didn't get it would ask others to let them see it."

In a segregated employment world, the *Defender* was one of the few outlets for black reporters and editors who in later years would have been recruited quickly by the most prestigious newspapers in the country. There was nothing in any of the Chicago papers as clever as the column Louis Martin wrote every week on the editorial page of the *Defender*. In the mid-1950s, after the white Mafia had seized control of South Side gambling from local black interests, Martin wrote that Bronzeville was in the worst possible situation. "We have kept the sin," he said, "and lost the syndicate."

Some of the *Defender*'s trademarks were transparent efforts to boost morale for itself and the larger black community by linking the paper to the white press. The *Chicago Tribune* called itself "the world's greatest newspaper"; the *Defender* was the self-proclaimed "world's greatest weekly." The *Tribune* talked about "Chicagoland"; the *Defender* liked to call its territory "Defenderland."

But much of what appeared in its pages was simply unavailable anywhere else—news about the personal lives of black athletes, such as the Cubs' new double-play combination, Ernie Banks and Gene Baker, or about the black entertainers who were appearing at the South Side nightclubs and trying to crash the television or movie mainstream. Much of the language sounds embarrassing now, with references to "sepia stars" and "tan sluggers." But there was some punch to it as well. The *Defender* agitated incessantly for a regular television show for Nat King Cole, a product of the South Side streets. It complained that there weren't nearly enough guest slots for black talent on the *Ed Sullivan Show.*

It can be fairly said that the *Defender's* militance increased with the distance from its home territory. It was a passionate supporter of the new African nations, sending a reporter to the independence ceremonies in Ghana and stationing Louis Martin in Nigeria for the better part of 1959. It angrily criticized the Reverend Martin Luther King, Jr., and Roy Wilkins of the NAACP for agreeing to concessions on the 1957 civil rights bill in Congress.

But the paper tread very carefully in Chicago politics. Whereas Robert Abbott had kept up a fierce independence for the thirty-five years of his stewardship, his nephew and successor, John Sengstacke, maintained a firm alliance with the Daley machine and with the Democratic boss of the black South Side wards, Congressman William L. Dawson. Political advertising at election time was a crucial source of revenue for the *Defender,* and it was purchased not so much to influence votes but as an outright gift in exchange for the paper's support. Dawson helped arrange the financing for the paper's capital needs; he also got Sengstacke appointed as a U.S. commissioner for the Virgin Islands. However tough the paper chose to be on other subjects, its return to the Daley–Dawson corner before the election was required. Sometimes it went a bit overboard. "Richard J. Daley," it wrote in 1959, "has provided Chicago with a type of progressive leadership that the city had never known before. Daley's four years in the City Hall as chief executive have been the most rewarding in the history of Chicago."

None of this, odd as it might seem, prevented the paper from taking regular shots at the mayor's school superintendent or police department. Throughout the years of the Daley first term it admired so much, the *Defender* was waging a weekly crusade against police harassment of black citizens. "South Siders," it complained bitterly in 1957, "can scarcely tell the difference between professional stick-up men and some police officers." It went on to recite a litany of "complaints from motorists as well as pedestrians about illegal searches, unprovoked beatings, abusive language, and shake-downs by Chicago police."

■ ■ ■

But the *Defender's* most lasting impact came not from crusading but from nurturing other community institutions. Holidays and cele-brations, a competition for "mayor of Bronzeville," a full-fledged scouting program for black children—all of them were instruments of mass participation deliberately set up to be parallel to institu-tions that existed in the white community. "You had to create par-allel institutions," Timuel Black says. "People in order to survive have to create institutions. The things the *Defender* created and sus-tained were vital to the health of the community. It gave folks something to look forward to. It gave some belief that there was a land beyond this one, and hope beyond this life."

Of all the projects of this sort that the *Defender* came up with over the years, none was more interesting than the elaborate con-test to select a shadow government of Bronzeville every two years. There was a mayor, a deputy mayor, a fire commissioner, and a health commissioner. The mayoral winner received a free Ford Thunderbird and led members of the community on a group vaca-tion each summer.

The contest was, in part, an excuse to sell papers. The only way you could cast a vote was with a ballot printed in the *Defender*. But each election attracted dozens of candidates—ministers, storekeep-ers, insurance salesmen—some running to advance their business prospects, but others in it simply for the fun and prestige. Every ballot in the paper counted for a hundred votes; it usually took more than a million votes to come in first.

The *Defender* worked hard to sell the candidates and voters on the importance of the decision. "The mayor is more than a figure-head," the newspaper assured its readers. "His counsel and advice are sought by city officials, community leaders and youth group leaders."

A whole crew of former mayors backed up those assertions. "I knew that for a whole year, I would be living in a glass cage," one of them recalled afterward. "That every action, practically every word would be weighed and measured by the people who had placed their trust in me. I knew that the Chicago *Defender* would be depending on me. I knew that the *Defender* would bring all its tremendous influence to bear in order to support my efforts."

It was all a little exaggerated, to put it mildly. As far as the larger city was concerned, the mayor of Bronzeville had no real role to play. His influence stopped at the borders of the black ghetto. Within that ghetto, though, the mayoralty meant a great deal and it was a powerful unifying force. "It was symbolic at best," says Dempsey Travis, who was starting out as a South Side realtor in the 1950s. "But you were respected. When you went into a nightclub, they said, 'The mayor is in the house.' "

The 1957 campaign attracted a huge field, but in the end, the winner was the incumbent, John Earl Lewis, proprietor of the Kim Lounge at Forty-seventh Street and Drexel Boulevard. Lewis was the ultimate neighborhood politician, shaking hands at virtually every party and reception that took place and sponsoring a free cha-cha party every Thursday in his nightclub. He was inaugurated at a *Defender*-sponsored Mardi Gras masquerade ball at the Parkway ballroom, with Sammy Davis Jr. as the guest of honor.

An even bigger event, however, was the paper's Bud Billiken parade, an annual celebration of community pride invented by a *Defender* city editor, supposedly in honor of an ancient Chinese deity that watched over children. In a typical year, thirty thousand marchers, fifty bands, and seventy-five floats wound their way through Washington Park, with as many as half a million lining the streets to watch them—more than half the black people in the entire city. The grand marshal was always a sports or entertainment figure: Duke Ellington one year, Sidney Poitier the next. A Miss Bronze America was chosen. After the parade, thousands of people picnicked all day and all evening in Washington Park. It was perfectly safe to do that.

The parade was a one-day event. All year long, however, the *Defender* attracted thousands of South Side children into its Bud

Billiken kids clubs, a network set up deliberately parallel to the Boy Scouts at a time when scouting was still essentially a segregated enterprise. Each week, the paper devoted an entire page to news, games, and contests aimed at the Billiken clubs, of which there were said to be four thousand worldwide. This institution went back to the 1920s; Nat King Cole and Lionel Hampton had been members as children. John Sengstacke, the *Defender* publisher, was said to be "the pal of all Billikens."

Growing up in this organization was not exactly training for an adulthood of social activism. "The big purpose of the Bud Billiken club," the *Defender* explained, "is to make boys and girls better sons and daughters and more useful to the community." Still, it got a few points across now and then. It liked to remind kids that the country was founded on protest, that the civil rights movement and the American revolution actually had quite a bit in common. "The institution of slavery has made the Negro different cultur-ally," Sengstacke explained, "but his aspirations and his values are wholly American. He wants the same as other Americans, from soup to citizenship."

For decades, the *Defender* had been the news and advertising vehi-cle for a thriving Bronzeville nightclub and entertainment scene. At one point in the 1950s, it printed a column called "While the Squares Sleep," offering gossipy tidbits about the performers play-ing all the important black clubs. And there were dozens of such places, featuring entertainers with national reputations: Nat King Cole, Duke Ellington, Count Basie, Cab Calloway. The list was endless.

In the first few weeks of 1957, the hot act on the South Side was Pearl Bailey at the Regal Theater. The Regal may not have been quite what it was before the war, when there was no television for its shows to compete with, but it was still an impressive landmark, in a building that everyone who entered still marveled at. It was a huge rococo palace built in 1928, with a Moorish lobby that held

1,500 people comfortably, a chandelier with 69,000 crystals, and a main theater with gold walls and 3,500 plush red seats.

The Regal and some of the larger theaters and clubs were white-owned, but there was also a significant black-owned entertainment industry in Bronzeville in the 1950s. There was, for example, the Roberts Show Lounge, at Sixty-sixth and South Park, often described as "the biggest Negro-owned nightclub in America." The Roberts had 1,000 seats and a chorus line with eight girls. It booked Sammy Davis, Jr., Sarah Vaughan, and Billy Eckstine; the comedian Dick Gregory got his start there as master of ceremonies.

Something was going on at the Roberts every day of the week. Even more important than its big-name entertainment policy was its status as party center for the plethora of social clubs that existed in Bronzeville through the 1950s. Dempsey Travis estimates that there were more than two thousand such clubs, covering most of the economic spectrum from the working class to the elite, and the Roberts was in effect their clubhouse. It was booked months in advance for Sunday afternoon fashion shows and cocktail parties sponsored by one club or another.

At the upper reaches of Bronzeville society were the 40 Club, the Chicago Assembly, the Green Donkeys, the Snakes, and the Druids. The 40 Club held a black-tie dinner dance every winter and a picnic in the summer; the Assembly sponsored a winter formal, a spring formal, and a smoker. The Green Donkeys had an annual talent show. Membership in any of these clubs was a badge of status for the ambitious doctor, minister, or insurance executive in Bronzeville society.

But the majority of the clubs, Travis recalls, were for ordinary working people—"post office clubs, bartenders' clubs, Campbell Soup clubs, U.S. Steel clubs, and Packinghouse Worker clubs." There were literally hundreds of women's clubs with names like the Amethyst Girls, the Debonairs, the Wild Rose, and the Sapphire Civic and Social Club, whose motto was "Life can be beautiful and worth living." Even the most modest of these clubs usually managed to have one formal or semiformal event a year.

"Twenty men were in the Foxy Cats club," Gwendolyn Brooks wrote in her Bronzeville novel, *Maud Martha*. "All were good-looking. All wore clothes that were rich and suave. All 'handled money,' for their number consisted of well-located barbers, police-men, 'government men,' and men with a lucky touch at the tracks. . . . Each year they spent hundreds of dollars on their wonderful Dawn Ball, which did not begin at dawn but was scheduled to end at dawn. 'Ball,' they called the frolic, but it served also the purposes of party, feast and fashion show."

It was the role of the *Defender* to provide coverage for these events and the other activities of the social clubs, and it did this with relish and at great length. Each club had a member with the responsibility to get stories into the paper and to provide pho-tographs, all of which were duly printed. Several pages of each week's paper were devoted to the club scene. "The middle-class social club world," Cayton and Drake had written, "thrives on pub-licity." It was as true in the late 1950s as it had been before the war. The clubs may have been a make-believe world, and their preten-sions were easy to poke fun at, even for the members themselves. But they provided thousands of people with a lifeline, an opportu-nity even for those whose living conditions were constricted and discouraging to nourish a sense of personal importance. In this respect, as in so many others, the *Defender* was the voice not only of community but of hope.

CHAPTER 7

Pillars of Optimism

n Bronzeville, hope and authority tended to come out of the same package. If the ultimate authority figures were wealthy white people somewhere far away, the most familiar and important ones were right there inside the community. They were people who had maneuvered their way through the currents of segregated life, made careers and often fortunes for themselves, and remained in the neighborhood, hammering home the message that there were victories to strive for. They were employers and entrepreneurs of all sorts: businessmen, politicians, and entertainers, gambling czars and preachers of the Gospel. They were people whose moral flaws and weaknesses were no secret to those around them, and those weaknesses were a frequent topic of discussion in the community. But they were leaders nevertheless. They led by command, sometimes rather crudely, and they also led by example.

It is easy to forget, forty years later, just how many successful black-owned businesses there were in Chicago. There were black entrepreneurs all up and down the commercial streets in the 1950s, able to stay afloat because they were guaranteed a clientele. They provided services that white businesses simply did not want to provide to blacks. They ran barber shops and beauty parlors, restaurants and taverns, photography studios and small hotels. Many of them were mom-and-pop operations but quite a few evolved into sizable corporations. "Business," as Dempsey Travis says, "was the pillar of optimism."

The nation's largest black-owned bank was at Forty-seventh Street and Cottage Grove Avenue. Parker House Sausage Company, at Forty-sixth and State, called itself the "Jackie Robinson of meat-packing." At Twenty-seventh and Wabash, S. B. Fuller operated a giant cosmetics business that touted three hundred different products, maintained thirty-one branches all over the country, and employed five thousand salesmen. "Anyone can succeed," Fuller used to say, "if he has the desire."

But the great symbols of the entrepreneurial spirit in Bronzeville were the funeral parlors and the insurance companies. In many cases they were related businesses, a legacy of the burial insurance associations that had existed among black sharecroppers in Mississippi and Arkansas early in the century. Undertakers were the largest single source of advertising in the *Defender;* they were also, like their white counterparts elsewhere in the city, mainstays of every community organization: lodges, churches, social clubs.

The opening of a new funeral parlor was a community event in itself. In the spring of 1957, the Jackson funeral home opened a state-of-the art facility on Cottage Grove Avenue, complete with three large chapels, slumber rooms, a powder room, and a smoking lounge. On the first day, 3,000 people came to see it. The Jackson family also owned Jackson Mutual, the fifth largest insurance company in Bronzeville, employing 120 people and writing nearly $2 million worth of policies every year.

Insurance actually was a service that white corporations were willing to provide to black customers. Thousands of Bronzeville residents had policies with Metropolitan Life, paying a dollar or two every month to an agent who came by door-to-door to collect. But this was one case where black firms could compete fairly easily. Met Life charged black families more than it charged whites for the same policies, its agents didn't like to come at night when customers were home, and they often seemed to resent having to be there at all. There were billboards all over the neighborhood urging people to buy their insurance from a Negro company.

The result was that by the mid-1950s, the five largest black-owned insurance companies in Chicago had nearly $50 million in assets and more than two thousand employees among them. "Negro life insurance companies," said Walter Lowe, one of the leading agents, "represent the core of Negro economic life. It is the axis upon which are revolved the basic financial activities of a world constricted by the overpowering forces of discrimination."

But it was more than that. It was the underwriter of the extended time horizons that made life in Bronzeville tolerable in the first place. It was the primary symbol of hope for people burdened with a difficult present but unwilling to abandon their focus on the future. In 1954, *Ebony* magazine, published in Chicago, took a survey of its black readership and found that 42 percent owned washing machines, 44 percent owned cars, and 60 percent owned television sets. But 86 percent said they carried life insurance.

The *Defender's* tribute to the life insurance companies was reprinted every year to coincide with National Negro Insurance Week: "I am the destroyer of poverty and the enemy of crime," it said. "I bring sunshine and happiness wherever I am given half the welcome I deserve. I do not live for the day nor for the morrow but for the unfathomable future. I am your best friend—I am life insurance."

At least half a dozen insurance companies were crucial institutions in Bronzeville, but one was the most important of all: Supreme Liberty Life, with $18 million in assets, the largest black-owned business of any kind north of the Mason-Dixon line. In 1956, Supreme Liberty had thirty-six offices in twenty-eight cities, 600 employees in all, 125 of them working in Bronzeville at the main headquarters at Thirty-fifth Street and South Park Way. A brand-new headquarters building opened that year—"streamlined in appearance," the company said, "and modern in every respect."

The founder of Supreme Liberty, T. K. Gibson, then in his mid-eighties, was sometimes called "the grand old man among Chicago Negroes." A native of Georgia with a degree from Harvard, he was on close personal terms with much of the white business and political elite. He and Mayor Daley were on a first-name basis. But he was extremely reluctant to invest any of his personal capital in any sort of protest or public controversy.

The chief executive of the company was a much different sort of man, one of a remarkable number of genuine leaders and authority figures that Bronzeville was capable of creating. Born in Mississippi, Earl Dickerson had graduated from the University of Chicago Law School and had been an assistant attorney general of

Illinois in the prewar days when it was tortuously difficult for blacks to do those things. He had argued the case against restrictive covenants before the U.S. Supreme Court. He had been alderman of the Second Ward, actually defeating William L. Dawson for the job. He was written about in black newspapers all over the country—"the eloquent, dashing Earl Dickerson," a West Coast paper once called him.

But the most remarkable thing about Earl Dickerson was that he managed to be a capitalist role model and an angry radical at the same time. He served as president of the leftist Lawyers Guild and ran for Congress in 1948 on Henry Wallace's Progressive ticket, demanding the impeachment of Chicago's mayor, Martin Kennelly. He was as militant on race issues as anybody in a position of influence dared to be. When his daughter was denied a table at a restaurant in the Palmer House Hotel, he sued the hotel and won. "I want to devote the best part of my time and training," Dickerson said, "to fighting against the inhuman attempt to jam my people into ghettos." And yet he was not only a tough corporate executive but a pillar of the Bronzeville social elite, president of the 40 Club, the gathering place for those who had made it in business, politics, and professional life. He was the first black person to serve as the director of a white Chicago bank.

Bronzeville and the business opportunities it created had made Earl Dickerson what he was, but he left no doubt about what he wanted for the future. "We must not only desegregate our schools," he insisted, "but desegregate our businesses and every vestige of separate status. Ultimately, the stream of free enterprise is going to be so vigorous in an integrated society that all businesses will be engulfed. We can no longer hope to leave the Negro market to ourselves. But if we had the genius of organization and perseverance and leadership to maintain separate business then we can meet the challenge of integrated business."

It wasn't just the separate businesses of Bronzeville that Dickerson was eager to sweep away—it was the community itself. "We must give up our provincial-mindedness," he said, "forget the neighborhood and city in favor of the nation."

Others in the same situation sounded a bit more ambivalent. "Integration is indeed the order of the day," insurance man Walter Lowe wrote at that time, agreeing with Dickerson. "Old traditions are being shaken and rooted up by the percussion of new ideas. Negro life insurance companies will be in precarious circumstances. Race pride is not enough to overcome the urge for great and greater returns. We have reached the end of an economic era which but a few years ago seemed omnipotent and eternal."

Lowe's uneasiness actually turned out to be a better gauge of the future than Dickerson's optimism, at least when it came to the insurance industry. In 1956, Dickerson had predicted that by the year 2000, Supreme Liberty Life would have $300 million in assets and would be writing a billion dollars worth of policies. But long before that, the company had ceased to exist at all.

One reason leaders such as Dickerson chose not to worry about the impending disappearance of black economic institutions was the fact that the job picture in Bronzeville was gradually improving throughout the 1950s, even for those toward the bottom of the ladder. Jobs in manufacturing, closed to most blacks before the war, were much more freely available. In 1940, 67 percent of Chicago blacks worked in some form of personal service and only 9 percent in manufacturing; as early as 1950, the figures had jumped to 30 percent in manufacturing and 34 percent in service, and were continuing to increase. Between 1950 and 1956, black family income in the city had increased by 42 percent, compared to 28 percent for whites, although the black number was still nearly a third lower. "Chicago's a better town for a Negro to make a living in, if he could find someplace to live," an editor of *Ebony* had said early in the decade. "There are more jobs in heavy industry than there are in New York."

In the stockyards—the one industrial facility that had always employed blacks in large numbers—they were no longer being confined automatically to the most distasteful jobs: the wool, glue, and sausage departments, or the "sweet pickle" department, where they pulled slimy bacon bellies out of a tank and loaded them on a truck. The work force at the stockyards was as much as 40 percent black in many departments in the 1950s; the real problem was the decline in the yards themselves, as the meatpacking industry gradually abandoned Chicago and moved further west.

Increasingly, the issue for blacks was not so much where they could work but how far they would be allowed to rise once they were there. There was clearly a ceiling at the Chicago Post Office, where the force had been more than a quarter black since the 1930s, but where the postmasters had been notoriously slow to move blacks into supervisory positions. There was a ceiling at the downtown department stores, where the first black salesgirls had been hired during the war, but had found promotion to better positions largely impossible. And there were many leading Chicago institutions, such as the First National Bank, that were still refusing in the late 1950s to hire blacks even as tellers. In 1958, civil rights groups had to picket First National to get that policy changed. "These lords of the Loop are compared to the bosses of the Kremlin in Moscow," Louis Martin wrote bitterly that year in the *Chicago Defender.* "They are master propagandists, with a mouth full of peace and goodwill and a fist full of iron and steel."

So if opportunities were expanding for blacks in Bronzeville in the 1950s, there were still far too few of them to match the supply of breadwinners who needed steady jobs. And that was the real importance of the Democratic political machine on those South Side streets. It was the largest employer in the community. There is no way to say precisely how many of the roughly sixty thousand city and county patronage jobs were held by blacks, but upward of five thousand is a reasonable guess. The machine was an economic lifeline. That, more than any personal or ideological affinity, was the basis of the enormous Democratic majorities that Bronzeville always turned out.

And virtually every one of those patronage jobs was ultimately under the control of a single man: a one-legged native of Georgia who had been carefully accumulating power on the South Side since the 1930s, serving on the city council and then in Congress, assuming control of the Second Ward and then expanding to take over five others in which he could pretty much handpick the alderman and committeeman. "William Dawson," the *Defender* wrote in 1956, "enjoys today more actual political power than any other Negro in modern history. His work inside the Democratic organization can make or break ambitious men on both sides of the color line."

Dawson was a figure of enormous authority on the South Side in the 1950s—not so much moral authority, which he didn't really claim, but sheer personal control and influence. He was a one-man symbol of the importance of organization, hierarchy, and discipline. "A church is highly organized, isn't it?" Dawson used to say. "So is a business. Why not politics?"

Dawson didn't seem to worry a great deal about money, and he positively detested publicity. The one thing he absolutely craved was control. "Power was Bill's passion," said Earl Dickerson, who fought him in South Side politics for twenty years. "It was all he cared about and lived for, really." Dawson wouldn't have denied it. He once explained matter-of-factly that "God gave me the key to understand men and to know them."

Nobody could accuse Dawson of being a back-slapping politician. To nearly all white people and to blacks who were not close to him, he was a man of very few words, gruff, taciturn, and profane. In front of his minions, however, he could turn into a preacher. He addressed them that way every Friday night at the meetings of "Dawson College" at his headquarters on Indiana Avenue. "Walk together, children, and don't get weary," he nearly always concluded, "for there's a great camp meeting in the promised land." Then the group adjourned to the nightclub in the basement and listened to the music of Jimmie Noone, the man who taught Benny Goodman how to play the clarinet. "It was a great social thing," John Stroger recalls. "Parties on Friday nights, then more meetings on Saturday morning." The Dawson machine was an important social institution as well as a political one.

The ultimate source of its influence, of course, was the votes it provided to favored white politicians. But it could be plausibly argued that Dawson had done something even more important than that for the new mayor.

Dawson had never gotten along with Mayor Martin Kennelly, who had been hostile to blacks in general, stingy with patronage, and prone to ordering intermittent raids on South Side gambling parlors. "We don't need you," Dawson lectured Kennelly in 1951. "You need us. Who do you think you are? You treat us like lepers." Dawson balked at supporting Kennelly for reelection that year, but ultimately agreed to back him for one more term. In 1955, however, that term was over, and Dawson knew the man he wanted in City Hall as Kennelly's replacement: Richard J. Daley, the South Side native who, as county clerk, had made it a point to stop by Dawson's Second Ward office every once in a while on his way home to Bridgeport in the evening. Dawson's wards gave Daley 87 percent of their vote, three-fifths of his citywide plurality, as Daley unseated Kennelly in the 1955 primary.

That Dawson did a great deal for Daley was beyond dispute. Whether Dawson and his constituents got their money's worth is another question. Though patronage jobs did continue to flow to the South Side, virtually all of them were at the lowest levels; the machine was very tight when it came to posts that carried any real prestige or political importance. In 1958, for example, there were thirty-six municipal court judges and forty-eight superior court judges in Chicago and Cook County, all of them under Daley's direct control. Only three of them were black, at a time when the black population of the city was approaching 25 percent. Dawson never made much of an issue about this sort of thing. "Dawson made Daley, and Dawson never really got his cut of the cake," Dempsey Travis says. "He was satisfied with a lot of menial jobs.

He'd take a hundred menial jobs over ten judgeships. He counted numbers."

In return for those jobs, Dawson was expected to turn out the vote for the organization for whatever office was at stake—even, on occasion, for a white candidate against a black opponent. In those situations, precinct captains were sometimes instructed to give each voter a dollar bill and a photograph of Dawson, reminding them that this was what he wanted them to do. "It has been charged," Louis Martin wrote, "that Dawson is an organization Democrat before he is a Negro. He sincerely believes, however, that whatever the organization decides is best for the Negro."

Dawson's relationship with Daley raises the question of how much of a leader he was, for all his status as a community legend and patronage godfather. There were always critics in Bronzeville willing to charge that Dawson was simply unwilling to fight when it really mattered. In 1958, for example, he drew a challenge in his congressional district from Dr. T. R. M. Howard, a social activist who had crusaded for black voting rights in the South and protested the Mississippi lynching of the Chicago teenager, Emmett Till. Howard accused Dawson of ignoring police brutality and, even more ominously, of wanting to slow down the pace of integration in order to keep his political machine intact. "Our people have grown tired," Howard said, "of leaders who are lions among Negroes, but lambs among others." But Dawson won easily.

It wasn't just patronage that made Dawson ultimately immune at the polls to that sort of charge: it was status as protector of the Bronzeville policy games, the illegal gambling industry that created almost as many jobs for South Side blacks as the Democratic machine did. For decades, ever since his emergence as Second Ward committeeman, Dawson had taken a cut from the policy operators and redistributed much of it to police and politicians so the games could continue undisturbed. Estimates of the number of people who worked in policy vary widely, but there were certainly several thousand of them manning the wheels that churned out the winning numbers, doing the clerical work, and taking bets on the street.

Dawson routinely denied that he had anything to do with the policy game. "I have never been in a position to give gamblers protection," he insisted. "That is the province of the mayor and the police commissioner. I have never taken money from a gambling place in my life for personal or political purposes." That may have been half true. Dawson's closest associates have always maintained that he didn't like to pocket policy money, that the only illegal enterprise in which he had a personal interest was the jitney cabs that operated without a license along South Park Way and the other major Bronzeville streets.

But the fact that Dawson's lieutenants took protection money from gamblers, and used some of it to keep the machine functioning, was really beyond dispute. Early in 1955, one of the gamblers' payoff men, Claude "Loud Mouth" Murphy, testified to prosecutors that Dawson's organization was raking in between $10,000 and $12,000 a month from the policy games, in addition to the bribes that went directly to police officers in the four South Side police districts where the games flourished. Murphy said that captains got $10,000 a month income from policy protection, while the lieutenants in a district split $5,000, and the sergeants divided $4,200. As a result of Murphy's testimony, Kinzie Blueitt, the one black captain on the entire Chicago force, spent more than a year defending himself against bribery charges, though in the end he was acquitted.

Murphy's allegations also brought Dawson a rare burst of attention from the white press. "Dawson has long been a force for evil within the local Democratic organization," the *Chicago Sun-Times* editorialized. "He is a political overlord of a district where policy rackets and narcotics peddling flourish as they do nowhere else in the city." In the 1955 campaign, Kennelly took every possible advantage of the gambling issue, staging well-publicized raids on selected policy wheels and seeking to rally white support against the evils of gambling on the South Side. But the effort seems to have had largely the opposite effect, galvanizing the black community in defense of its own industry and leader.

Policy was much more than an economic enterprise. For tens of thousands of Bronzeville residents, especially for the poorest among them, living in kitchenettes and barely scraping by, it was the transcendent social institution. Well into the 1950s, there were more than fifty different policy wheels operating in the community, some with exotic names like Monte Carlo and Royal Palm, some with more mundane ones like Harlem and the Bronx. There were perhaps five hundred stations where bets could be placed. Sometimes these were legitimate businesses—barber shops, cigar stores, laundries—and sometimes just basements with a light over the entrance and customers coming in and out eighteen hours a day. "It is the Wall Street Stock Market to the masses," the *Defender* said.

It was a simple game, a matter of guessing which numbers would appear on a few steel balls drawn from seventy-eight balls sitting in a large drum. There were three drawings a day—in the morning, afternoon, and at midnight—and the drawings were public events with big crowds gathered around some of the wheels. Once the winning numbers were drawn, they were printed up and distributed all over the neighborhood to the thousands of hard-core players who couldn't rest until they knew the result. "Policy is not only a business, it is also a cult," Cayton and Drake wrote. "It has an element of mystery and anticipation. It has developed an esoteric language. It organizes, to some extent, the daily lives of the participants."

The most popular bet was the "gig," an attempt to guess a three-number combination, with the numbers appearing in any order. The bet cost a dime and generally paid $20 to the winner. A gig wasn't a very good investment; the odds against getting it right were up in the thousands. But most of the people who played weren't doing it as a matter of calculation. They seemed convinced that there were means of divining just which numbers would fall. For most of them, playing a gig was an exercise in numerology.

At the simplest level, it could be a matter of betting on a combination that had just come up in the course of everyday life: a church hymn number, a license plate on a car in an accident, a streetcar transfer. More often, though, the numbers came out of a dream the player had had the previous night, and there were printed pamphlets available all over the neighborhood to translate the dreams into winning numbers. These books had a number for almost everything. In one of them, for example, a dream about a crippled man dictated a bet on 594 or 698. A dream about a man swimming was a hint to play 591.

Who produced these dream books? In most cases, the *Defender* said, "some 'wiseman' from the South who has come north with the idea of escaping race prejudice by placing a Hindu turban on his head and portraying himself as an East Indian."

This process sounds like an elaborate exercise in duping the gullible. But to say that is to miss the point. Policy was mass entertainment, a form of theater for the poor that cost only a dime to buy into. Even most of the raw newcomers up from rural Mississippi suspected that the man with the turban wasn't really an Asian swami. And most of them knew that the odds of winning a gig weren't all that good. But policy was fun, it was a diversion from the realities of ghetto life, and it did represent hope. It was a token of optimism that could not be extinguished. The odds might be long, but the possibility was always there.

And policy served one other important purpose: it created genuine leaders, people who were, in an odd sort of way, role models to much of the community. In the 1930s and 1940s there had been the Jones boys, sons of a Vicksburg minister who put together a network of thirteen policy wheels and drew so close to the regime at City Hall that they never had any trouble with the police. In the heyday of the Jones operation, there were 250 people working in their headquarters at Forty-seventh and Michigan, including some black lawyers and accountants who had had trouble finding work downtown.

The Joneses prided themselves on putting a large chunk of their winnings back into the community. They opened a small department store at Forty-seventh and South Park, the first black-owned store of any real size in the heart of Bronzeville. The grand opening was a major event, with Joe Louis and Bill "Bojangles" Robinson on hand for the dedication. "You have the Jones Brothers with one of the finest stores in the world. Patronize them and do everything you can to be satisfied," Bojangles told the crowd.

The Joneses had made a fortune without violence or fraud—their game was universally assumed to be on the level—and they were willing to share the blessings. Few questioned their leadership status. "Kids could emulate the Joneses," says Truman Gibson, Jr., a young lawyer in Bronzeville at the time. The *Chicago Tribune* went further. It once called Ed Jones "the Boss of Bronzeville, the Negro Santa Claus, and the colored Robin Hood."

Unfortunately, Ed Jones made a mistake that was to cost him and the community a great deal. Imprisoned briefly on a federal tax evasion charge in the late 1940s, he met the white gangster Sam Giancana, who happened to be detained for similar reasons. Jones described candidly to Giancana just how lucrative the policy game was.

Until then, the Mafia had never shown a great deal of interest in this particular form of illegal enterprise. Al Capone had called it a "nickel-and-dime hustle" and seemed content to leave it under local black control as long as blacks stayed out of bootlegging.

But in the decade after World War II, the mob gradually muscled black entrepreneurs out of the way and took over the management of Bronzeville gambling operations for itself. Ed Jones was kidnapped near his house one day, paid a $250,000 ransom, and moved immediately to Mexico, ending his family's reign as policy kings. By the mid-1950s, Giancana and Tony Accardo were said to be taking 40 percent off the top, and the salaries of the black employees who continued to handle the day-to-day work had declined. One midlevel white informant, Jake "Greasy Thumb" Guzik, told a U.S. Senate investigating committee that he had made $279,000 in a single year from policy alone.

In the early 1950s, though, there was still one bona-fide black policy king operating on the South Side: Theodore Roe, who had started out in the business before the war, working for the Joneses. Roe was independent; some said he was reckless. He refused even to discuss cutting the white Mafia in on his business. He was also, to many of the regular policy players, a model of personal rectitude. He not only kept his game fair, forcing others to play straight or lose customers, but he pressured competitors who didn't pay off on their bets promptly. Roe never denied bribing police and politicians, but it was said that on one occasion, when he gave an alderman $1,000 and was offered exclusive control of his territory, he turned it down. He said all he wanted was the freedom to do business along with everyone else.

On the night of August 4, 1952, Theodore Roe was killed by a shotgun blast in front of his house at Fifty-third and Michigan. Within a few minutes, there were thousands of people in the nearby streets. "Housewives in night clothes, stick-pinned gamblers and wine-drunk punks gathered to see where their Robin Hood fell," the *Defender* reported. "He said he'd never let the Mob take him over and he became a hero. He will be missed by the scattered remnants of the policy barons. Nothing stands between them and the octopus arms of the syndicate."

More than five thousand people attended Roe's funeral at the First Church of Deliverance. There were eighty-one cars, including four cars for flowers alone. The pastor, the Reverend Clarence Cobb, admitted that he had taken some criticism for holding services for a criminal in his church. But he said he was honored to do it. "I want every one of you to hear me," Cobb proclaimed. "When I was building this church, and didn't know whether I was going to get it finished or not, Ted Roe gave me a check."

Another neighborhood minister, the Reverend Richard Keller, placed the whole affair in a larger context: "Theodore Roe contributed greatly to the hopes and life of a people," said Keller. "We call men like Theodore Roe kings."

Calling Ted Roe a king may have been a little fanciful, but calling him a sinner seemed, to most of the residents of Bronzeville, a little ridiculous. As far as they were concerned, policy was a victimless crime; its only offense was that it had been declared illegal. "Betting is a human frailty," William Dawson used to say, "but it isn't an evil in itself. If anybody is to profit out of gambling in the Negro community, it should be the Negro." Indeed, what was disturbing about the Mafia invasion in the early 1950s was not the idea of white gangsters preying upon the inner-city poor but the loss of Bronzeville's biggest private employer. "We need all the capitalists we can find," Louis Martin wrote. "Now the gambling profits are making the wrong people rich."

That so many people took pains to defend gambling as less than sinful does, however, point up one important reality: Bronzeville was a community that thought about things in moral terms, in the language of good and evil. Like most of America in the 1950s, but even more than most of it, Bronzeville sorted the life around it into one category or the other.

It was pretty much forced to do that. Within a compact geographical area there were five hundred policy stations, eighty poolrooms, and two hundred taverns. All the residents of the community lived in their midst: the undertakers and the insurance agents just as much as the drifters and policy runners who worked for Ted Roe. Segregation kept the "respectable" people in direct personal contact with an underside of life they would have escaped had they been allowed to live elsewhere. Tavern fights and kitchen stabbings, bigamy and desertion, all were a central element in the kitchenette subculture throughout the South Side neighborhoods. They were the staple of the *Defender* front page. And even the most stable and affluent families were just a few doors away from them.

The situation was not the best, but it did provide a context for daily moral reflection that many of these families lost when they left Bronzeville in the 1960s and 1970s for more comfortable and quieter streets. The churchgoers of Bronzeville, Cayton and Drake wrote in *Black Metropolis,* are "in the world of sin but not of it." To them, "sin is a malevolent reality. It is the cause of all our present woes, individual and collective."

And this was the inescapable theme of what they heard in church on Sundays—the need to live in the midst of personal sin, individual weakness, and yet to rise above it. "Every human life is exposed to good and evil," the Reverend A. Lincoln Jones, of Greater Bethesda Baptist Church, told his congregation. "When a room is filled with foul air, we do not get a club to beat it out, or a broom to sweep it out, but rather we raise the windows and let the fresh air come in. Be not overcome with evil, but overcome evil with good."

CHAPTER 8

City of Faith

DR. JOSEPH H. JACKSON
PREACHER, PASTOR, PATRIOT
AND
INTERNATIONAL RELIGIOUS STATESMAN

Overcoming evil was a job at which most of Bronzeville worked very hard every Sunday, in congregations that ranged in size from tiny to immense. There were five churches whose sanctuary had a seating capacity of two thousand or more, and at least two churches had more than ten thousand people on their membership rolls. But a majority of the churches in the community, even in the late 1950s, were basically storefront operations—often a couple of dozen worshipers or even fewer than that.

In the bigger churches, Sunday worship was an all-day affair: Sunday school at nine in the morning and the main service at eleven; an evening musicale later on, with the full choir and Gospel chorus; and then, for many of the faithful, a radio sermon from one of the big-name Bronzeville preachers before retiring for the night. Music was at the heart of the experience. Most churches had choirs that accompanied the pastor when he preached as a guest in another pulpit, which all of them did. Some choirs spent considerable time traveling outside the city.

Between Sundays, the odds were that a larger congregation would be busy with some social activity every single night. All these churches had a wide variety of auxiliary organizations— youth groups, missionary societies, sewing circles—and some had as many as two dozen different ones in existence at the same time. Of all the Bronzeville social institutions of the 1950s, the churches were the most uniformly successful and self-reliant. "In their own churches in their own denominational structures," the historian C. Eric Lincoln was to write in retrospect, "black Christians had become accustomed to a sense of dignity and self-fulfillment impossible even to contemplate in the white church in America. . . . To be able to say that 'I belong to Mount Nebo Baptist' or 'We go to Mason's Chapel Methodist' was the accepted way of establishing identity and status."

The storefront churches had to make do without the elaborate network of groups and social involvement. But the key distinction was not the size of the facility; it was the style of worship and particularly the level of emotion. Many of the storefronts, perhaps most, were Holiness or Pentecostal churches—Holy Rollers, as the outside world had already come to know them. The service combined shouting, faith healing, and speaking in tongues; as much as three hours of singing, accompanied by guitar, drum, and tambourine; and vivid story-telling sermons about such things as the fiery furnace or the prodigal son. Some churches employed attendants in white uniforms to calm the shouting worshipers when they became too excited. In a liturgy that devoted a great deal of its time to discussing the nature and consequences of sin—and the specific sins of alcohol, tobacco, profanity, gambling, and adultery—there was intense joy as well. "I have known the sisters and the brothers to become so happy," one woman told Horace Cayton and St. Clair Drake in *Black Metropolis*, "that persons around them are in actual danger of getting knocked in the face."

The popularity of these storefronts was something of a problem for the mainline Baptist and African Methodist Episcopal (AME) congregations that aimed for what they saw as a higher level of decorum and dignity. Some ministers used to upbraid their worshipers for becoming too emotional during the service. By the mid-1950s, however, the liturgical distinction between the storefronts and the mainline institutions was blurring. Dozens of preachers who had begun with nothing had built their churches into successful operations, all without departing significantly from the Holiness or Pentecostal script.

The mid-1950s were an exciting time for Bronzeville churches of all varieties. Congregations were growing, debts were being paid, and churches everywhere seemed to be moving into larger, more elaborate facilities: the shouters as well as the elite.

Moses Cross was a good example. Born in Mississippi, he had opened his first church in an empty store on the South Side in 1941, preaching to a flock that consisted of his wife, his twelve children, and virtually no one else. Later he moved the church into an abandoned factory. By 1956, he had two hundred members, a vibrato Hammond organ, a senior choir, a gospel chorus, and a sewing circle. The following year, he bought a four-story building and set up a sanctuary seating three hundred people, a banquet hall for two hundred fifty, and a youth center and library upstairs. His church was still very small by mainline standards, but it was a thriving concern. And yet it was a singing, shouting congregation just as it had been in the old days.

The moving of a church from one location to another was a memorable event. In November 1959, for example, Fellowship Baptist, which had grown to five thousand in membership, moved from its old home at Forty-seventh and State to a new one at Forty-fifth and Princeton that it had purchased from fleeing white parishioners. On the Sunday of the move, a parade of five hundred cars made the eight-block trip, with fifteen hundred members of the congregation waiting in front of the new building for services to begin. When the motorcade arrived, church dignitaries made their entry in a carefully prescribed order: the officers, then the mothers' board, then the ushers, then the choir. William L. Dawson was the guest of honor; a telegram from Richard J. Daley was read aloud to everyone.

At that very moment, a similar ceremony was taking place at the building that Fellowship Baptist had just vacated. It had been claimed eagerly by Omega Baptist Church, whose members were happy to be able to move up from the storefront that they had outgrown. Omega had its own motorcade of fourteen blocks from the place it was leaving behind. The church didn't have a telegram from the mayor of Chicago; it had to make do with an appearance from the mayor of Bronzeville, Cora Carroll. But it was not less hopeful or exultant for any of that.

A few weeks later, another nearby church, Antioch Baptist, held an event of the sort that was becoming familiar all over Bronzeville in the late 1950s: a deed service. Antioch had paid off its mortgage, wiping out a debt of a quarter-million dollars in less than a year and a half. As part of the ceremony, every member of the church got a copy of the deed before it was destroyed. As an added touch, all married members of the congregation repeated their nuptial vows simultaneously in a gesture of personal and institutional commitment.

Not every aspect of the church relocation frenzy of the 1950s was quite so idyllic. Black congregations taking over bigger buildings in previously white neighborhoods almost always had to overpay to get them. In many cases, the *Defender* complained, "the conditions of sale imposed on our ministers are such as to make it impossible for them to get out of debt." This frequently meant more heavy-handed fund-raising tactics that parishioners did not appreciate, and caused resentment against the ministers that did not exist in the simpler, poorer days.

But even where those resentments existed, the status of the ministers as figures of authority and respect was not really in doubt. They were the preeminent leaders of Bronzeville in the late 1950s as they had been before World War II. They played a role more important than the businessman, the newspaper editor, even the machine boss. They were the indispensable coordinators of the community. They were into everything, acquainted with everybody, able to make the connections and the contacts between one set of institutions and another. "I am a part of every organization in the Baptist Church," one minister had told Cayton and Drake. "I am secretary of the Apex Funeral Parlor, Incorporated, and I own a half interest in the business and the funeral cars. I am a Mason and also the sponsor of a boy scout troop. I own a three-flat building and a vacant lot. I also have a two-car garage."

More than virtually anyone in Bronzeville, the pastors were free agents, beholden to no larger force or interest. And this alone was a source of a great deal of their authority. "The preacher was the one independent person in the community," recalls Timuel Black. "He wasn't bound for his livelihood to the outside world. He could afford to be independent. And the congregation expected him to be independent and honest with them." Nearly all the congregations accepted, if somewhat grudgingly, a comfortable style of life on the pastor's part that ended up costing them money at the collection box every Sunday. They were paying to maintain an authority figure they could trust.

Under these circumstances, the pastor was not only permitted to give political advice but was expected to do it. "If the Reverend said who you should vote for," Timuel Black recalls, "it was gospel. It might get included in the Sunday morning sermon."

As different as the ministers were from each other, they were nearly all models of some sort, casting a bigger-than-life impression on those who grew up in their congregations. Luther Hylton, for example, was the model of a clergyman as entrepreneur. He was pastor of Hylton Temple Church, referred to invariably as "Bishop Hylton," but he was a Bronzeville capitalist par excellence. In the course of a couple of decades on the South Side, he had been in the rug-cleaning business, invested in a radio station, and run a school that taught people how to make lamp shades. And none of these connections detracted from his prestige either as a man of the cloth or as a pillar of the community. He was always a strong contender for mayor of Bronzeville; in the 1957 contest, he held a huge campaign rally and invited virtually every local celebrity, including the most illustrious of all, Joe Louis.

As might be expected, Bishop Hylton preached a gospel of free enterprise, self-discipline, and self-confidence. "Without confidence there is no power," he told his congregation. "Achievement, the fruit of hard work, never rises higher than one's self-faith. Strong faith in one's own ability is a prerequisite of success." Hylton was also immersed in Chicago politics, and he was a Daley man. "Under the Daley administration," he insisted, "little men have been given jobs and are now working and bringing home salaries sufficient to support their families and educate their children."

The most impressive model of the pastor as machine politician was Clarence Cobb of the First Church of Deliverance, the church where Theodore Roe's funeral was held in 1952. First Deliverance was William Dawson's church, the religious headquarters of the Bronzeville Democratic machine, and Cobb used it every election year to turn out massive majorities from among his flock. "Good politics has an affinity with religion," Dawson used to say, and Clarence Cobb seemed to be living proof of that affinity.

He was also a symbol of the way a pastor could gradually transform his image in the community. In the 1940s, Cobb had been known as a Spiritualist, ministering almost exclusively to the lower class and presiding over a shouting brand of worship that the more respectable elements wanted little to do with. By the mid-1950s, however, he had made it into the mainstream, as the presence of Bronzeville's leading political figures in his congregation made amply clear. He still commanded a loyal following among the poor, however, especially with his Sunday night radio program, on which he came across not only as a voice of authority but as a possible instrument of divine intervention. "You in the taverns tonight," Cobb would say to his audience, "you on the dance floor; you in the poolrooms and policy stations; you on your bed of affliction—Jesus loves you all, and Reverend Cobb is thinking about you, and loves every one of you. It doesn't matter what you think about me, but it matters a lot what I think about you."

Of all the ministers in Bronzeville, however, the thoughts of one mattered more than the rest, and those were the thoughts of Joseph Harrison Jackson, pastor of Olivet Baptist at Thirty-first and South Park, fifteen thousand members strong, and president of the National Baptist Convention (NBC), which claimed to be the single largest black organization in the world, with nearly 5 million members and thirty thousand affiliated churches all over the country.

Of all the clergymen in the community—of all the leaders of any sort—Jackson was the one who found it easiest to speak to white power and make himself heard. Often he did not have to start the conversation. "When the white establishment wanted to find out what was going on," longtime civil rights activist John McDermott remembers, "they consulted J. H." In the early 1950s, when the establishment decided to tear down thousands of old apartments at

the north end of Bronzeville to make room for a middle-class
housing project, it didn't dare touch Olivet, even though the
church sat right in the middle of the land it wanted to build on.

Like William Dawson, J. H. Jackson faced his share of complaints
that he didn't use his position to do enough for his people—that
he cared more about his access to City Hall than about his influence over it. But there is no evidence that this troubled him. A
short, stocky, almost Churchillian bulldog of a man, Jackson never
hesitated to instruct his congregation in how to vote, think, or
behave. "The people there," says Timuel Black, "were bound to
their church." When the pastor's advice differed from the advice of
a parent, members usually went along with the pastor.

It would have been difficult for Jackson not to see himself as a
man of special gifts, or even destiny. He had been a child prodigy
in the Mississippi Delta, a boy preacher in rural Coahoma County,
and then had been plucked out of the Delta and sent to divinity
school at Colgate. He had been a pastor in Omaha and Philadelphia, and had come to Olivet in 1941, when the Depression had
left it $20,000 in debt. Jackson liquidated the debt in a year, and by
the end of the war the church was thriving again, the biggest and
most impressive in Bronzeville.

As striking as Jackson's personality and accomplishments were,
they didn't please everyone at Olivet. The congregation had a distinguished history that dated all the way back to its founding before
the Civil War, in what was now the Loop, and for most of that
history it had been a bastion of Lincoln Republicanism. Jackson's
immediate predecessor, the Reverend L. K. Williams, had been on
a GOP campaign tour with Wendell Willkie when he died in a
plane crash in 1940. Even in the 1950s, there were elders and deacons at Olivet who saw themselves as guardians of the Republican
tradition. They didn't care for Jackson's ties to Daley and Dawson,
and especially his willingness to deliver the invocation at the
Democratic National Convention in Chicago in 1952.

The Old Guard did not give up easily. They tried to oust him from the pulpit in 1953, charging that "a disproportionate amount of the church assets were spent on the purchase of a home and furnishings" for the pastor and for the Cadillac that picked him up and brought him to church every Sunday. Jackson offered $1,000 to anyone who had evidence of any impropriety. Then, when no one stepped forward, he allowed that he had been "the target of a campaign of lies and trickery" designed to destroy him, but that he bore no ill will.

Jackson could afford to be conciliatory for two important reasons. One was that he had the loyalty of nearly all the Olivet Baptist rank and file. The other was that he was about to become the head of the National Baptist Convention.

He had wanted for years to be president of the NBC, as Olivet's L. K. Williams had been before him, and he had shown remarkable ingenuity in pursuing the position. In 1952, it appeared the incumbent would retire, prompting an open contest. A month before the vote was to take place, Jackson conspicuously offered an assistant pastorship to the son of the man who was to preside at the balloting. His rivals all charged improper influence, which Jackson indignantly denied. Under the circumstances, the incumbent president chose to stay on for one more year.

By 1953, however, Jackson's time had come. He was elected NBC president and assumed a role he was to hold for more than a decade as an international religious figure and stubborn conservative voice on race questions in Chicago and at the national level.

Jackson was nearly as inventive holding office as he was gaining it. In 1957, when the rules of the NBC dictated that he step down from the presidency after four years, Jackson declared from the podium in Louisville that the term limit was unconstitutional because it had been passed on the wrong day of the previous meeting. A majority of the delegates from twenty states appeared to be against his point of view, but a vote was taken and Jackson announced the count as five thousand in favor of the chair's ruling to sixteen against.

The official minutes of that meeting of the National Baptist Convention report that when the decision was announced, "joy and satisfaction radiated throughout the vast auditorium." This account ignores, however, the fact that sizable numbers of delegates were fighting with their fists in the aisles. One Chicago minister returned from the session and painted a much darker picture. "This has set us back ten years," he lamented. "The fact that Louisville let down all color bars and admitted Negroes to hotels only to have riots and fistfights doesn't do us any good." In the aftermath of the dispute, ten of Jackson's opponents within the NBC brought suit against him for cheating. Jackson denounced the legal challenge as "a moral and spiritual attack upon the Baptists of the world," and it never went anywhere.

By the closing years of the decade, Jackson was more secure than ever, both in the National Baptist Convention and as pastor of Bronzeville's most important black church. At the NBC meeting in Chicago in 1958, he was given a forty-five-minute celebration in his honor, a Chrysler Imperial, and a money tree with $3,000 on it. Mayor Daley showed up as well, to present him with the keys to the city. The following year, the members of Olivet voted to make him pastor for life, "to protect him from the forces of uncertainty and insecurity."

They could not protect Jackson from the judgment of the generation that followed. By the end of his career, in the 1970s, he had come to symbolize a distasteful brand of black authority, one that could be imperious, even arrogant, to people of his own race, while cultivating a carefully staged subservience to the white elite. He spoke with lofty eloquence about "common moral ground" and "accepted standards of value" while playing politics as enthusiastically and manipulatively as William Dawson ever did. To his angriest critics, J. H. Jackson was a real-life version of Dr. Bledsoe, the infamous college president in Ralph Ellison's *Invisible Man,* who boasted that "the only ones I even pretend to please are big white folk."

More than anything else, Jackson's reputation was to suffer from his feuding with the Reverend Martin Luther King, Jr. Jackson had had Dr. King ousted as an officer of the National Baptist Convention for staging a public demonstration at one of the NBC meetings, accusing King of conducting a "militant campaign against his own denomination and his own race." After King's assassination, in what seemed an extraordinary gesture of pettiness, he changed the official address of Olivet Baptist Church to Thirty-first Street so its letterhead would not have to bear the new name of South Park Way: Martin Luther King, Jr. Drive.

But if J. H. Jackson was a manipulative and sometimes vindictive man, he was a serious thinker as well. One can take Jackson as a frightened protector of his own personal and political turf, but one can also take him as a man who saw clearly the impending disappearance of a larger community, and worried legitimately about what sort of bargain that was.

"All human beings who have tasted bondage," Jackson wrote, "and have known the bitter experience of servitude in any form, hate the chains that bind the bodies, souls and minds of mankind, and they will pay the greatest price to dismiss their fetters and to loose their chains. But all the citizens in this democratic republic have more to lose than their chains. They may lose . . . their community with all its values and social endowments."

"We believe," he said in another context, "that a voluntary togetherness of the race based upon constructive and creative ventures is desired and should be encouraged in the interest of the preservation of racial values. There is nothing wrong with Negroes undertaking to make any community where they live as great as any other community. Now that the walls of segregation are crumbling, what is left to bind the Negro people together? Or do we wish to be together?"

If Jackson was a reactionary, he was also an economic nationalist of sorts, one who liked to talk about gaining control of the tools of production and the organization of capital. "Protest has its place in our racial struggle," he was fond of saying, "but we must go from protest to production."

And on that issue he had something strangely in common with another black preacher who was operating on the South Side at the time. J. H. Jackson would never have admitted any affinity with Elijah Muhammad: he considered the black Muslims dangerous and they considered clergymen like Jackson to be worse than useless. But the Muslims were the only other significant voice in Bronzeville still talking about racial self-sufficiency in those days of Montgomery and Little Rock. "Know yourself (and your kind)," Muhammad told his followers. "Protect yourself (and your kind). Do for yourself (and your kind)."

The Muslims had bought an old synagogue on Greenwood Avenue in the early 1950s, made it into the Temple of Islam No. 2, and a few years later were operating not only the temple itself and the University of Islam next door but also a grocery, clothing store, dress shop, bakery, and restaurant. "The white man spends his money with his own kind, which is natural," the Muslim leader wrote in his newspaper, *Muhammad Speaks*. "You, too, must do this. Help to make jobs for your own kind."

Moreover, the Muslims were questioning integration itself in a way that J. H. Jackson, whatever his private feelings, would never have dared to do. "Today's world is floating in corruption," Muhammad said. "Its complete disintegration is both imminent and inescapable. Any man who integrates with the world must share in its disintegration and destruction."

Such comments and references to "white devils" and the inevitability of eventual race warfare had gained the Muslims national attention by the late 1950s, with alarmed coverage in all the important newspapers and magazines. It is fair to say, however, that they were primarily a national story rather than a local one; on the South Side, they were never more than a fringe institution. At the end of the decade, when the Muslims claimed sixty-nine different temples of Islam in twenty-seven different states, Cayton and Drake wrote that while Elijah Muhammad "can fill the Chicago Stadium at nationwide conventions of the Black Muslims, the number of people in Bronzeville who have actually joined the movement would hardly fill the auditoriums of the two largest Baptist churches."

The *Defender,* which initially displayed a tolerant curiosity to the new religious movement in its midst, had turned unequivocally against it by 1959. The paper was calling Elijah Muhammad "a shrewd master of mob psychology" who "lives like a potentate in a pretentious mansion," and it was expressing its approval of an FBI probe into the organization's finances. The views of the Muslims, the paper said, with some understatement, "can never be reconciled with the accepted Negro leadership provided by the NAACP and Urban League."

Actually, those establishment organizations were themselves in the midst of a protracted identity crisis in the late 1950s, divided over their proper role in the cause of civil rights. In the early part of the decade, the Urban League had gone through a highly militant phase and had lost its white financial backing. After it had been effectively shut down for a brief period for lack of funds, sponsors brought in a new director, Edwin F. Berry, who managed to straddle the fine line between agitation and respectability. Berry cultivated white business leaders and worked with them amicably enough to remain a figure of influence and respect in Chicago politics for twenty years to come, even as he fought the banks to win jobs for black tellers, protested the conditions in South Side public schools, and called Chicago "the most segregated city in America."

Meanwhile, the NAACP was enduring its own turmoil, also going through a period of angry militance during the early and middle years of the decade. After the lynching of Emmett Till in 1955, it called upon the federal government to launch a military occupation of Mississippi and to take away the state's voting rights. The NAACP attacked William Dawson for failing to make a vigorous enough protest in the Till case, and for accepting a weak civil rights plank in the Democratic Party's national platform of 1956.

"Mr. Dawson has finally revealed himself," the NAACP said, "not as a statesman, not as a leader, but as a tool of the Democratic National Committee."

The following year, when the presidency of the Chicago NAACP chapter was up for election, Dawson decided to stage a dramatic reminder of his continuing authority over the politics of the South Side. He ordered all his precinct captains to take out NAACP memberships, which at that time cost two dollars each. Six hundred Dawson allies joined up on the last day permitted for qualification. On the night of the election, December 13, 1957, Dawson's men voted as a bloc to oust the incumbent NAACP president and install in his place Theodore Jones, an executive of Supreme Liberty Life and pillar of middle-class Bronzeville respectability. The militants were outraged. "This is no time," one of them warned, "for the Chicago branch to move backward or stage an Amos and Andy routine." But the outcome was never really in doubt.

Nor was it in doubt in the subsequent NAACP election, when Dawson helped realtor Dempsey Travis defeat the militant faction one more time. Travis was no pushover on civil rights issues, but he also was realistic about where the real authority lay. "There was no way in the world you could have been president of the NAACP without the blessing of Dawson," he recalls. "It was a controlled situation." Dawson himself phrased it a little differently. "I'm not interested in controlling the NAACP or its policymaking body," he said. "However, I do want to see the 'right man' as president."

Nineteen fifty-seven, the year that Dawson packed the NAACP and J. H. Jackson engineered his own reelection as head of the National Baptist Convention, was also the year that the sociologist E. Franklin Frazier, perhaps the nation's most distinguished black scholar, published his controversial book, *Black Bourgeoisie*.

Frazier had little use for either of these men or the leadership they represented. His book was an unrelenting attack on the urban black middle class and its community institutions. The mainstream Baptist churches were huge and sterile institutions that offered little warmth or comfort to the worshipers who came seeking them. The black business leaders had deluded themselves into accepting a myth—that black enterprise could ever be more than a pathetic shadow of white capitalism as long as segregation persisted. Black newspapers like the *Defender* recruited inferior and poorly trained journalists who displayed "plain ignorance of the nature of the modern world." The social clubs that were so important in Bronzeville were nothing more than "an effort to achieve identity with upper-class whites by imitating as far as possible the behavior of white society."

And Frazier went further. As far as he was concerned, the lives and attitudes of the black middle class in Chicago and other big cities were themselves a form of psychological illness. "The badges of inferiority and insecurity," Frazier wrote, "are revealed in the pathological struggle for status within the isolated Negro world and craving for recognition in the white world."

Nearly four decades later, perhaps it is time to be more charitable. Judged against the standard of what a black newspaper might have been, the *Defender* certainly had its shortcomings, but judged against the banality of the four white dailies, it had nothing at all to be ashamed of. Olivet and the other big churches must have offered some form of spiritual comfort and relief, or they wouldn't have attracted thousands of people every Sunday. Supreme Liberty Life was not Aetna or Prudential, but to dismiss it as a nonentity is to disrespect the work it did, the jobs it provided, and the leaders it generated.

That the institutions of Bronzeville lacked some of the strengths of those in the more affluent white society should be no surprise, but it should be no embarrassment either. Nor should it be embarrassing to admit, a generation later, that the decline of those institutions is a genuine loss from which it has been very difficult to recover.

Bronzeville's leaders were doing what leaders in any community are supposed to do: maintain a set of institutions that can give a semblance of order and stability to life. That they had to do this under the most impoverished circumstances gave the institutions a vulnerability and sometimes even a quality of desperation in comparison to what existed around them. And yet the effort was no less urgent for that—it was more urgent—and the creators no less worthy of respect for what they accomplished.

Moreover, Bronzeville's leaders were role models—flawed ones, to be sure, but role models, nevertheless. If William Dawson and J. H. Jackson did not practice unimpeachable candor or selflessness, they were still examples of genuine achievement and authority, known and seen all the time on the streets of the community. To say that their presence reached down to the furthest depths of Bronzeville, to the kitchenettes, taverns, and the "bed of affliction" that the Reverend Clarence Cobb used to talk about, is perhaps to go too far. But it is not too much to say that authority had an impact at the margins, that the presence of Dawson or Earl Dickerson or even Theodore Roe was a source of stability that any community, especially the most troubled one, badly needs. Nor is it too much to say that the absence of functioning institutions and leaders has been a calamity for those left behind on the streets of what used to be Bronzeville in the years since then.

In 1957, the year Frazier published *Black Bourgeoisie,* Lorraine Hansberry, a product of Bronzeville, was writing *A Raisin in the Sun,* a play whose opening on Broadway was to generate universal acclaim in 1959, and whose power remains undiminished thirty-five years later.

Hansberry's play is not about any of the larger community institutions but about a working-class Bronzeville family with middle-class inspirations crowded into a tiny apartment and living on hope and dreams. The son, supporting his wife and child on his salary as a chauffeur, dreams of opening a liquor store; the daughter, attending a local college, dreams of becoming a doctor; the mother dreams simply of moving into a "little old two-story" with a garden in the back. "Seems like God didn't see fit to give the black man nothing but dreams," Mama Younger quotes her late husband as having said.

A Raisin in the Sun has been the subject of decades of critical interest, including a vigorous debate over whether it is a play about the urban black experience or a more universal statement about families and their aspirations. But one point is inescapable: it is a play about hope, the commodity that permeated all of American society in the 1950s and is even more striking for its presence in places where reality might have seemed discouraging enough to extinguish it.

"Could a dream," Gwendolyn Brooks had asked years before in her poem, *Kitchenette Building,* "send up through onion fumes its white and violet, fight with fried potatoes/ And yesterday's garbage ripening in the hall? . . . We wonder." But the answer to her question, as she knew, was yes.

PART IV

SUBURB

CHAPTER 9

Close Quarters

Had race been no object, and the hard-pressed inhabitants of Bronzeville been free to let their dreams stretch as far as the mind could stretch them, they might have reached all the way to Elmhurst, fifteen miles outside the city, where white middle-class families were moving west into houses and lives that seemed, even to them, almost too good to be true.

Every Sunday afternoon in the summer of 1957, thousands were making the drive out from Chicago, across the Cook County line, just to see what suburban life might promise. One very hot weekend in July, there were more than five thousand curious visitors at a brand-new development in Elmhurst whose last few units were still available.

The promoters were ready for them. "Every room in all five magnificent model homes," the literature proclaimed, "is lavishly furnished to show you how rich, how happy family life can be. . . . Here in Elmhurst has been developed an entire community where the whole family can share a rich spirit of togetherness, based upon the soundest family values."

This community was Brynhaven, a collection of five hundred split levels and ranch houses less than an hour from the Loop, straight out Washington Boulevard. Some of the homes had been occupied for nearly two years, but the last hundred or so were now being completed, and the developers, the Dreyfus brothers, had been advertising them heavily in all of the Chicago papers.

When it came to advertising, Gene Dreyfus was not a man of subtlety. He had long believed that he knew the magic word in suburban home sales: *family*. "The most important room in any home is the family room," Dreyfus explained that year. "There, natural materials might be used—rich woods to capture warmth from controlled lighting—soft earth colors to carry the relaxed, informal atmosphere through full glass walls which lead to a huge patio area." And patios, he went on, "offer an opportunity for family togetherness which too often is lacking in modern-day living."

The people who bought in Brynhaven that summer, most of them putting down a couple of thousand dollars in cash on a

$20,000–30,000 investment, were actually buying into a suburban village that was more than a century old. Elmhurst had existed since the 1840s, when it took shape as a refueling stop for wood-burning locomotives heading west out of Chicago. The first settlers were Yankees, but most of the people who followed were German. The local train stops were called out in German as well as English and the north side of town was called "Little Berlin." It was at Elmhurst College that the theologian Reinhold Niebuhr, who grew up speaking German in a small town in downstate Illinois, received his undergraduate education. Carl Sandburg, who was not German but Scandinavian, liked the quiet streets and the elm trees so much he spent the entire decade of the 1920s in Elmhurst, and it was in his house on York Road that the first volume of his Lincoln biography was written.

But old Elmhurst was fading fast in 1957—it had been overwhelmed by postwar suburban development. The population was almost three times what it had been in 1940, and the local institutions that remained in place were in the midst of accommodating themselves to rapid and unsettling change.

At the start of the 1950s, pheasants could still be spotted within a half-mile of the ranch houses that were starting to spring up. Pupils at York High School walked to class across farmland. A blacksmith was in business on York Road as late as 1950. Just a few years later, those were folktales. Elmhurst was growing by eighty to a hundred families a month, most of them migrants from Chicago. In the summer of 1957, builders of the new expressway scheduled to run west from the city were negotiating to buy the very last farm within the town limits. Old-timers were complaining that the place was changing for the worse. When Brynhaven opened, one of them had lamented that "this is no longer a small town where you can be sure that there is no one on the streets who does not belong there."

The local newspaper, the *Elmhurst Press,* was too much into boosterism to denounce the revolution, but it did take up the responsibility of educating the newcomers in the customs and courtesies of suburban life. "Don't burn your leaves on the pavement," it warned them on the front page. "Unless, of course, you want a run-in with the police. . . . Do shovel your walk, please. It's better to get burning ears from the crisp, cold outdoors than from the comments of your neighbors who must plod along your unscooped thoroughfare."

The newcomers themselves, especially the refugees from Chicago apartments, seemed equally impressed by the strangeness and the attractions of the world they had just entered. "It's a new life in every respect," said Mrs. Hugh Kempner, shortly after her family had moved into a Brynhaven split-level. "It is wonderful," said Maureen Kelly, a pioneer Brynhaven resident, "to be able to see grass and trees, instead of hallways and speeding automobiles." And on that point, the *Elmhurst Press* offered total reinforcement. "For our newcomers coming from crowded city apartments," it editorialized, "their newfound suburban existence is a pleasant way of life and the fulfillment of a dream."

Who were the dreamers? They were salesmen and office managers, engineers, industrial chemists, and printing plant supervisors. Some of them were ethnic Catholics, usually the grandchildren of an earlier immigration: German, Irish, or Italian rather than the more recent East European. A larger number, however, were small-town Protestant midwesterners, products of farms and farm market towns in Iowa, Wisconsin, and downstate Illinois, the first in their families to attend college. Nearly all the men were World War II veterans, many were beneficiaries of the G.I. bill, and most had bought their homes with little or no money down on V.A. mortgages. Nearly forty years later, these are the people who insist with little prompting that the 1950s were their favorite time of life.

These new suburbanites remained tied to Chicago in several fundamental respects. The men drove in to work every day down Washington Boulevard or Roosevelt Road, not on expressways, as would be possible a few years later. Their wives still came into the Loop for shopping and for entertainment. They were, whether they

wished to be or not, bound up with the city's politics and problems in a way that later suburbanites would not have to be.

Still, they were fleeing the city, fleeing all the things suburbanites fled in the 1950s: landlords and cooking smells, neighbors one
flight above or uncomfortably close next door, physical surroundings that carried indelible reminders of hard times years ago. They
were giving up the grayness of Chicago for the pastels of Du Page
County.

And they were seeking something less tangible as well: a little bit
of sophistication and luxury—commodities that they had convinced themselves they could afford in small measure and that
Gene Dreyfus understood exactly how to promote. They were
seeking newness for its own sake, because they had been told and
they believed that new things were a good in themselves.

The new suburbanites were not fleeing community, or even the
particular communities they were leaving behind. In many cases
they felt genuine fondness, if not for the urban physical surroundings, then for the old friends and social connections. But they
believed, with the faith of the 1950s, that community was something they could simply re-create in the place they were moving to.
And they did everything they could to re-create it, with an energy
that sometimes bordered on compulsiveness.

Authority was something else again. Back in the city, it had
existed, for many of them, in vivid and unmistakable terms—in the
parish, in the school, in the family itself. Grafting authority onto
life in a wholly different physical environment was a tortuous
process. It may not have seemed so to the children, who almost
invariably recall a culture in which authority was tough, rigid, even
crude at times. But we will remember these suburbs more accu-
rately if we think of them another way: as places where natural
authority was eroding, in a new and unfamiliar world in which
rules were difficult to enforce, and where adults invoked it hesi-
tantly, less certain than in the old days of just what the rules were.
Authority was loud in these places often because it felt awkward

and artificial even to those charged with exercising it. That is one reason why the price we paid for it seemed—and still seems to many of us—unacceptably high.

Brynhaven was not the first dream the Dreyfus brothers had sold in Elmhurst in the 1950s or the greatest shock they had imposed on the community. In 1952, the Dreyfuses had come in from downtown Chicago, quietly bought Emery Munson's corn farm in the northwest part of the village, and proceeded to do something unbelievable—fill the land with row upon row of tiny ranch houses, brick veneer over drywall, boxes on stone slabs with a four-foot crawl space for a basement. It was a Levittown-style development, although much smaller, and it was brand-new at the time in Chicago and in the Midwest.

In a matter of months, the houses were built, models were furnished, a ribbon cutting took place, and Emery Manor, Elmhurst's first subdivision, had come into existence. "Walk the Street of Dreams" was the invitation the Dreyfuses made on the front of the first Emery Manor brochures.

Emery Manor had not been hard to sell. More than four thousand people came to the ribbon cutting on February 21, 1953, and for a while the real estate agent had to keep the models open twelve hours a day, seven days a week. All 365 Emery Manor homes were taken in less than a month. The cheapest went for $14,000, while the most expensive, the ones with garages, still sold for a little less than $20,000. If you were a veteran, all it took to buy one was a down payment of $700 or less. Eighty percent of the buyers came from the Chicago area, many of them from apartments on the West Side.

The Dreyfuses had included some amenities carefully calculated to appeal to the families who came out to look: stove and washer-dryer, double sink, matching bathroom fixtures, front and rear door chimes, oak floors. Still, what seems most striking about the Emery Manor homes today is how small they are. People with growing

families were buying two-bedroom homes that had no family
room, no basement, no attic to speak of. And the rooms themselves
were tiny. A typical Emery Manor living room was nineteen by
twelve feet, a master bedroom thirteen by ten feet, and a dining
room (if there was one) only nine by eight feet, so small that getting up from the table was a chore in itself.

Respectable citizens of Elmhurst drove by the Emery Manor
construction site in the fall of 1952, took a look at the site and the
tiny brick boxes, and concluded that it was going to be a slum. It
is easy enough to imagine what it must have looked like to them:
dusty, dirty, no streets, no trees, little boxes all alike—all this coming suddenly to a quiet and conservative village. It must have been
truly frightening. Mrs. Munson let it be known that she was
embarrassed about what was happening on the old family property.

"People called them 'shacks,'" remembers Charles Weigel, then
a local businessman and later Elmhurst's mayor. "Emery Manor was
a change—a radical change from what they had been used to. They
asked, 'What kind of people are going to buy these houses?'"

The Dreyfus brothers were worried about just this reaction.
When the model homes were ready, they prepared a special invitation for the town's existing residents. "Yes, indeed," they wrote
with some understatement, "all Elmhurst has noticed with interest
the beginning of a brand new community—Emery Manor—
inside the city limits of Elmhurst. You've watched, you've won-
dered—now you and your friends are invited out to see and
inspect this beautiful new community."

As it turned out, the attitude of established Elmhurst didn't have
any effect on the salability of the houses. But it did prefigure a
small-scale "class war" of sorts that lasted most of the decade. If
Emery Manor represented a new form of community to its new
residents, it symbolized the erosion of community to many who
had lived in the village before the war.

"We here in Emery Manor are considered to be the upstarts of
Elmhurst," one of the new homeowners complained shortly after

the development opened. "We are the city slickers on parole and we have to prove our worth to the old-timers in town. . . . Why must we hear old-timers in stores whisper about 'those people up in Emery Manor'? . . . Why can't we have water wells and sewers and decently paved streets?"

The old-timers tried to explain it all to them. "It is only natural," one of them wrote in the *Elmhurst Press,* "that we who knew Elmhurst when it was a much smaller town, in which we could know personally large numbers of our fellow residents, and in which there were no problems of congestion, become vexed at the conditions we face today."

One person even called herself "Old Timer" and tried to be conciliatory. "I feel positive," she said, "that we can all live very easily in peace and contentment—whether it be Emery Manor or Elmhurst proper." But the words themselves were ominous. Emery Manor might be inside the town, but it wasn't proper.

In retrospect, the situation seems very silly. It is hard to imagine anybody much more proper than the salesmen and engineers and factory supervisors who moved out from Chicago to their first homes in Emery Manor in the 1950s. The houses were their obsession.

The home of the Tewell family, at 323 West Fremont, was as good an example as any. On the outside, all the colors were pastels, to create a casual, outdoorsy look: pink brick, pink gable, pink entrance, aqua paneling. Like every house in Emery Manor, it had a picture window in the living room facing out to the semi-finished street. Framed in the window, at floor level, was a huge philodendron. The colors of the living room were forest green, cocoa brown, and beige, accented by the blond wood of the end tables and the console television. There was a wall-to-wall beige cotton shag rug. The kitchen was decorated with rainbow square linoleum and green fishnet curtains.

The Tewells were unusual, however, in one respect. They had

moved to Elmhurst from California. Charles Tewell was in Chicago setting up a new office for the Industrial X-Ray Engineering Company.

A more typical Emery Manor family was the Frantz family—Peggy, Rod, and their two-year-old—escapees from an apartment in Berwyn, a working-class suburb on the border of Chicago. Peggy and Rod had met right after the war, in a boarding house for singles on the North Side. Rod Frantz was a mechanical engineer who had graduated from Purdue; one of his fraternity brothers had told him about Emery Manor. It took just about all the money the Frantzes had to make the move.

The Linanes lived around the corner on Highland Street. Mr. Linane was a biochemist for the American Can Company; the family had lived in an apartment in Oak Park, the older suburb that was the second most common source of migration to Elmhurst after Chicago itself. There were no single-family houses to be had in Oak Park in the early 1950s, even for those who could afford one. The Linane family bought one of the three-bedroom Dreyfus models in Emery Manor for $18,000. "We had a hard time affording it," Jo Linane recalls. "My husband didn't think we should have a mortgage. He thought houses should be paid for."

By 1954, the Dreyfuses were ready for something bigger. They bought 132 acres south of downtown, on the other side of Elmhurst from Emery Manor, and launched a development of larger, more expensive homes, roomier ranches and split-levels, three and four bedrooms. They chose the name Brynhaven.

The homes were aimed in part at the veterans and their families who had moved into developments like Emery Manor earlier in the decade and now found themselves unexpectedly with enough money to move again. In the mid-1950s, the Elmhurst Bank was running ads that showed cartoons of a father sleeping in his station wagon because his small ranch house was jammed with children. But Brynhaven was also aimed at a second migration from

Chicago, not at victims of an acute housing shortage, because that shortage was over, but West Siders driven out by the prospect of racial change.

Either way, the buyers were more upscale, if equally nervous, and the Dreyfuses pitched their whole campaign for Brynhaven on the idea that these families could afford more than they might realize. "New financing," they insisted, "makes it possible for any family with a yearly income of approximately $7,500 from all sources to own a spacious-luxurious Brynhaven home. . . . The very same families who, up until now, have been restricted to homes in the $16–19,000 category, can now live a life of luxury in Brynhaven." The names of the models had the right sound of traditional elegance: the Stuart and the Winston, the Malden, the Hampton, and the Lamont.

The word *luxury* was stretching the truth a bit. The Hampton, smallest of the Brynhaven split-levels, was only 1,143 square feet—not much more floor space than an Emery Manor box. One of the most troublesome problems of the postwar ranch house had not been addressed—the bedrooms remained tiny, some of them as small as nine by eleven feet.

Still, a Brynhaven split-level, selling in the high twenties, was a significant step above Emery Manor. The living rooms were much larger, and some of them had fireplaces. There was a big open basement with space for the kind of family room Gene Dreyfus loved to promote. "The family room is going over big," Brynhaven's real estate agent, Tom Myers, remarked shortly after the homes went on the market. "An extra room that could be used as a family room takes their eye." It was possible to buy one of these homes for less than $3,000 down and $130 a month, and they sold almost as easily as the first development.

Selling Brynhaven to Elmhurst was considerably more difficult. When the city council took up the issue in the summer of 1954, it had to deal with the hostility of longtime residents who thought another big subdivision full of newcomers was the last thing they needed. "Prior to the construction of Emery Manor, we had no flooding," one of them told the council. "Now we have quite a bit of it, and it seems to be getting worse. Now you are considering another project."

Nevertheless, the project was approved, in part because it had the support of Mayor Earl Ogden, who told the council that limiting development might be illegal, and in part because the Dreyfuses themselves kept the lowest possible profile. They never advertised their name in any of their business documents or promotional literature, avoiding any questions about them as Jewish real estate promoters from downtown Chicago. For purposes of building Brynhaven, they were Cooperative Home Builders Inc.

And the council took a few steps toward squeezing some extra cooperation out of them. It required, for example, that Brynhaven come preequipped with streets, sidewalks, and water mains—amenities that were a little slow to appear in Emery Manor. "The plans for Emery Manor had caught the city council with no background of previous experience to fall back on in attempting to see potential difficulties," the *Elmhurst Press* advised its readers. This time, the newspaper assured them, "both the city and the developers of Brynhaven are being businesslike. The city . . . is well on the way to avoiding a repetition of some of the errors of the past."

Even so, the carping continued through the two long years of construction and sale. "Why should a builder," asked one old-timer, Mrs. Donald English, "throw up such a tremendous growth of houses, with what must surely be a vast net profit, with no responsibility toward the educational facilities needed almost immediately." She thought a flat $1,000 should have been added to the cost of each Brynhaven house to pay for the schools Elmhurst would have to build to accommodate it.

In 1957, the Brynhaven issue and the council's obviously close relationship with the Dreyfus family were to cost Earl Ogden the Elmhurst mayoralty. By that time, however, the development was virtually finished, the last few models were going on the market, and residents of Brynhaven were hard at work in their basements, putting in the wood panels for the family rooms that had been the development's crucial selling point. "Ask anybody in Brynhaven what is next on the project agenda," the *Press* noticed, "and the answer will be 'the recreation room.'"

Ginny Harmon and her husband were among the Brynhaven newcomers in 1957. Mr. Harmon was a salesman for Hair Arranger, the hair tonic that sponsored Cubs baseball on television; his wife was active in the Elmhurst evening women's club and the Marmonettes singing group. Ginny had liked Brynhaven the moment she saw it. "I liked the modern look of it," she remembers. "I just liked the idea of split-level." Still, the open layout took some getting used to. Because there was no wall separating the bedroom corridor on the second floor from the living area below, many of the routine chores of daily life were considerably less private than in a more traditional house. "You could be entertaining people," Ginny Harmon remembers, "and there your kids would be tromping on the railing upstairs."

By 1957, the split-level home had become a national icon for middle-class aspirations to luxury. Its popularity had spread remarkably fast: In 1953, 88 percent of the new houses built in America had still been ranch houses, many of them Levittown-style slabs or slabs plus a crawl space like those in Emery Manor. Three years later, split-levels had overtaken them.

American Builder magazine had helped launch that fashion in 1954 by proclaiming the split-level best "for the large family with a modest income. Economical construction and architectural ingenuity combine to provide maximum living space at minimum cost." The next year, the *Small Homes Guide* had informed its readers that "millions of families who bought or built basementless homes in the post–World War II economy craze have found out too late they made a mistake. . . . An expenditure of 10–20 percent more than a slab structure can make your house essentially twice as big."

Because of the trend to split-levels, the average size of the newly built American house was increasing rapidly. In 1950, the average had been 983 square feet—12 percent less than before the war. By mid-decade, as the split-levels came in, the average grew closer to 1,200 square feet. The Federal Housing Administration liberalized its lending rules in 1955, allowing buyers to borrow more, sellers to charge more, and builders to build larger. In 1956, a building survey of the Chicago area found that eighty-three of ninety-two home builders had given up two-bedroom houses for three-bedroom models, and most of those were split-levels.

There was no question that the split was an ingenious invention. With the living-dining area and kitchen on one level, the bedrooms four or five steps above, and the family room four or five steps below, it could be described reasonably enough as a three-level house. And yet it didn't require the materials or other building costs of an old-fashioned three-story house. To those who bought the split-level, it was a miracle of 1950s architecture, more room without taking up all that much territory. And that was just what promoters said. "Spaciousness," *House Beautiful* promised, "and not simply the illusion of space . . . soaring, singing spaces that have been made possible in our time."

But the design was, if not an illusion, at least a manipulation. All that space had been made possible essentially by the elimination of boundaries. The levels, just a few steps apart, flowed right into each other. The rooms flowed into each other as well: the living area into the dining area, the dining area into the kitchen, with only a counter between them. The entire inside of the house was designed to look more spacious through the use of movable glass that all but brought the back yard into the living room. "Wide sliding glass doors," *House Beautiful* said, "give all the rooms visual spaciousness as well as direct access to outdoors . . . by rolling aside the door, interior and exterior melt into one."

House Beautiful, in fact, envisioned far larger possibilities. "Wouldn't it be wonderful," the magazine asked, "if life was so simple that it could all take place in one large room?"

Critics occasionally raised the question of whether all this free-flowing space was what the consumers had really asked for, or merely a design that architects had managed to impose upon them. A 1957 survey by the U.S. chief of housing asked housewives to critique modern housing design. Many of them responded that they missed having a genuine dining room.

But even those who questioned the popularity of the split-level house seemed to agree that in some deeply felt way it reflected the values and aspirations of postwar America. "I wonder," the social critic Russell Lynes wrote, "if the modern house, so open, so transparent, so free from dark corners and hiding places and secrets, is not a reflection of the influence of psychiatry in our generation. . . . We believe in the open mind, in the open plan, in the importance of the facts of life, and not of the myths of childhood."

Forty years later, there are equally challenging questions to ask about the homes built in the 1950s in Brynhaven and in developments like it all across the country: In erasing the physical boundaries of the house, what did they do to the boundaries among the people who lived there?

The family room was the citadel of togetherness—it belonged to everyone and accommodated everything. *Parents* magazine urged homeowners to treat it as a "Don't Say No" room where children would be free to romp as they pleased. It was nearly always the television room and usually the adult game room as well, the three-ring circus of almost every split-level house. In 1957, family room linoleum could be purchased with a shuffleboard court designed right onto the pattern. One architecture critic, Bernard Rudofsky, called the family room a "no-man's land where all may enter and no one, parent or child, feels comfortable." Meanwhile, the living room, the only traditional room of the house that had grown larger with postwar construction, frequently sat unused unless guests were present.

The master bedrooms were not the adult retreats they had been in middle-class homes built before the war: at ten by twelve feet, or nine by fourteen feet, they were simply too small. Russell Lynes

called them "pigeon holes for sleeping." Children wandered in and
out all evening, as most experts advised parents to let them do.
"Parents," Rudofsky wrote, "enjoy in a bedroom about as much
privacy as on a sidewalk."

Rudofsky may have been impossible to please, but even the
staunchest defenders of split-level life seemed to notice that it
lacked places of privacy. *House Beautiful* advised homeowners to use
the bathroom for this purpose. "Here for a brief time each day," the
magazine urged readers, "shut out all others and salve your ego
with the balm of warm waters and perfumed air . . . make it the
restorative, pampering refuge you deserve."

One can overdo this idea of declining privacy. The Brynhaven
newcomers, settling into split-level suburbia after childhoods spent
in walk-up Chicago apartments or Wisconsin farmhouses, had lived
in close quarters all their lives. They were accustomed to it. But in
the old days, their limited privacy had merely been something to
endure, an unavoidable consequence of urban poverty or big rural
families. Now they were living in circumstances of middle-class
comfort in which erasing the physical boundaries between people
was thought to be a good in itself, a matter of ideology. The split-
level house was advertised as a temple of spaciousness and in some
ways it delivered. But it was not advertised as an advance in privacy.

One has to assume that, contrary to the implications of critics
such as Rudofsky and Lynes, most of the adults who moved into
these houses adjusted to them and did not find them too bad a bargain. Otherwise the houses would not have continued to be built
in great numbers through the 1950s and into the 1960s. There
would not be so many of the early Brynhaven buyers still there as
empty-nest families in the 1980s and 1990s. The more interesting
question is how split-level homes affected the values of the children who grew up in them.

One thing nearly all these children had that they would not have
had earlier—even in the Emery Manor ranch houses—was a room
of their own. That was almost universally applauded as a good
thing. Lewis Mumford believed every member of every family

should have a private room to develop his or her individuality. The popular press agreed. "Young people," the paper in Elmhurst wrote, "get a sense of independence and self-confidence if they have their own domain."

And yet it was an odd sort of domain: tiny, with paper-thin walls, in the midst of an almost boundaryless house whose inhabitants were constantly being urged to keep themselves fused together as a household and as a family. It is not too difficult to draw a mental picture of the twelve- and thirteen-year-olds of the late 1950s, sprawled on the beds that took up virtually all of their ten-foot by ten-foot split-level bedrooms, listening defiantly to Alan Freed or Dick Biondi or some other 50,000-watt disc jockey, and see at least a few of the physical roots of hyperindividualism in the generation that followed.

One does not produce a generation of rebels by architecture alone. The early baby boomers were not just crowded at home— they were crowded in school and in most of the other things they did. Still, architecture had an influence. Raise children in surroundings that deliberately play down the importance of boundaries and privacy; raise them at the same time to be proud of their individual identities and specialness; and it should be no surprise if you end up decades later with middle-aged adults talking endlessly about "personal space" and sustaining publications with names like *Self* magazine.

CHAPTER 10

The Joiners

I t is safe to say that in 1957 very few people were concerned about the Elmhursts of America producing a generation of hyperindividualists. The fear among the elite was that the suburbs were stamping out individualism altogether and that it might never appear there again.

To many of the social critics of 1957, the suburban house, whether split-level or ranch-style, was just a miniature version of suburbia itself: a place where meaningful boundaries did not exist and identity was rubbed out. It was, the critics said, a parody of community, like the togetherness that was supposed to prevail within the home.

The bible and the primary source for that view was William H. Whyte's *The Organization Man,* which had spent much of the preceding year at the top of the national best-seller lists. Whyte drew a picture of an America in which middle-class suburbanites had forgotten how to think and act for themselves, and had become obsessed with adjusting to whatever the crowd happened to believe. The Protestant ethic of individualism and personal achievement had disappeared in America, replaced by the much flimsier values of merely belonging. "It is indeed an age of group action," Whyte wrote. The American who prized individualism so highly "is in a collective as pervading as any ever dreamed up by the reformers, the intellectuals, and the utopian visionaries he so regularly warns against."

It is hard to overstate the impact of Whyte's work. His was far from the first book of the decade to take on postwar conformity—David Riesman had done it effectively in *The Lonely Crowd* as far back as 1950—but no other writer achieved the penetration that Whyte did. The popularity of his book by the summer of 1957 explains in large measure why the graduation speakers that June all warned their audiences about the dangers of conformity and submissiveness, sounding a bit conformist about the idea themselves.

Whyte spent the better part of a year hanging around Park Forest, Illinois, a built-from-scratch early 1950s suburb at the southern end of the Chicago area, thirty miles from Elmhurst. Its newly minted developments weren't much different from Emery Manor and Brynhaven; many of them housed junior corporate executives and their young families spending a few short years in the Chicago office on the way to a higher position in their companies somewhere else.

On the whole, Whyte's criticism is controlled and even sympathetic to the people whose lives he talks about, making his analysis all the more devastating. Park Forest is not an unhappy place, but it is an outpost of compulsive belongingness, prying neighbors, and stifling conformity. "You belong in Park Forest," Whyte quotes the real estate company's advertisements as saying. "The moment you come to our town you know: You're welcome. You're part of a big group—you can live in a friendly small town instead of a lonely big city. You can have friends who want you—and you can enjoy being with them. . . . Coffeepots bubble all day long in Park Forest."

To Whyte, this is the obsessive friendliness of people who have left their extended families and childhood roots behind, who have no sense of where they are going geographically or personally, who cling to their fellow suburbanites for clues to what they should wear, eat, say, and believe. It may not be an unhappy place, but it is a scary place. Suburbs like Park Forest, Whyte wrote, "are not merely great conglomerations of mass housing. They are a new social institution. The values of Park Forest, one gets the feeling, are harbingers of the way it is going to be." Americans in the future will seek to blend into the group at all costs—and think for themselves only when there is no alternative.

Where Whyte was rational in his approach, many of the other people who were attacking the suburbs in 1957 were hysterical. The architecture critic Mary Mix Foley, for example, fulminated on the Park Forests and Emery Manors of the world in *Architectural Forum*. They were, she wrote, "row on row of identical small boxes marching across a denuded landscape, sprouting TV aerials like insect feeders. . . . Probably never in history . . . has a culture equalled ours in the dreariness and corrupted fantasy of a major part of its building." Worse yet, the people who live in these places "are eminently satisfied with the established ugliness. They do not even know it is ugly."

Others had been saying the same thing for several years. To Lewis Mumford, the American middle-class suburb of the 1950s was "a multitude of uniform, unidentifiable houses, lined up inflexibly at uniform distances, on uniform roads, in a treeless communal waste, inhabited by people in the same class, the same income, the same age group, witnessing the same TV performances, eating the same tasteless prefabricated foods from the same freezers, conforming in every outward and inward respect to a common mold."

Even these perorations pale by comparison to those of John Keats, the journalist who spent much of the 1950s shouting at the top of his lungs that suburbia was the closest place on earth to hell itself. In the summer of 1957, thousands of Americans were still reading his book, *The Crack in the Picture Window,* published in hardback the previous year, which found few midcentury social problems not traceable, one way or another, to the indignities of suburban living. The modern tract house developments, Keats said, were "developments conceived in error, nurtured by greed, corroding everything they touch."

And the center of the corrosion was conformity. "More insidious and far more dangerous than any other influence," according to Keats, "is the housing development's destruction of individuality . . . we're constantly being badgered to look around us and make sure we're doing and saying and thinking what the mass of our neighbors will accept. The closer we huddle together, the greater this pressure for conformity becomes . . . breeding swarms of neuter drones. . . . When all dwellings are the same shape, all dwellers are the same shape."

Keats was not urging any sort of political action or social protest, let alone encouraging the generation then growing up in suburbia to rebel. Few of the baby-boom children who grew to angry maturity in the 1960s ever read him. And yet they were his followers nevertheless—young people who found the suburban community of the 1950s so fraudulent that almost any excess in the name of individualism could be justified.

To accept Keats in his time, however, one had to swallow some rather awkward propositions. One had to agree with him, for example, that there was some logical connection between uniformity of architecture and sterility of thought. Nobody had argued this seriously about the working-class row houses of South Philadelphia, or, for that matter, about the upper-class row houses of Philadelphia or Boston. The evil influence of architectural standardization upon the human personality was, to say the least, a point that remained to be proved.

As did the larger notion that the residents of these new suburbs were somehow miserable without knowing it. They did not sound miserable; they sounded grateful for a modicum of physical comfort after two very rough decades. There is no question that the social critics of 1957 had tapped into the sources of future adolescent rebellion; what they made light of were the small but hard-won satisfactions of the grown-ups.

In one of the chapters of his book, Keats tells the horror story of a woman named Mary who lived in one of the new suburban developments: "She had moved into a house that could never be a home. She had moved into a neighborhood that could never be a community." As far as Keats was concerned, there were lonely and alienated people in all the cul-de-sacs of Elmhurst and every suburb like it all over America.

If Keats was right, however, the victims seem to have forgotten, at least in Elmhurst. What strikes most of them as remarkable about the early days, looking back forty years later, is what an adventure it all was, what pioneers they all felt like in their brand-new brick boxes. "Everybody had the same problems," Peggy Frantz recalls about her first summer in Emery Manor, in 1953. "We didn't have much money. We relied on each other. We all had to plant our lawns. We spent that whole summer in the yard weeding." The costs of the yard work were shared. One family bought the mower; another one bought the wheelbarrow.

On summer nights, she says, "We'd put them to bed and then the parents would all play volleyball in the back yards. All the bedrooms faced the back yard so we could hear if the kids cried." The universal beverage of those evenings, warm as they must have been, was coffee; nobody on Ridgeland Street seemed to drink anything stronger.

Around the corner, on Highland Street, social life was a little naughtier. "We had great parties," Jo Linane remembers. "We had parties at least every weekend. We'd have the greatest progressive parties, moving from one house to another. And everyone would drink. People would call the police when we had our parties. We were out in the yard doing our choo-choo train. The police would tell us not to worry about it."

The common desire to share burdens was about the same on the Linanes' block as it was where the Frantzes lived. When a woman came home with a new baby on Highland Street—which was very often indeed in the mid-1950s—a different neighbor cooked dinner for her family every night for a week.

One does, however, have to concede a point to Whyte and the other critics about the sense of community in Emery Manor and its clone developments around the country. There was something compulsive about it, something too intense to be natural. These people not only shared lawn mowers and cooked dinner for each other but joined and volunteered for clubs and social organizations with an energy that seems in retrospect to have bordered on the manic. Rod Frantz was a typical example. He ran the Halloween carnivals and the Fourth of July parades; he was a coach in Little League and a chief of the Indian guides.

There were PTA meetings in Elmhurst in the evening *and* in the afternoon in those days. The evening sessions were for business; the afternoons were reserved for tea parties, fashion shows, and flower demonstrations. "Everybody was in the PTA," recalls John Stoddard, who moved to Brynhaven in the early days. "Everybody seemed to join in the thing."

As with decisions in so many different settings in those years, there was little practical choice. Participating in group social life was a requirement that young suburbanites ignored at the risk of virtual ostracism. "There was pressure to go to PTA," recalls Millie Smith. "You were kind of expected to be on a committee, be a room mother, go on the field trip."

Millie Smith and her husband Ray were people who found themselves swept up in the fervor to participate even though, on their own, they might have chosen a more solitary life. The Smiths had moved to Elmhurst in the early 1950s from the South Side of Chicago; Ray was a mechanical engineer like Rod Frantz, an employee of the Continental Can Company. Unlike Frantz, he was no extrovert. Shy and serious, he had been affected emotionally by his combat experiences in World War II, and he returned home more reserved and withdrawn than ever. Still, he soon found himself a scout leader. "He joined," Millie says. "The pressure was on you to do it." Ray Smith was of one of those who paid a high price for living in the world of limited choices in which Elmhurst was located. This was the majority culture in a dictatorial mood.

Millie Smith, a quiet, bookish woman who had taught high school English, found her own way to be a joiner. She enlisted in the Great Books discussion program. In the fall of 1957, while Ray was coming home from Continental Can to his duties as a den father, Millie was going out in the evenings to group discussions of *Richard III*.

For those in Elmhurst who found Shakespeare too heavy at the end of the day, there were dozens of other opportunities. In 1957, in a community of about thirty thousand people, there were three competing square dance groups: the LT's, the Dos-a-do's, and the Kurly Kues. "With so many new people moving into the area," the *Press* reported, "square dancing is a good way to get to know your neighbor. . . . Migration to the suburbs seems to be one of the reasons why callers are tapping feet, clapping hands, and calling—'Everybody jump up, and never come down.'"

Perhaps volleyball in the street and choo-choo lines in the back yard, Great Books and square dancing at night, are not specimens of genuine community, the old-fashioned sort that existed in small midwestern towns and urban apartments. One may choose to find something coercive and sinister about a suburban social ethic that took a quiet, brooding man like Ray Smith and made him into a reluctant scoutmaster. Or one may see something artificial about a form of community that requires so many clubs and organizations to bring people together. St. Nick's parish didn't need all those formal groups: people there knew how to relate to each other on the simple basis of common background and interests.

But all these years later, when a new generation of suburbanites seems to have time for very little except working and retreating into a private world at home every night, one is tempted to say that artificially created community is, at least, a form of community. Given a choice between Great Books and the Dos-a-Do's on the one hand, and the modern neighborhood of strangers on the other, it is difficult to be quite as caustic about suburban values as the social critics of the 1950s were at the time.

For the young husbands and fathers of Elmhurst in the 1950s, one organization stood far above all others as a symbol of fellowship and civic pride—the Jaycees, then known officially as the United States Junior Chamber of Commerce. This was the nerve center of the new suburban generation.

The Elmhurst Jaycees started in 1950 with 36 men as charter members; by 1955 they were up to 176, with 100 enlisting that year alone. It took lots of new recruits to keep the membership up because everyone had to leave the organization on his thirty-fifth birthday, moving to "exhausted rooster" status. Thus, there was a great deal of turnover.

There was also an enormous amount of energy. It was the Jaycees who revived the moribund Elmhurst Fourth of July celebration, with a parade, a fireworks display, a freedom flame pageant, and an Iwo Jima tableau. They held a soapbox derby, and bused children from school to the circus on a Friday afternoon each spring.

In December, the Jaycees launched a "Put Christ back in Christmas" campaign, crusading against the "Xmas" vulgarization and the creeping secularism it represented. In the winter of 1953, there were "Put Christ back in Christmas" stickers and signs all over Elmhurst—on postal machines, on buses, on every tree sold for the holidays anywhere in town. Residents were urged to send only cards that had a religious theme and merchants were pressured to place biblical scenes in their store windows. The Boy Scouts were enlisted to distribute eight thousand pamphlets door-to-door, explaining the significance of the crusade. "Many of our youngsters," said Robert Bosworth, the former Jaycees president, "are far more conscious of civic responsibility than we adults realize." That year, the Elmhurst Jaycees were named the most outstanding chapter in the entire state of Illinois.

By then, however, the Jaycees were doing something more important than the anti-Xmas campaign or the soapbox derby. They had built a political organization and were taking over the local government.

Through the early 1950s, the leadership of the community had been in the hands of the People's Party, its dominant alliance for the preceding thirty years. They amounted to a collection of village elders, men who had lived in Elmhurst in the Sandburg years, who had been too old to fight in World War II, who were suspicious of postwar suburbanization and especially of using public money to pay for the extra public services required.

The Jaycees were their polar opposites: men in their twenties and early thirties, war veterans, virtually all newcomers to the community. "We wanted schools, parks, we wanted to build things," says Jack Knuepfer, one of the Jaycee stalwarts. "And they had to pay for them. They saw this whole new group of people coming into town and raising hell out of their taxes."

The Jaycees, unlike their political predecessors, were sensitive to the interests of the tract homeowners pouring into Emery Manor and Brynhaven. A good number of the Jaycees came out of the subdivisions. Others simply wanted the community to face up to the costs of growth.

Jack Knuepfer was one of those. He didn't live in Emery Manor, but he lived on the border of it, and when the three hundred Emery Manor houses were placed on his sewer line, he was faced with the continual problem of flooding in his basement. In 1955, he decided to run for the city council on a platform of more money for sewers and traffic control. He had never run for office before—never shown any interest in politics—but he was a Jaycee, he got Jaycee support, and he organized the residents of Emery Manor, for whom flooded basements were an equally important issue. The Emery Manor vote elected him. "It was the first time in many years," the *Press* reported, "that the city had felt the impact of a vote from a newly developed area."

One of the first things the Jaycees decided was that a modern suburb needed a modern form of government—it needed a city manager to replace the old haphazard village stewardship of the prewar years. The People's Party was dead set against that sort of change, so the Jaycees simply took over the People's Party. It proved remarkably easy to do. Not only did the Jaycees have in their ranks at any given time 100 to 150 of the most energetic, self-confident young men in the community—they were building a large alumni group composed of even better-established men, still young, still full of drive, eager to maintain contact with the ones still participating.

Of all the bonds that brought these men together and gave them the self-possession to take over the government and declare themselves its leaders, one bond was preeminent: their common experience in World War II. It was a confidence builder unlike anything that any generation of American political leaders had experienced. It led them to the conclusion that they were the natural wellspring of leadership and authority in the community, no matter how young they might be, and that the citizens would accept them. "You came back and it was almost a fraternal group," recalls Charles Weigel, who had fought in Africa. "You didn't do a lot of talking about it, but if a guy was a veteran, you knew he was a pretty good guy. . . . People were glad to be back and they felt any challenge could be overcome if they put their minds to it."

The Elmhurst Jaycees would have been horrified to hear their organization called a political machine. To them, the word *machine* symbolized just the sort of politics they had hoped to leave behind in sinful Chicago. A machine meant stuffed ballot boxes, bloated payrolls, bribes to cops and building inspectors. It meant coercion of voters, employees, and an entire community. It was authority of the most heavy-handed and offensive sort.

Suburban politics, they felt, could be something else entirely. With a city manager in place to run local affairs on a nonpolitical and businesslike basis, with a cohesive group of council members making the larger decisions in consensus fashion, there was no need for anyone to be coerced at all. There was no call for a Daley, or a Dawson, or anyone who might be tempted to resort to their tactics. A town like Elmhurst was well rid of that sort of leadership.

It must be said that, for most of the 1950s and for a while afterward, places like Elmhurst got along quite nicely with these non-coercive governments infused by the community spirit of the

Rotarians, Kiwanians, and Jaycees. In retrospect, however, the political changes made in those suburbs in the postwar years stand out as one more element in the erosion of local authority—something that, a generation later, less homogeneous and more contentious communities would find missing, and very difficult to restore.

For one group of young Elmhurst families, the all-consuming challenge of the mid-1950s was the making of a church. In 1953 they had sat around a living room and willed Elmhurst Presbyterian into existence. Since then, most of their spare time and energy had gone into its development.

Indeed, there was an explosion of church-making in Elmhurst in those days. The *Press* lectured its new suburban readers every fall on the importance of regular church attendance. "With vacations over," the newspaper declared one September, "with the 'too hot to go to church' excuse soon to be nullified by fall weather, area congregations will be looking forward to crowded sanctuaries. Is support of your church a part of your plans for fall? It should be."

Clarence Fralick was fairly typical of the young men who did the church building in places like Elmhurst in the mid-1950s. He was a small-town midwesterner, from Wisconsin, a war veteran, and a mechanical engineer at International Harvester. In 1951, with three small children, he and his wife moved out from a duplex to a three-bedroom home in the Crescent Park section of Elmhurst, built in the years just before the war. Fralick was not a deeply religious man—he never had an easy time keeping his mind on sermons—but he was a community builder. Building a congregation out of nothing was just the sort of human engineering task that interested him.

It was a project worthy of the best organizing talents. Fralick and a handful of other charter members had started by knocking on doors all over Elmhurst, interviewing people who had declared themselves in a religious census to be Presbyterians. When they found a hundred prospects, they began holding services in an American Legion hall. Then they moved to an auditorium at Elmhurst College. By 1957, they had a thousand members and plans for a gleaming new building spacious enough to accommodate an even larger crowd, at the corner of Spring and St. Charles in the center of town.

Elmhurst Presbyterian was a huge success, and a good part of that success was due to Fralick's efforts. As chairman of the building committee, he had roamed the streets looking for the ideal church site. He made phone calls at work on the acquisition of the property. Most of the others were just as enthusiastic. In 1956, after they hired their first permanent pastor, a dozen men showed up every Saturday morning for weeks to decorate the church manse for him. "We had a lot of energetic parents in their twenties and thirties," Fralick says. "There was tremendous enthusiasm."

There was also a certain amount of tension between these church-makers and the members of Yorkfield, the one Presbyterian church that had existed in the village before World War II, before Fralick and his generation had ever heard of Elmhurst. The people at Yorkfield were struggling to find new blood themselves—they didn't understand why these newcomers wanted to set up a rival church. As far as they were concerned, all the Presbyterians in Elmhurst could simply worship together.

In practical terms, however, that was impossible. Nobody in Fralick's group wanted to come out and say it, but Yorkfield, located at the far southern end of town, was not the kind of place young middle-class families felt attracted to. Its members were mostly tradesmen and blue-collar workers. Worse, Yorkfield had a fundamentalist tinge. The minister, Lester Dacken, was a fire-and-brimstone preacher and an authoritarian to boot. Smoking and drinking were frowned upon. So was dancing for young people. "They just took the word very literally," says Jack Knuepfer, one of the members of Fralick's group. "That didn't set well with some of us."

As dedicated as they were to creating a church, the new suburbanites of Elmhurst did not want to hear about sin in the same language that Chicago's blacks were hearing about it at Olivet Baptist, or Catholics at St. Nick's. It was not that they really disagreed about the world being a sinful place; it was that they wanted to view sinfulness, to the greatest extent possible, as something they had left behind in their previous location. Elmhurst was fresh, clean, and bursting with optimism. Why dwell on the past?

In some ways, the objection to Reverend Dacken's fundamentalism was a strange complaint, because reliance on "the word" had traditionally been the central tenet of Presbyterianism, both in Great Britain and in the United States, differentiating its followers from Anglicans and Episcopalians, whose primary loyalty was to the dictates of a priest or bishop, and from Methodists and Baptists, who centered their worship more on the feelings of the individual believer. Presbyterianism was founded as a denomination of the word.

In the social life of most American communities, however, Presbyterianism played a different role. Regardless of its theology, it was the middle path of the Protestant mainstream, perched between the status pretensions of the Episcopalians and the downscale emotionalism of the Methodists and Baptists. This perch was not always easy to occupy; Presbyterian leaders and thinkers were constantly warning of the dangers of losing their flock to the competition on either end. At the beginning of the twentieth century, the denomination's main legislative body officially urged congregations to "guard against the contrary evils of confusion and ritualism." A leading Presbyterian official, fearing a slow erosion of believers into Episcopalian ranks, asked, "Why do we abuse the papists and then imitate them?" Those sorts of troubled self-appraisals marked Presbyterian writing for decades.

Still, for the Protestants of postwar suburbia—for people like Clarence Fralick—the Presbyterian identity crisis was no issue at all. Placed as it was in the center of the denominational spectrum, Presbyterianism was the ideal form of worship for the middle class in the Midwest at midcentury. It was dignified without being stuffy; it was impressive without having to be authoritarian.

The years in which Elmhurst Presbyterian was founded were a time when religion, perhaps more than at any point in the twentieth century, had become enmeshed with wider American popular culture. Billy Graham, Bishop Fulton J. Sheen, and Norman Vincent Peale were not only national celebrities but television stars. Peale's book, *The Power of Positive Thinking,* had sold well over two million copies by the mid-1950s. Sheen's *Look Up and Live* was one of the highest-rated network programs in prime time; he explained that he was "doing it all for his sponsor, the good Lord." Religious songs were even, in those last days before rock and roll, familiar fixtures on the top forty charts: both "I Believe" and "This Old House" had been there in 1955. Jane Russell, Marilyn Monroe's co-star in *Gentlemen Prefer Blondes,* described her religious faith to film magazine readers by proclaiming that "God is a livin' doll."

In the fall of 1954, at President Eisenhower's urging, the words "under God" were added to the Pledge of Allegiance. Eisenhower, who had never been a devout churchgoer, summed up the nation's widespread but not particularly intense religiosity that year in a puzzling but somehow appropriate way: "Our government makes no sense," he insisted, "unless it is founded on a deeply felt religious belief—and I don't care what it is."

Spiritual leaders of virtually all the organized denominations found the marriage of religion and pop culture to be disturbing. Whether the pop preachers were rural, like Graham, or urban, like Peale, or simply creatures of network television, like Sheen, they all seemed to offer religion as something comfortable and almost effortless, a pleasant reassurance against personal doubt and insecurity.

"People turn to religion," complained Archbishop Patrick O'Boyle, "as they would a benign sedative to soothe their minds and settle their nerves."

The focus of this criticism, more than any other religious phenomenon, was the suburban church. To traditionalists like O'Boyle, or to Will Herberg, author of *Protestant, Catholic and Jew,* the new parishes and congregations sprouting up in suburban territory were little more than social clubs, satisfying the need for belonging in a confused world. Religion was ceasing to be a matter of faith and becoming a matter of social identity. Stanley Rowland explained the situation in the most acerbic terms in an article in *The Nation* in 1956: "Dedicated to a heaven scrubbed in detergent, adjusted by psychologists, serviced by your friendly Esso dealer and brimming with baby food and pre-digested opinion, the suburb turns to the church and demands more of the same . . . in the middle of this amicably nihilistic, low-keyed non-believing situation of casual this-worldliness, it is a miracle to see one man of faith."

There was a grain of truth in what Rowland was saying, and yet there was something ironic and misleading about it. By the standard definition of faith—as trust in a divine plan for human life, or unquestioning reliance on the preacher in the pulpit—congregations such as Elmhurst Presbyterian had far less than their counterparts in the city. And yet they had a profound faith in so many things: in American capitalism, in democratic government, in the technology that had made prosperity possible and given most of them their livelihoods. To describe these people as faithless is to miss the point of the decade.

The members of Elmhurst Presbyterian, needless to say, did not accept the notion that they had altered the terms of American religion. They had never had the slightest intention of doing that, and they considered themselves to be religious people. Still, it is impossible to dismiss Rowland's point that in moving the church to the suburbs, they had made it a substantially different institution. In religion, as in politics, it makes sense to recognize the Elmhursts of America as the beginning of something new.

In 1956, Clarence Fralick and his cohorts brought Clare Tallman out from Pueblo, Colorado, to become the first permanent pastor of the Elmhurst Presbyterian Church. Tallman's personal views were on the strict side. He didn't much care for smoking or drinking. On the other hand, he didn't really try to impose those standards on his parishioners. He was reserved and even a little distant; he was always referred to as Dr. Tallman, even by those who knew him best, and he maintained his study in a remote choir loft high above the main sanctuary, where he would not be disturbed too often. His sermons offered little in the way of emotion or charisma.

To contrast Dr. Tallman with the Reverend J. H. Jackson or Father Joseph Lynch—or the Reverend Lester Dacken of Yorkfield Presbyterian—is to state the obvious. They commanded; he presided. There was simply no place for a traditional authority figure in the pulpit of the suburban Protestant Church of the 1950s, any more than there was a place for one in the suburban town hall. Had Clare Tallman wanted to play that sort of role, he wouldn't have been selected pastor in the first place.

What Dr. Tallman was very good at was business. He came recommended by his Colorado church as a preacher who "has possibly made more of a real impact upon the social and business community in Pueblo than any other minister who has ever been here." He had increased benevolent giving among his Pueblo flock more than fivefold in a period of eight years.

Once settled in Elmhurst, Tallman lost no time in establishing his reputation as a clergyman who was comfortable in business circles and understood the bottom line. He joined Rotary and Kiwanis. He plunged into the campaign for the new church building. "Here again," he reported on the progress of the building fund, "is tangible evidence that you mean business so far as the Kingdom of God is concerned."

Clare Tallman was just the sort of pastor that the engineers and salesmen of Elmhurst understood and appreciated. They had never been uncomfortable mixing theology and commerce in one denominational package. Their annual reports reflected that mixture. "Blessed are those who use the offering envelopes," the founders of the church had reported to the congregation in 1955, "for their contributions shall be recorded, and shall be deductible from their income tax. Blessed are the systematic givers, for there shall be order in their lives and in their quarterly statements."

The new church building, the focus of so much work and planning for so many people, opened in 1958. The church deacons had interviewed a series of architects to find the one they wanted and had chosen one who advertised his style as "conservative contemporary." His signature touch was the thin silver spire that rose from the center of the building's slanted roof. It was a religious icon in anodized aluminum that managed to resemble a space needle at the same time.

There were stained-glass panels at the entrance to the main sanctuary, and inside the sanctuary, exposed brick on the side and squares of stone at the back—materials that reminded worshipers of the construction of their own new ranch-style and split-level homes. The pews were blond wood. There was a vaulted ceiling with wooden beams.

The sanctuary seated 400 people, not a particularly large number, but the room was filled twice every Sunday morning, at 9:30 and again at 11. There were 525 children enrolled in Sunday school, and the Sunday school had a staff of 50.

The new church was exactly what Clarence Fralick and his friends had wanted to build and knew without a flicker of doubt that they would build. It was the vehicle through which their sense of community expressed itself. "It was the center of our life," says

Jack Knuepfer. "It was our social group, the people we were comfortable with on Saturday night."

Actually, Elmhurst Presbyterian Church was a hub of activity almost every night of the week, every week of the year. The church spawned a major event for every season. In 1957, there was a Spring Fair, a Fall Fair, and a series of potluck suppers. There was an array of softball teams for the men and basketball teams for the boys. If an event was not being held at the church on a given night, it was being planned.

And there was a proliferation of smaller clubs and organizations covering almost every station in life: Young Mr. and Mrs. Club, Singles, Women's Association. The people who joined these clubs were the young businessmen and their families who were populating Brynhaven and Emery Manor, whose occupations symbolized the expanding consumer society of the mid-1950s. One of the officers of Young Mr. and Mrs. was a steel salesman, another was a civil engineer, and another identified himself as sales manager, Midwest Region, Photoflash Division, Sylvania Corporation.

In 1957, its second year of operation, the Young Mr. and Mrs. Club held gamefest nights, a treasure hunt, bridge parties, and square dances. The next year the club put on a minstrel show. The Singles Club, in its first year, went bowling and visited the planetarium. It sponsored a discussion of problems in the television industry. The Women's Club held a benefit baby shower. "Fifteen layettes were assembled," a member explained, "which will go to foreign lands to help keep warm the little ones who are so underprivileged."

On the tenth anniversary of the church's founding, with the membership at well over thirteen hundred, the officers held a banquet to celebrate and to congratulate themselves on what they had accomplished. "You've had ten astounding, wonderful years," they told each other, "ten gratifying productive years." They showed slides to recall the new building under construction and marveled that "nobody will ever forget the thrill of the groundbreaking." They passed out gag gifts—the senior Sunday school teacher got a giant lollipop; Clarence Fralick, who had taken the responsibility to feed the choir every time it rehearsed, was given a doughnut cutter. It was a wonderful evening. They were celebrating something important—not only a church and a social center but the confidence and the innocence that had made it all possible. Even then, one has to assume, in the early 1960s and in their own early middle age, they must have realized it was starting to slip away.

CHAPTER 11

The Taming of the Young

For a brief time in Elmhurst in the late 1950s, it was fashionable to enroll in a course called "Parenthood in a Free Nation," a series of ten evening classes sponsored by the local PTAs and the Board of Education, and based on materials supplied by the Parent Education program of the University of Chicago.

The idea was that in democratic postwar America, the authoritarian child-rearing techniques of earlier years were no longer appropriate—families and schools needed to work together to implement the most modern scientific methods. The leader of the group in Elmhurst, Mrs. Herbert W. Suckow, explained that once a family had been exposed to its theories, "children will receive the same discipline in the home and in the school rather than jumping from one type of discipline to another."

Millie Smith was one of those parents who enrolled in the course in Elmhurst. She felt it taught her not to suppress her children's natural ideas and inclinations. Other graduates said the same thing. "I don't yell as much," said one. "There is more democratic living in our house," another insisted. A third reported that "I now consider more—whether it's the child's fault or the parents'."

The advertising that urged Elmhurst families to sign up for "Parenthood in a Free Nation" made it starkly clear just how high the stakes could be. "No one wants to rear a delinquent," one ad said. "The fear that one's method may not produce the mature citizen of tomorrow haunts the most conscientious parent."

In the late 1950s, Elmhurst residents were as terrified of delinquency as parents everywhere else, despite the fact that there was virtually nothing going on that would qualify as delinquency by today's standards. During the summer of 1957, an Elmhurst boy concealed himself in the open trunk of a car, poured ketchup on his arm so it would look like blood, and dangled the arm from the trunk while one of his friends cruised through town. They were both charged with disorderly conduct and given a stiff fine.

It was consensus opinion around town that much of the teen misbehavior problem had to do with the absence of an adequate social facility. The mayor's wife took charge of the effort to find one. "It may be that we need a community building," she said, "a roller rink, a place to play handball. Something is missing. What it is, we haven't been able to pinpoint, but we're working on it."

The occasional incident of petty vandalism brought a thunderous response from the civic establishment. One winter, as the Jaycees were laboring to "put Christ back in Christmas," a group of teenagers stole and broke some lights that had been hung on the homes in one of the residential developments. "It is difficult to imagine a more vicious kind of behavior," the *Elmhurst Press* editorialized a few days later. "These vandals can't leave alone the decorations which residents have created in order to add to the festive atmosphere." Then the newspaper unloaded on the parents: "Their offspring may already be such badly warped personalities that they can't be reclaimed. But the parents of youngsters on their way into their teens had better be sure of what they are doing in raising their children, and if they are uncertain of their techniques, they had better get expert advice."

It is a cliché these days to talk about the 1950s family as an outpost of traditional values, a deeply rooted institution whose stability is symbolized by the situation comedies written on the memory of nearly everyone now middle-aged. A brief visit to the Elmhurst of those days serves as a reminder that it was not that simple, not in the suburbs at any rate. In subdivisions such as Brynhaven and Emery Manor, the suburban family was regarded, like the physical setting, as something very new: an experiment in fulfilling personal needs and solving personal problems that used to be the province of the larger community.

Many of us who were raised in such places look back on a family life that we perceive as having been authoritarian in style: a father who made decisions confident in his ability to make them stick, and wives and children who knew their role and carried it out accordingly. This is largely a creation of memory. It was widely believed in suburban America in the 1950s that the authoritarian family was already a relic, a casualty of change in the unraveling postwar world. If the era of unquestioned discipline was still more or less alive in the school systems of the time, it was fading in the precincts of the middle-class family.

Moreover, its decline was seen by much of the popular culture as a good thing. The American family, it was said, could never succeed in meeting massive new obligations in the old patriarchal way. The family had to be reborn on a more egalitarian basis for the demands of postwar suburban life. It had to become a partnership. That was the idea behind "togetherness."

As a word and as a concept, togetherness was just over three years old in the summer of 1957. That can be said with precision because the theme was born all at once, in the pages of *McCall's,* as an article and an advertising campaign in the spring of 1954. Its launching was entirely commercial. But it was a brilliant, and as it turned out, a long-lasting appeal to the nervousness of the American people about the quality of their family lives.

American families, wrote *McCall's* publisher Otis L. Wiese in April 1954, "are creating this new and warmer way of life not as women alone or men alone, isolated from one another, but as a family sharing a common experience. . . . From this day forward, *McCall's* will be edited to meet the needs and excite the interests of all of you who are or wish to be partners in this way of life."

To explain what togetherness was, *McCall's* introduced its readers to a modern suburban family: the Richtscheidts of Pines Lake, New Jersey—Ed, Carol, and their two children. "Had Ed been a father twenty-five years ago," the magazine explained, "he would have had little time to play and work along with his children. Husbands and fathers were respected then, but they weren't friends and companions to their families. Today the chores as well as the companionship make Ed part of his family. He and Carol have centered their lives almost completely around their children and their home."

In building a partnership rather than a patriarchy, the Richtscheidts were merely doing what most of the family advisers and child-care experts told them was best. It was time for the authoritarian Father to yield his place to the more genial and sympathetic Dad. *Parents* magazine led the chorus. "Today," it reported in the fall of 1956, "Dad finds families function best on a partnership basis. He shares in the daily care and companionship of small-fry— all sizes. As for discipline, he's replaced the woodshed with a do-it-yourself workshop where everyone has fun."

These anti-authoritarian ideas were reinforced by specialists with impeccable social science credentials. Sidonie Matsner Gruenberg, of the Child Study Association of America, reassured families that "modern psychology backs up the common sense of parents by proving through actual studies how much unhappiness is caused when parents . . . are too autocratic and severe."

This was, in addition, the doctrine of Benjamin Spock, who admitted in the pages of *Baby and Child Care* that he wanted to end "the long repressive reach of tradition." He did not like anything about the authoritarian family, its way of raising children or its way of governing relations among the adults.

By 1957, the disappearance of the traditional father was an idea taken for granted in much of middle-class America. Russell Lynes wrote about it that year in his volume of cultural criticism, *A Surfeit of Honey.* "The roles of husband and wife are becoming less sharply differentiated," Lynes said. "The man, once known as the 'head of the family,' is now partner in the family firm, part-time man, part-time mother and part-time maid."

The truth was that by then the disappearance of Father and the emergence of the egalitarian family was already beginning to create a backlash. Even *McCall's,* which was still celebrating the trend in its advertising, was warning that it could go too far. "No one wants fathers to go back to acting like tyrants," the magazine declared. "But they should wield more authority in their families than they are currently doing. The family needs a head. This means father, not mother."

In the summer of 1957, this backlash was being given prominent play all over the women's pages of American newspapers. "Father Is Slipping as the Head of the House," one *Chicago Daily News* headline announced. Another one a few weeks later was even worse: "We're Raising a Generation of Little Sissies." Underneath the latter headline, feature writer Lois Wille reported that "a combination of over-protective parents, weak fathers and new suburban developments is breeding an effeminate little boy. . . . The strong and mighty dad, once idolized by little boys, is disappearing in a maze of apron strings and commuter trains."

So where were the authoritarian parents so much of the baby-boom generation grew up to rebel against? What about the tyrannical father who drove his son to suicide in *Dead Poets Society?* Are all of them merely creatures of literary imagination?

For anybody who grew up in the 1950s, that is too much to believe. Memories of arbitrary authority are disturbingly real, in family life as in school or in the neighborhood. But it is fair to say that they are likely to be less real—less intense, at any rate—if you grew up in a suburban split-level than if you grew up in a bungalow in St. Nick's parish or an apartment in Bronzeville. It's not that fathers weren't raising their voices in the subdivisions of Elmhurst; they were. It's that they were beginning to doubt their own legitimacy in doing it, and they betrayed those doubts, and that made their efforts at authority seem all the more arbitrary and capricious.

In September 1957, while young mothers and fathers of Elmhurst were learning how to parent in a free society, the community was honored by a visit from Dr. James B. Conant, former president of Harvard University, who was in the midst of what was to be a landmark study of education in America.

Conant spent two full days in town as an official guest of York Township High School, the all-purpose public high school serving Elmhurst and surrounding territory. Conant liked York. He had liked it even before he arrived, which was why he included it on his itinerary. "One of the very best," he had written in his notes before setting out.

Conant thought high schools should bring their communities together, and York did that. More than 90 percent of the eligible teenagers in the township went there. He liked large institutions, and York was huge. In the fall of 1957, the enrollment was 3,266, including 998 in the freshman class alone.

In truth, York was not just huge—it was swollen. The school was on double shift that September, with continuous classes from 7:45 A.M. to 4 P.M., with five lunch periods, starting at 11, and with separately marked "up" and "down" staircases to avoid traffic jams. A freshman student, asked the previous year to give her first impression of the place, answered, "the way you get trampled."

Still, the crowding didn't bother Conant very much. He labeled the size of the school "acceptable." He appreciated the fact that it seemed to mean business academically, with four years of English required, and German, Latin, Spanish, and Italian all available. He liked the whole curriculum. "Good social studies," he wrote down in longhand. "Good senior problems course, good summer session, good guidance department."

What Conant saw was a massive institution struggling to make useful citizens out of a diverse array of raw material. This was what he admired and had come to see. It was more important than any particular form of academic instruction. "I am committed to the general idea of a comprehensive high school," he wrote, "meaning by that a school which enrolls all the youth of a given area. . . . I am a believer in the theory of the use of various devices to break down social barriers between different types of students in such a school with the hope of engendering a spirit of democracy and a respect for all forms of honest labor."

Conant's visit to Elmhurst occurred two weeks before the launching of *Sputnik,* at a moment that was later to seem a turning point in postwar secondary education. Even before *Sputnik,* the "life adjustment" theorists who played down the importance of academics had been losing ground in the curricula of schools like York; science and foreign languages had already begun their comeback. Still, a principal like York's Bruce Allingham, with more than three thousand teenagers on his hands, could be excused for a little ambivalence about just what to teach them. Was it really possible to focus on science and math and still do justice to the hundreds who had no academic interest and would not even have been in high school in the years before the war? In 1890, only 6 percent of all fourteen- to seventeen-year-olds in the United States were enrolled in high school. In 1930, the proportion was still only about half. But by the late 1950s, it was more than four out of five. Everyone was there, even if they had no idea why. It was a confusing place to try to run.

The one theme that seemed to permeate the high school experience, however, was character building. York's administrators were all but obsessed with character, citizenship, and the molding of polite adults. In their rhetoric, even before *Sputnik*, character building was linked inextricably with patriotism and the Cold War. "Let us be intelligent patriots," the students were urged by one assembly speaker, Dr. Henry Dinkmeyer, the president of Elmhurst College. "In that way we may become true Americans." The township school superintendent, Hal Hall, urged students on with the exhortation that "we are today in a race for knowledge, which we must win if we are to keep our place in the sun and on the moon."

The formation of character and citizenship were not left to chance. Every spring, teachers rated students on a detailed personality and character inventory that was sent to college admission offices. Among the categories were emotional health—retaining poise and self-control under varying conditions; personal appearance—neatness and pleasantness in person and in dress, and courtesy—exercising tact and good manners in daily relationships.

It had its effect. One week in February 1957, for example, was a student-enforced Courtesy Week. The school newspaper, the *York-Hi,* explained that "watchbirds, little birds who go around pointing out all the wrong things people do, will be watching discourteous people all over school . . . posters and slogans will try to point out to students that such discourteous acts as tripping people in the hall, shoving in a crowd or pushing a girl's face into the water fountain are also unsafe practices." At the end of the week, the two students judged to have the school's best manners were named Mr. and Miss Courtesy. Marise Rader, the cheerleading captain and president of the girls' club, was named Miss Courtesy for 1957.

However, the authorities did not rely on gimmicks such as Courtesy Week to maintain discipline and order at York High School. They worked at enforcing it every day, from the first bell until dismissal. Life at York was an endless series of rules and restrictions that brought real penalties for their violation. The dean kept a collection of ropes in his office for boys who failed to wear belts to school. Forgetting gym clothes was grounds for detention; so was talking during an assembly. Athletes who failed to keep their hair short risked expulsion from the team. The school day was punctuated by a steady stream of sarcastic comments from teachers about gum chewing, posture, and other petty issues that were the currency of discipline at a big public high school in those days.

Every year in the 1950s, the York High yearbook published, next to the name of each faculty member, a few words that the student editors associated with that particular teacher. To read those "teacher sayings" now, forty years later, is to be thrust back into that particular world in a vivid and sometimes chilling way.

"Shut up, peasants." "Spit that gum out or down to the office." "Did your mother dress you this morning?" "You're going to keep doing it over until you do it without any noise." "We always have showers unless I tell you differently." "I demand absolute silence."

Some of this was the legendary tyranny of the gym teacher and the shop class, but it seemed to reach up through all the academic departments. One gets an idea of its pervasiveness by examining the year-by-year entries of Leon Benson, a veteran mathematics teacher and a York institution. Benson's yearbook quotations suggest a drill sergeant rather than an educator. His saying for 1953 was "Stay where you are." It was "Did you get your pass stamped?" in 1956; "Just throw that gum out!" in 1957; "That's uncalled for" in 1958. In the twelve years that the yearbook sampled Benson's comments, not one of them dealt with mathematics or any aspect of education at all.

And that was more or less typical. There were a few exceptions—a science teacher who used to ask, "Isn't nature grand?"; a math teacher who said "this problem is so beautiful I could cry"—but by and large the hundreds of comments published over more than a decade suggest an institution where discipline ranked far ahead of learning as a priority.

Most of the male teachers at York in those days were veterans in their thirties and forties, secular counterparts, one might say, of Father Lynch of St. Nick's. They had lived through adolescence in a relatively bleak time for the country and had gone to war right after high school. In many cases they had received their education degrees on the G.I. bill, working and raising families at the same time, not even getting started on a career until age thirty or later. They had little patience with a collection of postwar teenagers they almost invariably saw as pampered.

"It was very controlled," recalls Richard Webber, who entered York High as a transfer student at the end of the 1950s. "You couldn't walk down a hall without a pass. You couldn't enter a hall without a pass. These people were constantly trying to reiterate their stature and position. They had to establish control. There really was an authority problem."

Were the teachers of this generation obsessed with maintaining absolute docility? Or were they struggling somehow to preserve minimal control in an overcrowded institution in which chaos seemed to lurk frighteningly close to the surface?

Even at the time, there were social critics who saw the high school disciplinarians of the 1950s as the embodiment of mindless tyranny, if not outright evil. "About one teacher in four," Edgar Z. Friedenberg wrote in *Coming of Age in America,* "is an embittered martinet, snarling, whining, continually ordering the students to stand closer to the wall and threatening them with suspension or detention for real or fancied insolence. What high school personnel become specialists in ultimately is the control of large groups of students even at catastrophic expense to their opportunity to learn."

On the inside, however, things looked a little different. Joe Newton joined the York physical education faculty in 1956 as a recent college graduate. "A kid would mouth off to you and you'd grab him," he says. "You had to maintain your own discipline. You had to survive. If you were tough enough, you survived. There was a camaraderie among teachers. We had to stick together. It was us against them. . . . You were sitting on a powder keg." His recollection of those days is of an institution grown frightening in its sheer size and forced to cater to the needs of rebellious adolescents who, unlike the prewar high school population, had no particular academic reason for being enrolled.

Those on the receiving end of authority at York High remember it as intimidating; those on the other end remember it as fragile. There is a simple explanation for that: it was both.

Even in a prosperous suburban school like York, the trend toward high school education for the masses created social distinctions between the middle-class and upper-middle-class kids who were headed for college and most of the working-class kids who were not. York in those days encompassed not only Elmhurst but neighboring Villa Park, a blue-collar town where an Ovaltine factory was the leading employer. One result was a clear class boundary between the children of affluent Elmhurst, from Crescent Park and other prewar neighborhoods, who dominated all the activities and honors, and the blue-collar kids who resented them, sulked, and fed the faculty's preoccupation with discipline.

In the parlance of 1957, there was a clear-cut split between the JDs and the White Bucks set. The JD boys, also known as hoods (rhymed with "foods," distinguishing them from true hoodlums in Chicago and other genuinely sinful places) liked to wear leather jackets and unbelted blue jeans slung low over their hips. The girls wore black skirts and blue jackets with white striped sleeves. They rarely participated in sports or extracurricular activities of any sort; they referred to the athletes as "rah-rahs."

But they stayed in school. The dropout rate at York was under 5 percent. There was no official tracking program; everyone at York started out, in theory, on an academic track. The ones who could not make it on that track, or did not try, simply drifted off to shop, typing, driver education, and auto repair. And they nursed their resentments of the suburban social elite. "Don't tell me the White Bucks boys don't do anything wrong," a self-described greaser wrote to the school paper in 1957. "They just play it cool while any teachers are nearby."

The greasers knew instinctively, even if they weren't always able to articulate it, just what they were rebelling against. They were challenging a culture of Mr. and Miss Courtesy, sermons on citizenship, expectations about college and a lifetime of routine employment. That was the majority culture, and the rebel essentially elected to be on the outside. He was different and he knew exactly who he was different from. Teenage hoodiness was not an effort to overthrow the system; it was actually a sullen way of acknowledging its hegemony.

A generation later, that sort of rebellion is impossible. There is no real majority culture to rebel against. We have not only lost the ability to enforce standards of conduct but we have lost any clear sense of what standards we would wish to enforce. In high school, as in most areas of American life, we have enshrined choice, and all choices are supposed to be treated with equal respect.

The first requirement for either playing by the rules *or* rebelling against them is to have a set of rules in the first place. In the high school and in the culture of the 1990s, one has to begin by questioning not whether the rules are being fairly enforced but whether they exist at all.

Whatever the inherent social tensions, York High School was a place that, in James B. Conant's words, enrolled "all the youth of a given area." It was in fact the only form of educational institution that did so. Elementary schools each drew from a small and usually homogeneous neighborhood; college, for those who went, was the preserve of the elite. Only in high school did all the social elements of the broader suburban community come together, compete, and manage somehow to coexist.

However one may choose to view that situation, there is little question that it made discipline the focus of school life every day, more important to student and teacher alike than anything in the academic curriculum. In fact, one gets the impression that, whatever Conant may have found at York in the fall of 1957, learning was essentially a by-product of the process.

Earlier that year, the student newspaper had solicited suggestions for improving the quality of life at the school. Most of them had to do with food: "Lunch period should be longer; more selections in the à la carte line; a coke machine in the main hall." One student had a practical recommendation for making entry into the building less unpleasant. "Rubber strips," he pointed out, "might keep the doors from slamming."

During the same months that James B. Conant was touring American high schools to assess them academically, the young sociologist James Coleman was studying them from a different angle altogether. Coleman's extensive research into life at a wide range of secondary schools led him to conclude that it was a mistake even to think about these schools primarily as academic institutions. They were social institutions—places where young people educated themselves in the adolescent subculture of the 1950s.

"Academic achievement," Coleman went on to write in his book, *The Adolescent Society*, "counts for little in the culture, and does not give a boy or girl status in the eyes of his fellows. . . . Adolescent subcultures exert a rather strong deterrent to academic achievement." Coleman found that "the intellectuals of such a society, the best students, will not in fact be those with the most intellectual ability" but those kids willing "to work at a relatively unrewarded act." That was as true of the affluent suburban schools as of the less prestigious ones in urban neighborhoods and small towns. In one wealthy North Shore Chicago suburb, which he called Executive Heights, Coleman asked forty-four girls what they would like to be remembered for at the end of their high school careers. Not one said she wanted to be remembered as a brilliant student.

What most adolescents actually did in high school, as far as Coleman could tell, was look for mates. The median marriage age in the United States was barely above twenty years in 1957. An extraordinary number of young people married upon high school graduation or shortly thereafter, so the high school years were a time to take socializing seriously—a time of making decisions that were supposed to be irrevocable, to be commitments for life.

To Coleman, this in itself made it very difficult for the high school to serve any ambitious educational function. "It seems unfortunate," he wrote, "that so much of adolescents' energies must be spent in acquiring skills that serve them at only one point in life—in playing the courtship game." The girls, he thought, were essentially taking an extended course in attractiveness to males, as if all of them were training to be "chorus girls, models, movie and TV actresses, and call girls."

York was no different. Teachers were constantly needling female pupils about their obsession with makeup. One of the health teachers had a reputation for being something of a broken record on the issue: "Girls, put your beauty aids away"; "Girls, this isn't a beauty parlor."

During the 1957–1958 school year, Betty Lou Hamilton, a speaker from the Patricia Stevens modeling agency in Chicago, came to talk to the members of York High School's Commercial Club, an organization of the less academically inclined female students. "Your best friend is your brush," Hamilton told the girls. "The hair style for you is the hair style that will make your face look more nearly oval." She warned them that only three pieces of jewelry should be worn at any one time.

At another point that year, there was a makeup scare among these students at York. There were rumors that the dean of girls was going to ban long hair and black skirts. The dean had, in fact, issued a warning that the most recent makeup styles "have been exaggerated to the point where they have become almost garish." But no official makeup code was promulgated and the crisis passed.

Most of the members of the Commercial Club stood on the lower rungs of the social ladder among York girls; the cheerleaders stood at the other end. They were the elite, at York as at all of its counterpart high schools all over suburban America.

In the generation since then, the cheerleaders of the 1950s have become an object of ridicule, a token of the decade's hypocrisy. Symbols at once of sexuality and virginity, prissiness and temptation, they seem perhaps the most graphic exhibit of a culture that did not quite know what to think about the most sensitive issues of its time. "What does it do to the mind of a sixteen-year-old to be Marilyn Monroe one moment and Little Goody Two Shoes the next?" a cheerleader of this period was to write in *Ms.* magazine in 1973. "Half the time in real civilian life I had to keep pulling those gray flannel skirts down, making sure 'nothing showed.' The other half the time, as a cheerleader, I dropped a skimpy red costume over only bra and panties and got out there in the middle of a gym full of screaming spectators to wiggle my hips all over the place."

Her testimony raises an issue that the 1950s raise on many other levels: Was the life of the cheerleader merely a burden of deceit that made people uneasy about themselves and miserable later in life for their deceptions? Or was there some legitimate value to promulgating a formal societal standard even if it was honored, as cheerleader virtue sometimes was, mainly in the breach?

The truth is that it is hard to have any sort of public value system without generating a fair amount of hypocrisy; the mere existence of social virtues guarantees a class of citizens who will preach them but not be able to practice what they preach. Do we declare a culture indefensible simply because it breeds its share of hypocrites in conspicuous places?

In the 1957–1958 school year, most of the cheerleaders at York High School had boyfriends; most of them, in fact, were going steady. It was a moment when steady dating had become the norm in American high schools and a subject of controversy for educational and social thinkers. Many of them did not know quite what to make of it. On the one hand, going steady seemed a conservative, stabilizing institution, an imitation of adult married life at the adolescent level. "Teenagers, traditionally promiscuous, have become monogamous," Russell Lynes reported. "The convention of going steady threatens to change the sex mores of the nation."

The Catholic Church, however, saw going steady as a sure step in the direction of illicit sexual activity and overall moral laxity. Boys and girls who went steady, according to *Information,* a Catholic magazine, "start making bad confessions, then no confessions, followed by no sacraments, no mass, finally no faith." In the parochial schools of Lynn, Massachusetts, students who went steady were not eligible for honors.

Scholastic magazine published a forum on the subject. "Does it mean prestige and security, or dangers and monotony ahead?" *Scholastic* leaned in the latter direction. It quoted Marilyn Van-Derbur, Miss America of 1957, who confided that, "I've always dated several boys at a time, myself . . . it is the only way to find the right husband." Then the magazine summed up: "Going steady does not necessarily mean going sexy, but there is no denying the drift in this direction."

Steady dating was a major issue at York in 1957. By and large, a girl who had reached her junior year either had a steady boyfriend or could not attend the prom in the spring. Not all of them liked that; not all the boys liked it either. "At today's dances," one boy wrote to the school paper, "we dance with our dates and with no one else, not even the couple with whom we double date. What do I want? I want to be able to go to a dance and spend most of the time with my date, yet feel free to ask any girl present to dance. . . . I'm sure sorry I'm growing up at a time when tying yourself to one person is the rule, not only of our dances, but of teenage social life in general."

The parties were remarkable events—exercises in the manufacture of fantasy and illusion about adolescence and about the middle-class suburban universe in which the students lived. The themes were always exotic. In 1956, the theme of the fall homecoming dance was "Coral Mist," and "seaweed, mermaids, starfish and fish nets adorned the walls." The girls got a bid book in which, on the last page, they were invited to note down whether their date had been "Check One—precious pearl, fair fish, or cold clam."

The junior-senior prom in the 1957–1958 school year was held in the gym, as all the events were in those years, but it had a celestial theme. "If it's ok'd," the newspaper reported—and it was—"white gauze will hang overhead, coming to its highest peak in the center, where a large chandelier will appear. If gauze is ruled out, angel hair will take its place to form wisps of clouds overhead. The gym will take the shape of a circle formed by white columns in two arcs. The columns will be accented with gold at the top to depict age." The bid for that year's prom closed with a poem: "We entered a mystic fairyland, upon a moonlit night."

There were students who complained about all this exotic pretending. One wrote to the school paper suggesting that the theme of the next prom be "Gymnasium," so the job of preparation could be made easier. By and large, however, the York students wanted the fantasies. In the late 1950s, for what may have been the last moment in American life, suburban adolescents possessed the ability to pretend for a few hours that a gym really was some sort of South Sea island, or a place in the clouds. And they were able to maintain ambitious fantasies about each other. On homecoming night, the paper reported, "we're taking those steps up the walk to see a princess who last night was a blue-jeaned bobby soxer hanging decorations in the cafeteria." In a decade of faith, the willingness of suburban adolescents to believe in all that gauze and crepe paper is as graphic a demonstration of credulity as anybody could ask for.

The mood was so romantic and innocent that one has trouble imagining these parties leading to any trouble at all. But the adult authorities were constantly worrying about keeping things under control, warning of the dangers of letting adolescent enthusiasm get out of hand. In 1958, it did, or so Principal Bruce Allingham felt. He called a special assembly and lectured the entire student body on the embarrassing fiasco that the previous week's homecoming had turned into.

The event had started off quietly enough, with the traditional pep rally, but after the rally was over, several hundred students snake-danced through the streets of town, surging onto the Elmhurst College campus, destroying the football goal posts and performing numerous other acts of minor vandalism. Allingham condemned "the destructive pranks and the mob spirit which . . . bring indignant reproach and criticism upon the school."

"When the mob spirit takes over," Allingham told the students, "reason and good judgment go out the window, and we all must stand up to the criticism of the community. Perhaps we need an 'agonizing reappraisal' at the grassroots of our student body." Allingham did not wait, however, for the results of the reappraisal. He declared there would be no homecoming the following year— no pep rally, no parade, no party, no king and queen. "I am tired," he said, "of apologizing for our misbehavior."

Eventually he relented. By the next fall, Allingham had agreed to hold homecoming with tight control by chaperones and a Stunt Night program after the pep rally to forestall any repetition of the disastrous snake dance. Student leaders waged an intensive campaign urging classmates not to get out of control again. "Support the student council and homecoming," the council president urged, "by being a constructive force, not a destructive force." The school paper warned that "this weekend will show whether or not we can be adult enough to have a homecoming that doesn't infringe upon the rights of others. Many Elmhurst citizens remember last year's disgraceful romp through the town and general displays of childish behavior."

In the end, all went peacefully. There was no vandalism or other embarrassment during the rally, the parade, or the football game on Friday night. Self-control was maintained even during the halftime show, which may have been a challenge for the boys, judging from the advance description of the event in the school paper. The paper explained that the show was to have a jungle motif and that "thirty-six tigresses will perform to the Wildcat Swing . . . camouflaging themselves from the great masculine hunters, the girls will wear short green skirts and white blouses. And they'll be shaking some kind of green and white leaves."

The next night, all went smoothly again at the homecoming dance, whose theme was, appropriately enough, "Taboo." Bruce Allingham was pleased. "I was deeply proud," he told the students, "as I observed the earnestness and the vigor and the honesty with which you all worked."

■ ■ ■

One can, if one wishes to be gentle, treat all this as simply one more irony of growing up in the 1950s: going to a dance called "Taboo" and watching girls pretend to be jungle tigresses while promising the principal not to depart from strict school decorum.

Or one can portray it as the outright hypocrisy of the decade. Either way, we are reminded of what a life full of contradictions those suburban teenagers lived. More than almost any other generation, they were forced to grow up in two cultures at the same time: the sexually provocative, genuinely rebellious peer culture fed by rock and roll and the prurience of 1950s entertainment in general (the required initiation for the French Club at York High in 1959 was a Brigitte Bardot imitation); and the conservative middle-class family culture they were expected to master and, at crucial moments, imitate perfectly, even as teenagers.

As students in high school, most of them were only a few short years away from marriage and the responsibilities of work and raising families, but they were disciplined essentially as children by school authorities who saw no other means of maintaining order in a crowded and confused environment. The student paper summed it up in a cryptic but telling way at the end of the 1956–1957 school year: "When you leave, you are almost an adult, and adult things are expected of you—not just in the brain department, but in all areas, including fun."

It was, unlike youth in more recent times, a life of role-playing, and of constant switching between one role and another. That it might be a difficult act to bring off was noticed by the more perceptive observers even at the time. "The contrast of tight pressures and permissive freedoms," Max Lerner wrote in *America as a Civilization,* published in 1957, "might seem confusing to the young American and produce in him a sense of being boxed in and of being left bewilderingly alone."

It might even, to take Lerner a step or two further, produce a generation that spent the better part of adult life rebelling against those unpleasant confusions—at the nervous authorities that forced all that role-playing upon them and at the sanitized atmosphere of community those authorities seemed to be trying to produce. It might create a generation determined to keep permissiveness and unfettered self-expression at the top of its list of values long after they turned into corrosive forces for the society as a whole.

PART V

THE PAST AND THE PENDULUM

CHAPTER 12

Beyond Nostalgia

I n St. Nick's parish on the Southwest side, the octagon bungalows still stand as they did in the 1950s, their bay windows
thrusting outward to the street. And many of the couples
who raised big families in them are still living there, alone now
in small houses more comfortable for two people than for six or
seven.

But much else is gone: the sociability of the front stoop on summer evenings, the camaraderie of the back alley as an athletic field,
the network of at-home moms who provided an instant neighborhood bulletin board seven days a week. On weekdays now, for long
stretches of time, no one walks down the quiet residential streets.
That is in part because the older people worry about crime and
fear the streets almost as much as they took sustenance from them
in the old days.

Violent crime in St. Nick's parish is still very low by urban standards, certainly by the standards of the city in which it is located.
In 1992, the Southwest Side as a whole reported thirteen violent
crimes per thousand residents, barely one-third the rate for Chicago
citywide. And St. Nick's is near the low end of the statistics even
for the Southwest Side.

But the perception is what counts, and the perception among
older people in the parish is that the streets are dangerous. These
same people certainly thought about crime forty years ago, worried about juvenile delinquency, and exchanged concerns about
tales of mayhem reported in the *Southwest News-Herald*. But in the
1950s they considered the streets to be their home, an extension
of their property, whereas today the streets are, for many people,
an alien place. A block is not really a community in this neighborhood anymore. Only a house is a community, a tiny outpost
dependent on television and air-conditioning, and accessible to
other such outposts, even the nearest ones, almost exclusively by
automobile.

Most people don't walk to Sixty-third and Kedzie anymore;

there isn't a great deal there to justify the walk. Most of the commodities of life are still available at or near that corner, but not from a neighborhood merchant. The dutiful clerks at Slater Shoes have yielded to the self-service racks and boxes of a Payless shoe store. The grocery stores are mostly convenience stores now, and the old Chicago Savings and Loan, a smaller and more intimate version of Ben Bohac's Talman Federal, is a branch office of Citicorp. It has been a long time since people trudged there on Friday nights to meet each other, listen to music, and record their deposits; by far the busiest feature of this bank is its automatic teller machines. And when the residents need to make a major purchase—a piece of furniture or a big appliance—they drive either to Ford City mall, at Seventy-ninth and Cicero—more than a hundred stores under one roof—or to one of the newer malls beyond the city limits, in Oak Lawn, Evergreen Park, or Palos Hills.

On the western border of the parish, things haven't changed quite so much. There is a family-owned coffee shop at Sixty-third and Pulaski, and a cigar store on the opposite corner, with the same grotesque wooden Indian that was there in the 1950s. A block down the street, Nick Bertucci is still selling pork loin and hamburger, although he has added so many extraneous items in recent years that his butcher shop is itself beginning to resemble a convenience store. He has gradually had to change the nature of his operation and expand his hours just to keep his head above water. "The loyalty just doesn't exist anymore," he complains. "In the old days, you were part of the family. Where you lose that personal relationship today is over cost. Nobody wants to pay for that relationship."

That the streets were safe and crime nonexistent in a big city a generation ago; that butchers were treated like family members; that an entire working-class neighborhood was a sort of innocent Eden—all these thoughts could possibly be, if not fantasies, then at least distortions generated by a mischievous mental process. But when it comes to the core of neighborhood life, the church itself, we no longer have to worry that we are trafficking in illusion. Vatican II was a real event and its consequences are all around.

In place of the ethereal Monsignor Fennessy and the dictatorial Father Lynch, in the early 1990s, there was the friendly Father Goergen, who preferred to be known as Father Mike and to dress during the week in casual pants and a sweater. It has been a long time since any priest at St. Nick's walked the streets of the neighborhood in a long black cassock, as Lynch and Fennessy once did. Mass continues to be celebrated on weekdays as well as Sundays, and there is good attendance from the older residents, as well as among Hispanics who live at the eastern end of the parish. But the older people make no secret of their preference for the old Latin mass with the priest speaking for the congregation. "There was an awesome presence of the Lord, even though it was in a language the people didn't understand," Father Goergen says. "They miss it."

Confession is still heard, but compared to the old days, very few parishioners step forward to make it. The long lines have disappeared. The only confession booths in operation are the ones in the basement; the carved wooden booths near the altar in the main church upstairs are now used for storage. Only 6 percent of the Catholic adults in America confess their sins even once a month anymore and St. Nick's is probably not too far from the national average.

The vast majority of the people at confession are children of the parish school, preserving a ritual that is so terrifyingly familiar to the middle-aged adults who went through it in the days of Father Lynch. But so much about the school has changed. There are no tyrannical nuns firing erasers at misbehaving children; in fact, there are no nuns at all. The last Adrian Dominican sister, the school's principal, left in the late 1970s, and the convent is now a social service center. The children receive ample portions of religious instruction, as they always have, but in matters of discipline, style of teaching, and overall atmosphere, St. Nick's now resembles a good public school more than it does the fearsome parochial school from pre–Vatican II days.

One can dispute the loss of community that the older residents of St. Nick's parish feel when they think about their world of a generation ago. It can be argued that the neighborhood was never the cocoon of relationships memory fills in, or, alternatively, that strands of community remain intact and are simply ignored in the service of nostalgia. Authority, however, has palpably eroded. There is no Father Lynch, no Sister Ellen Marie, no Ben Bohac. Outside the province of the individual family, there are no noticeable figures of authority at all.

Ten miles west, in Elmhurst, there is the same sense of physical continuity and social upheaval. Emery Manor fooled its critics—it never became a slum or anything close to it. More than forty years after the grand opening amid prophecies of disaster, it is quite a nice place. Rows of tall trees line the streets that seemed so bare and uninviting when the development was built. In that respect, Emery Manor now looks like the Old Elmhurst it was once said to be destroying. An Emery Manor ranch house sells for about $120,000, a respectable price but a decent bargain for a starter house in the close-in Chicago suburbs. The only real drawback is the size. "I show them to couples," one agent says, "and they tell me, 'I couldn't live in a place this small.' "

But if the streets are pretty, they are also empty just about all the time. Emery Manor, like nearly all the suburban subdivisions in America, is now a neighborhood of two-job families, so you don't see mothers with strollers on their way to and from the park the way you would have in the 1950s. Nor, for that matter, do you see many older children playing outside by themselves in the late afternoon. There are a good number of children in the neighborhood, but they are in extended-day programs, waiting to be picked up by their parents on the way home from work.

The social consequences of the two-job family extend far beyond the empty streets in the daytime. There is little time during the hours at home for the gestures of community that bound the original residents together. The idea of conga lines in the back yard or grown-up volleyball games on summer weekday evenings would strike most of the current suburban generation as bizarre.

To the extent that a feeling of community does exist in Elmhurst today, it is not geographical. It does not grow out of the shared experience of being members of a neighborhood. There are substitutes: the groups of friends from work that get together periodically at night, the social clusters that form around weekend tennis or racquetball or aerobics. But this is community of the most transient and attenuated sort.

Such an arrangement has one presumed virtue: it is based on choice. When we build friendships out of an exercise class, we can pretty much select them on the basis of personal taste. The original residents of Emery Manor essentially couldn't. Their community was, to a great extent, limited to the people who happened to buy houses near them on the same block, and they were expected to participate whether or not the match was compatible. If a newcomer family liked to drink and dance, and the preference on their block was for teetotaling volleyball games, they had to accommodate themselves accordingly. There were other opportunities to build friendships, of course—at church, or through the PTA or the Jaycees—but these served as a supplement to geographical community. They were not an alternative to it.

There is something to be said for having more choice in the selection of one's friends, just as there is something to be said for the freedom to choose one's employer, or political organization, or wardrobe. Few would argue nowadays that friendships ought to be included with the purchase of a house, as they were in Emery

Manor and Brynhaven in the 1950s. In that more constricted world, some inevitably found themselves out of place. On the other hand, people were obliged to make the best of the situation in which they found themselves and try to derive some comfort from it. That is a disappearing skill in the suburbs and practically everywhere else.

The church that the postwar suburbanites created, Elmhurst Presbyterian, remains open for business. The aluminum spire still soars like a space needle from the center of the roof, and the blond wood pews in the sanctuary are in fine condition after more than forty years. But there aren't nearly as many people in the pews as there once were. Membership, which rose as high as thirteen hundred in the early 1960s, is down to about five hundred now, mirroring the membership decline in mainline Protestantism nationally in the past twenty years. And while quite a few of the charter members are still active and as dedicated as ever, and the minister is youthful and energetic, one cannot escape the notion that the church's exciting days are over and its original function fulfilled.

What the church did, perhaps more than anything else, was provide its members with a tangible symbol of their faith in midcentury America and a place to express their gratitude for the affluent lives they felt privileged to live. Its creation from scratch was a test of their competence and commitment, and they passed that test, establishing a congregation and erecting a building that gave them a feeling of self-affirmation every time they entered it or even looked at it. That is not a feeling that can be passed on to the succeeding generation, no matter how solid and respectable an institution Elmhurst Presbyterian continues to be.

York High School has been similarly depopulated, but with more or less useful consequences. In the course of the last generation, its size has gone up and down like a yo-yo: up in the 1950s with the growth of Elmhurst; down in the early 1960s with the construction of other high schools in the area; up again as the peak of the baby boom moved through in the early 1970s; then down again in the 1980s as the boomers were replaced by the much smaller cohorts that succeeded them.

Walking the corridors these days, one sees few signs of the crowding that once seemed to define the place. There is plenty of room for everyone. Twenty years ago, the principal had to let students wander off campus for lunch just to create room in the building. Now everyone stays inside all day, making it possible to lock the doors for security purposes—something nobody thought necessary until only a few years ago.

Still, for a large public high school, York is on the peaceful end of the spectrum. Within the building, a rough sort of decorum prevails: rough not only in the sense that it is loosely enforced but in the sense that it permits a fair amount of physical aggressiveness, both boy-to-boy and, unlike a generation ago, girl-to-girl. One gets the feeling that the school's standard of behavior is based pretty much on what the students themselves can live with. The faculty simply is not in the business of enforcing norms of conduct the way it was in the old days. There are no Leon Bensons prowling the halls anymore to check on what students are wearing, to ask them for hall passes, or to tell them to spit out their gum. There are no more gym teachers or driving instructors willing to keep potential miscreants in line by the humiliation of calling them "peasants" or even "spastics," as was true a generation ago.

Given the form that authority took in the halls at York and similar schools in the 1950s, the disappearance of discipline by dictatorship is in many ways a blessing. Teachers and administrators who turned up the volume to camouflage their fear of a bewilderingly large mob of teenagers may represent the single least attractive memory of 1950s high school life.

As it has abandoned arbitrary discipline, however, the present-day high school has also abandoned the belief in the value of character building that gave it a sense of purpose in the postwar years. "The primary obligation of public schools," York principal Bruce Allingham told the school PTA in the fall of 1956, "is to teach democracy as we know it . . . essentially we are preparing our youngster to become a citizen, a homemaker, and a worker." No doubt this was a slogan more often than an actual practice. Talking about character building in a speech was one thing; thinking about character building in the halls on a day-to-day basis was something else.

Still, there is no question that most of the staff would have agreed with Allingham in 1956 about the purpose of the school—not only for public consumption but for real. Today, anyone who asked about purpose would get a disorderly mess of answers, many mouthed with little conviction. The most honest response might well be that the real purpose for students and teachers alike is simply to make it through: the day, the week, the school year, the four years to graduation, the decade left until retirement. In cleansing education of the windiness and frequent hypocrisy that plagued it in the 1950s, we have also cleansed it of much of its sense of mission. But to say that of high school is merely to say what is equally true of the larger society outside its doors. Somehow hypocrisy and values are intertwined with each other, and it is difficult to strip away one without threatening the other.

Change cannot be measured in Bronzeville the way it can be measured in Elmhurst or St. Nick's. Bronzeville no longer exists. That is not merely because no one would use such a name anymore, but because most of the buildings that comprised the neighborhood have long since been leveled. With the completion in 1962 of Robert Taylor Homes, the nation's largest public housing project and quite possibly its most squalid, the area once called Bronzeville ceased to run the gamut from worn-out but respectable apartment buildings to gruesome kitchenettes. It became a much more uniform high-rise slum, punctuated every half-mile or so by decrepit commercial strips, hosting intermittent taverns, barbecues, and convenience stores and suggesting only a remnant of the much more thriving business streets that once existed.

Bronzeville is long gone not only physically but socially; it passed out of existence as a community as soon as the middle class left, which was as soon as it was permitted to leave with the lifting of segregation. By 1960, the middle-class exodus had already begun, and by 1970, it was virtually complete. Thousands of families who had been the pillars of Bronzeville society returned at most once a week, for church on Sunday.

So much has been written about the impact of middle-class departure on the life of the ghetto that it seems unnecessary to belabor the point. Perhaps it is sufficient to say that Bronzeville was a community unique in America, that its uniqueness depended on the presence of people from all classes and with all sorts of values, living and struggling together, and that with the disappearance of that diversity, the community could not have continued to exist, even if there had been no physical changes at all.

In thinking about what has disappeared, however, there is no shortage of ironies to ponder. The policy racket is legal now, run neither by local black gamblers nor by the Mafia but by the state of Illinois, which calls it a lottery. The game that was once considered an emblem of sin by much of white Chicago is now depended upon as a contributor to the financing of public education. Policy is merely a business now, managed by a colorless bureaucracy far away—it is no longer a cult or a neighborhood institution. There is no demand for dream books anymore on the South Side, no circus-like drawings in crowded basements with a light over the entrance. People play the legal numbers game with a humorless compulsiveness that has little in common with the old-fashioned emotional experience.

Legal businesses have fared almost as badly as illegal ones. Notwithstanding Earl Dickerson's prediction that Supreme Liberty Life would thrive under integration to become a billion-dollar insurance business by the end of the century, the company was simply absorbed into United of America, becoming a piece of a gigantic white institution, and a rather small and inconspicuous piece at that. Not that there was anything racist about such a consolidation; plenty of smaller white-owned insurance companies suffered the same fate. But the cumulative effect on black economic life was powerful: the old life insurance companies were the one significant engine of capital in Chicago's black community, and by 1990, not a single firm was left.

The *Chicago Defender* remains in business at the same location it occupied in the 1950s, published by the same man, John Sengstacke. But it never really found a coherent role to play as a voice of its people in an integrated city. Once the white newspapers began printing news about blacks on the South Side, the paper lost its franchise as virtually the sole source of information within the community. It played a surprisingly passive role in the civil rights confrontations of the 1960s, serving neither as a conspicuous engine of militant activism nor as a persistent critic. By the 1970s, the *Defender* had essentially been superseded as a forum for political debate by the plethora of black radio stations that had sprung up on the South Side. The Bud Billiken parade is still held each summer in Washington Park, attracting a huge contingent of Chicago politicians, white as well as black, but it is no longer the signature event of a powerful black journalistic institution: it is a reminder of the influence that institution once had.

Of all the fixtures of Bronzeville life, the churches come the closest to having survived in recognizable form. Olivet Baptist stands as an impressive edifice at Thirty-first Street and King Drive, its front lawn dominated by a statue of the Reverend J. H. Jackson, pugnacious in stone as he was in life, along with quotations from some of his sermons and praise for him from around the world.

Olivet, South Park Baptist, and some of the other Bronzeville churches still turn out crowds at services on Sunday morning, attracting families who return from the far South Side and the suburbs, senior citizens who have remained in the neighborhood, and a sprinkling of children and adults from the projects nearby.

Some of the churches still maintain choirs, Sunday schools, Bible study groups, and social outreach programs, struggling rather heroically against the social disorganization that is all around them. But they have ceased to be voices of clear authority. No preacher can deliver instruction and expect compliance in the way that J. H. Jackson could in his prime. And while sin remains a familiar topic in the South Side black churches on Sundays—a more important topic than at St. Nick's or Elmhurst Presbyterian—the subject no longer has the hold over its listeners that it had a generation ago.

Only in politics can one really argue that Bronzeville has gained more than it has lost. William L. Dawson was a power broker and even a role model of sorts, but he was a leader whose rewards from the white machine were disappointingly meager, somehow not commensurate with the job he did in guaranteeing the election of Richard J. Daley and other white politicians. Dawson's machine yielded in the 1980s to something truly remarkable—a citywide coalition that made possible the election of Harold Washington as the city's first black mayor. Washington's victory in 1983, in a campaign with "Our Turn" as its most conspicuous slogan, was a psychological triumph far beyond anything the old Dawson organization could possibly accomplish, perhaps beyond anything blacks had experienced in any American city. And while the extent of Washington's tangible achievements in office can be debated, the fact that he died in 1987 with his heroic status in the black community intact, and his respect growing even among whites, represented a victory comparable in its way to the first one.

Black political power in Chicago, however, seemed to disappear almost as suddenly as it emerged. Ten years after Washington's first election, Chicago was again being governed by a white mayor, Richard M. Daley, son of the old boss, and by a majority coalition in which Hispanics, not blacks, were the significant minority partner. Meanwhile, the black community was deeply divided over whom to follow and how to proceed, seemingly years away from the level of influence it had had in city politics in the mid-1980s.

In the black community, unlike the white working-class neighborhoods or white suburbia, it may seem perverse—or at least misleading—to dwell on the losses of the past generation. At the individual level, there have been so many gains—in personal freedom, in job opportunities, in income. Today's black middle class is far larger in proportional terms than the one that existed in Bronzeville in the 1950s, much of it living comfortably in neighborhoods scattered all across the Chicago metropolitan area.

When it comes to community institutions, however, the losses are no less real for Chicago's blacks than for white ethnics or for the split-level suburbanites of the 1950s generation. If anything, they are more real. Nearly all of the things that gave texture and coherence to life in Bronzeville, demeaning as that life often was, are simply not reproducible in the freer, more individualistic, more bewildering world of the 1990s.

There are those who will insist that any return visit to the neighborhoods and values of the 1950s is merely an indulgence in nostalgia, a cleansing and oversimplifying of the past that makes it look beguilingly rosy and innocent from the vantage point of a few decades of history.

There is no doubt that nostalgia plays strange tricks on us. It plays them in our individual lives, filtering out the complexities of childhood and adolescence, so that we see them as uncomplicated even if they were not always very happy. Perhaps, it can be argued, our societal memory works the same way: we filter out the complexity so that life always appears to have been simple and then to have come apart in the last generation.

After all, the desire to escape from rigid authority and stifling communities is what this country has always been about. It is the force that brought millions of people here from Europe and drove them west across the continent, leaving behind extended families, close-knit villages, and clearer sets of social rules. Perhaps those who talk about the decline of community and authority have merely been noticing some of the downside of the American experience, and disguising those feelings in the mistaken notion that the country's values were somehow different a generation earlier.

One can argue quite plausibly that the modern history of Western civilization is itself a history of eroding community and authority, reaching back to the Reformation, if not further; that the West has spent the last five hundred years moving inexorably away from the values of tribe and hierarchy and village life and toward individualism and the market. Perhaps all we have done since the 1950s is play out the process one generation further.

It is a tempting proposition, and carries with it the potential to trump virtually all the arguments one can make about the losses of the past generation. It is a means of minimizing not just the eclipse of familiar social institutions but the transience of personal relationships and the decline of the notions of character and virtue. Relax, we are told. It is normal to worry about the quickening pace of society, the erosion of old standards, the depersonalization of everyday life. The task for the years ahead is not to nurse the memories of the old days; it is to prepare for the changed world of the twenty-first century.

The argument is seductive, but ultimately it does not work. It collapses in the face of all the tangible changes of the past forty years that we cannot live through a day without encountering.

Nostalgic illusion does not explain the disappearance of lasting relationships between merchant and customer in the commercial life of a neighborhood or suburb. It does not explain the willingness of profitable corporations to leave the communities that nurtured them in an aimless quest for a higher stock price. Those are genuine changes and genuine losses. What explains them is our worship of choice. It is true that in the 1950s, traditionalists were already lamenting that the corner grocery store was not what it had been a generation earlier. But that does not argue against the magnitude of what has transpired between the 1950s and the present, or suggest that it is somehow irrational to point out that some of the most important foundations of a stable neighborhood life are now gone.

Nor does nostalgia account for the public high schools where, in the 1950s, the principal passed out ropes to boys who failed to wear belts each day, but where today the most offensive displays of speech, dress, and conduct are now regarded as individual liberties and protected from discipline. Only a wave of individualism and disrespect for authority is powerful enough to explain that. There is no denying that the parents and teachers of the 1950s were already fearful of juvenile delinquency and youthful disrespect. But the realities of the 1990s dwarf those concerns, not because of any nostalgic illusions, but because the problem itself has expanded in geometric terms.

Memory may play tricks on all of us, but the flight from authority and the enshrinement of individualism and choice in the last forty years do not represent lapses of memory, personal or societal. They represent losses that it is altogether rational to mourn.

In June 1994, as in June 1957, college seniors all over the country suffered through a plague of unusual early summer heat as they sat outside in folding chairs and listened to the advice of the nation's elite on graduation day. The setting and the costumes were deceptively similar to those of an earlier day; it was the speeches that revealed the decline in American morale over thirty-seven summers.

The sermons delivered to the Class of 1957 dealt with the need for young people to avoid complacency and self-satisfaction; the sermons to the Class of 1994 sounded more like desperate pleas to stay out of the trap of nihilism and despair. "Cynicism drains us of the will to improve," Vice President Al Gore warned the graduates of Harvard. "It diminishes our public spirit; it saps our inventiveness; it withers our souls."

But as he spoke those words, it was difficult to think of a corner of national life in which cynicism had not taken root. The entire political system seemed corroded by it, and by a disrespect for leadership unparalleled in modern American history. Hostility to the president, and the willingness of his critics to subject him and his wife to personal abuse and ridicule, proceeded without the restraint of any larger belief in the authority of the office itself. One television evangelist, host of a program called *The Old Time Gospel Hour,* was playing tape recordings that month in which a man charged that "Bill Clinton had my father killed." No evidence was presented, although the tapes were being sold for $40 a copy.

Congress was an even more depressing story. As the month of June began, the chairman of the House Ways and Means Committee—an aging protégé of the old Daley machine—was indicted on seventeen different charges of milking his staff payroll and expense accounts for half a million dollars in personal profit over twenty years. Some of the charges seemed serious; others rather flimsy. But all of them contributed to the deepening national suspicion that no elected leader was worthy of trust or respect.

The suspicion was being fed further by an election season in which candidates for public office at all levels passed up serious debate in favor of playground name-calling of the most demeaning sort, berating each other on television as liars, charlatans, and petty thieves. The desire to discredit the opposition—and the knowledge that voters were willing to believe the worst about almost any political figure—had long since overcome any residual loyalty most candidates might have felt toward the institutions in which they served or the political system in whch they were operating. By the summer of 1994, American politics had come to resemble a stage on which all the worst individual traits of post-1960s America—egotism, incivility, disloyalty—were being exhibited with painful bluntness.

Politics was far from the only such stage, however. It was difficult to know where in the newspaper to turn to find relief from cynicism and disrespect. Certainly not the sports page—it had been filled all month with threats of a baseball strike, as wealthy players and even wealthier owners insisted they could not continue operating without protection against a drop in their income. The owners were preparing to impose a cap on players' salaries that appeared certain to bring the game to a halt indefinitely. "It is an act of people preparing for war," charged the spokesman for the players' union. But the leader of the owners said the dispute merely reflected "the decade and the era we live in."

Few disagreed. Baseball—the one emblem of summertime continuity and reassurance over decades of war, depression, and national upheaval—seemed unable to handle the decline in societal trust and stable relationships in the 1990s. The players, offered choices and rewards undreamed of in Ernie Banks' day, could not restrain their desire for more. The owners, playing a game of economic hardball that most of their predecessors would not have understood, lacked the self-discipline to draw the line short of catastrophe.

The business news that month was no better; it told a seemingly unending tale of eroding corporate commitment to the nation's work force. To cite one small example that made the papers in June, the Sara Lee Corporation announced that it was laying off thirty-eight hundred workers, 6 percent of its work force, despite solid profits and strong gains in sales and earnings during the most recent year. In the 1950s, Sara Lee had been owned and lovingly operated by Charles Lubin, a Chicago baker who insisted on using the most expensive ingredients even if they cut into his profit margins. In the 1990s, Sara Lee was merely a branch on the organizational chart of a multinational corporation. "We had a couple of areas that didn't do as well last year as they should," the company CEO said, "and we're dealing more aggressively with that now." The day of the layoff announcement, Sara Lee stock went up nearly a dollar a share.

Meanwhile, in Detroit, two thousand workers were on strike against General Dynamics. They were protesting the fact that the company, after a profitable year in which it awarded its executives substantial bonuses, was asking rank-and-file employees to accept reductions in life insurance, health insurance, and paid vacations. "You've worked here all your life planning on something because they've been telling you something would be there," said Gary Martin, a fifty-one-year-old assembly-line worker. "With the stroke of a pen, it can be gone forever."

What we have done in the last forty years is repeal a bargain that, if it was starting to unravel a bit at the margins in the 1950s, nevertheless was a fact of day-to-day life for nearly everyone in America.

The bargain provided us with communities that were, for the most part, familiar and secure; stable jobs and relationships whose survival we did not need to worry about in bed at night; rules that we could live by, or, when we were old enough, rebel against; and people known as leaders who were trusted with the task of seeing that the rules were enforced.

The price of the bargain was a whole network of restrictions on our ability to do whatever we liked. Thus, John Fary stuck with the Daley machine, Ernie Banks stuck with the Chicago Cubs, and the Lennox Corporation stayed in Marshalltown, Iowa. And thus bright young pupils chafed under the strictures of parochial school

education, and introverted suburban homeowners forced themselves to be scoutmasters because it was what they were "supposed"
to do.

That the price of this bargain was substantial is a truth we would
be foolish to deny. But that it was in fact a bargain, in which the
costs could not be repudiated without affecting the benefits, is a
reality that many of us are even now reluctant to admit.

It turned out to be possible to emancipate the individual and to
give him free choice in all sorts of decisions that were once
imposed on him by habit, custom, or authority. And we have done
that. But it has not turned out to be possible to make that change
without sacrificing many of the things that most Americans still
value as comforts of life.

Millions of us whose summer evening activities in the 1950s
would have consisted of a series of conversations on the front stoop
are now free to spend those hours using a remote-control device
as an ultimate weapon of personal choice, proceeding in the course
of an hour to select and reject dozens of visual entertainments
whose ability to satisfy us for more than a few minutes is crippled
by our suspicion that there may be something more stimulating a
couple of frequencies further on.

Channel surfing is not exactly a metaphor for life, but it isn't
a bad caricature of the larger predicaments of the 1990s. We are
trying to operate without a chart—at both the most profound and
the most mundane levels. Nowhere do we need a chart more
than in front of the television set, but nobody has figured out how
to make a decent one when there are dozens of channels and they
can't all be listed on a single page, let alone grasped simultaneously
by an ordinary human mind. The chaos of choice has made chart-
ing a futile effort and has reduced television watching to an aimless sequence of fragmentary stimulations. Channel surfing can be
addictive, and there are those who can do it night after night
and show few signs of weariness. For most people, though, it is

ultimately a depressing activity. There is too much choice, adding up in the end to dissatisfaction and insomnia.

Too many of the things we do in our lives, large and small, have come to resemble channel surfing, marked by a numbing and seemingly endless progression from one option to the next, all without the benefit of a chart, logistical or moral, because there are simply too many choices and no one to help sort them out. We have nothing to insulate ourselves against the perpetual temptation to try one more choice, rather than to live with what is on the screen in front of us.

CHAPTER 13

The Next Generation

America is full of people willing to remind us at every opportunity that the 1950s are not coming back. Ozzie and Harriet are dead, they like to say, offering an instant refutation to just about anyone who ventures to point out something good about the social arrangements of a generation ago—conventional families, traditional neighborhoods, more stable patterns of work, school, politics, religion. All of these belong, it is said, to a world that no longer exists and cannot be retrieved. We have moved on.

And of course they are right. If retrieving the values of the 1950s means re-creating a world of men in fedora hats returning home at the end of the day to women beaming at them with apron and carpet sweeper, then the idea is indeed foolish. It was an exaggeration even in 1957.

But the real questions raised by our journey back to the 1950s are much more complicated, and they have nothing to do with "Ozzie and Harriet" or "Leave It to Beaver." They are questions like these: Can we impose some controls on the chaos of individual choice that we have created in the decades since then? Can we develop a majority culture strong enough to tell children that there are inappropriate ways to behave in a high school corridor and that there are programs that eight-year-olds should not be free to watch on television? Is there a way to relearn the simple truth that there is sin in the world and that part of our job in life is to resist its temptations?

The quickest way of dealing with these questions is to say that the genie is out of the bottle and there is no way to put it back. Once people free themselves from rules and regulations, and taste the temptations of choice, they will never return to a more ordered world. Once they have been told they do not have to stay married—to their spouses, communities, careers, or any of the commitments that used to be made for life—they will be on the loose forever. Once the global economy convinces corporations that there is no need for the personal and community loyalties they once practiced, those loyalties are a dead letter. So we will be told many times in the years to come.

But is it true? Is the only sequel to social disorder further disorder? There are other scenarios, if we do not mind making a leap to look for them.

It is always dangerous to stack up decades one against the other, but it is remarkable how many of the laments and nostalgic reflections of the 1990s sound curiously like those of one particular time in the history of America in this century. They sound like the rhetoric of the 1920s.

Seventy years ago, the best-selling book in America was Mark Sullivan's *Our Times,* a fond chronicle of everyday life before the Great War and a lament for the lost community of those years. "Preceding the Great War," Sullivan said, "the world had had a status—an equilibrium." Since then, the most prominent feature of social life for the average American had been "a discontent with the postwar commotion, the turbulence and unsettlement that surrounded him and fretted him; it was a wish for settled ways, for conditions that remained the same long enough to become familiar and dear, for routine that remained set, for a world that 'stayed put.'"

More than anything else, Sullivan believed, the eroding values of the 1920s had to do with technology—with the automobile and the methods of mass production that had transformed the American factory in the first quarter of the twentieth century. So it is more than marginally interesting that the creator of those methods, Henry Ford, spent the 1920s mourning societal change and the loss of community as much as anyone. In 1926, he began the construction of Greenfield Village, a historic replica of the village in which he had grown up, complete with gravel roads, gas lamps, and a country store. "I am trying in a small way," Ford explained, "to help America take a step . . . toward the saner and sweeter idea of life that prevailed in prewar days."

Ford believed that the pace of living had somehow accelerated beyond easy comprehension or control. So did millions of other people who were less responsible for the change than he was. "In our great cities," the financier Simon Straus worried early in the decade, "people break down in health or reach premature senility because of late hours, loss of sleep, fast pleasures, and headlong, nerve-racking methods of existence."

The sense of debilitating change and collapsing rules was not simply an idea loose in the popular culture of the 1920s; it was central to the most sophisticated intellectual debate. Walter Lippmann talked about the "acids of modernity" undermining traditional truths and authoritative standards. Joseph Wood Krutch, in *The Modern Temper* (1929), argued that science had broken life loose from any moral compass altogether.

In the years since then, historians who have studied the 1920s have struggled to come to terms with its palpable tension and longing for a simpler time. Two decades ago, Roderick Nash set out to write a new book about the period after World War I variously described as the "Roaring Twenties" and the "Jazz Age." He ended up with *The Nervous Generation* as his title. "The typical American in 1927 was nervous," he wrote in one chapter. "The values by which he ordered his life seemed in jeopardy of being swept away by the force of growth and change and complexity."

It was a point reminiscent of one made a few years earlier, by William Leuchtenburg, in *The Perils of Prosperity*. Two things about the 1920s stood out most clearly to Leuchtenburg: the loss of community and the loss of authority.

"The metropolis had shattered the supremacy of the small town," Leuchtenburg wrote, "and life seemed infinitely more impersonal. It was proverbial that the apartment-house dweller did not know his neighbor. . . . In the American town of 1914, class lines, though not frozen, were unmistakable. Each town had its old families. . . . The world they experienced was comprehensible. The people they saw were the people they knew. . . . Moral standards were set by the church and by the family. Parents were confident enforcers of the moral code. By 1932, much of the sense of authority was gone."

It was easy to dismiss those who mourned the social losses of the

1920s by telling them that they were indulging in flights of nostalgic fantasy. The Great War was a social as well as a political watershed; the horse and buggy were gone, and so was the America that they represented. Anyone who bothered to point to the communitarian virtues of life before the war ran the risk of being trumped by the all-purpose Ozzie and Harriet rejoinder: "Forget it. Those days are over."

And they were, in the same sense that the 1950s are gone today. But nobody on either side of the argument had any clue to what lay ahead in the two decades that followed: extraordinary group effort and societal cohesion in the face of the massive challenges of a depression and another World War, back to back. The 1930s and 1940s not only produced real communitarian values but generated real leaders and authority figures whose arrival appeared as unlikely in the individualist era of the 1920s as it does amid the individualism of the 1990s.

It would be foolish to minimize the tensions and divisions that existed in America all through the Depression and war years, or to suggest that those years somehow represented a return to the innocence of the time before World War I. Still, it seems fair enough to say that, under the pressures of crisis, the country developed a sense of cohesion and structures of authority that seemed lost forever only a few years before.

Of course, suggesting that community and authority tend to return in times of crisis may not be a very reassuring or relevant argument for the 1990s, a time when both depression and world war seem remote prospects. But could the moral erosion of the present time be, in its way, a crisis sufficient to rival war or economic collapse? And if so, might a swing back to older values be a plausible response? Perhaps that is not so far-fetched.

There is an even more interesting case, if one is willing to cross the ocean to look for it.

Few of us have much familiarity with England in 1820, but here are some facts: It was a time of notorious disrespect for authority at the top of the social system. The king and queen were national laughingstocks, exposed as such by a sensational divorce trial that documented the stupidity of both. The political system was distrusted as a cesspool of corruption, with seats in Parliament bought and sold at the constituency level by private wealth, and the Church of England was widely regarded as a bastion of clerical privilege rather than religious devotion. The cultural superstars were artists such as Byron and Shelley, notorious for their rejection of what they considered obsolete standards of family life and sexual morality: Byron boasted publicly of having slept with two hundred women in two years, while Shelley was a wife-swapper and founder of a free-love colony. The country was in the midst of a widespread and poorly concealed wave of opium addiction that disabled some of its most promising talents.

England's conservative social critics of that time lamented the disappearance of authority, community, and all the bonds that had made the place livable in the eighteenth century. "The ties which kept the different classes of society in a vital and harmonious dependence on each other," William Wordsworth wrote, "have with these thirty years either been greatly impaired or wholly dissolved."

Wordsworth was referring to the thirty years since the events that triggered the French Revolution and launched a revolution in manners all over the Western world. To most thoughtful people, 1789 had been a watershed that marked "modern times" off from an old regime that grew fainter and more remote with each year that passed. To talk to them about a "return" to the arrangements that prevailed before 1789 would surely have struck them as an exercise in fantasy.

Certainly few of them believed that a generation later, England would be in the midst of a period famous to this day for its sexual prudery and obsessive concern with "family values," renowned for its national devotion to a frumpy widowed queen and marked by the reform and revitalization of its religious establishment. Victorian

England does not represent a reenactment of any previous historical time; it merely serves as a reminder that there is a pendulum at work in the manners and values of a society, and that it can swing when no one expects it to.

In 1820, it had been just three decades since the start of the French Revolution and the arrival of what was thought to be a permanent social transformation. In 1995, it is three decades since the events of the mid-1960s, the social and moral equivalent of Bastille Day in our own lives. There is nothing far-fetched about asking when the pendulum might begin to swing again.

One needs to be even more politically careful talking about the England of Queen Victoria than about the America of Ozzie and Harriet. Anybody who refers to this era in anything but the most caustic terms risks being labeled as an advocate of censorship and sexual repression. But it is nonetheless true, and revealing, that in the past few years a growing number of scholars have suggested that the Victorians have something to tell us about our situation.

"Contemplating our own society," the historian Gertrude Himmelfarb wrote in 1994, "we may be prepared to take a more appreciative view of Victorian moralism—of the 'Puritan ethic' of work, thrift, temperance, cleanliness; of the idea of 'respectability' that was as powerful among the working classes as among the middle classes."

Himmelfarb not only writes with approval of Victorian virtues; she comes close to suggesting that they will reappear on the stage sometime in the coming decades. "If in a period of rapid economic and social change, the Victorians showed a substantial improvement in their 'condition' and 'disposition,' " she argues, "it may be that economic and social change do not necessarily result in personal and public disarray. If they could retain and even strengthen an ethos that had its roots in religion and tradition, it may be that we are not as constrained by the material conditions of our time as we have thought."

As Himmelfarb points out, the Victorian era did not witness any national slowdown in the pace of societal change. Its cohort lived through a time of enormous technological upheaval, marked by the appearance of the railroad, telegraph, and camera, and the expansion of the British empire into a worldwide colossus that made immense fortunes and transformed the economy at home.

What can be said about the Victorians is not that they reversed the flow of societal change but that they searched for anchors to help them cope with it, and that they found them in the familiar places: family, religion, patriotism of the hokiest and most maudlin variety.

And that also seems a fair thing to say about the 1950s in America. They were not a period of stasis but of rapid and bewildering change: nuclear tension, population explosion, the creation of a new world in the suburbs, the sudden emergence of a prosperity and materialism that scarcely anyone had expected and few knew how to handle. The people who lived through this change looked for anchors to help them cope with it all, and found them, however imperfectly, where people normally look for such things: at home, in church, in the rituals and pieties of patriotic excess. They found them in "togetherness" and the basement family room, in the Holy Name Society and the Green Donkeys Social Club, in Bishop Sheen and Walt Disney. Some pretending was required—some hypocrisy, if you insist—but it served a purpose.

We are never going to return to the 1950s any more than we are going to return to Victorian standards of morality. And we should not want to return to them. What is past is past. What we badly need to do, once our rebellion against the 1950s has run its course, is to rebuild some anchors of stability to help us through times of equally unsettling change.

For that to happen anytime soon, the generation that launched the rebellion will have to force itself to rethink some of the unexamined "truths" with which it has lived its entire adult life. It will have to recognize that privacy, individuality, and choice are not free goods, and that the society that places no restrictions on them pays a high price for that decision. It will have to retrieve the idea of authority from the dust bin to which it was confined by the 1960s deluge. The middle-aged communitarian who yearns, in the words of Hillary Clinton, to "do what I used to be able to do when I was a little kid," must first develop a realism about the natural limits of life that most of the baby boomers have yet to demonstrate.

There is a good chance that this will not happen. It is difficult enough for individuals to correct the misconceptions of their youth once they have reached middle age; for the largest single generation in American history to do this in the years remaining to it seems highly problematical.

In that case, what really matters is what the next generation grows up believing—those who are children now, who are being raised by the creators of the deluge. What will they think about community and authority, habit and choice, sin and virtue? This generation will come to adulthoood in the early years of the next century with an entirely different set of childhood and adolescent memories from the ones their parents absorbed. They will remember being bombarded with choices, and the ideology of choice as a good in itself; living in transient neighborhoods and broken and recombinant families where no arrangement could be treated as permanent; having parents who feared to impose rules because rules might stifle their freedom and individuality.

Will a generation raised that way be tempted to move, in its early adult years, toward a reimposition of order and stability, even at the risk of losing some of the choice and personal freedom its parents worshiped? To dismiss that idea is to show too little respect for the pendulum that operates in the values of any society, and the natural desire of any generation to use it to correct the errors and the excesses of the one before.

NOTES

Chapter 1: The Limited Life

8   Career of John G. Fary: *Congressional Quarterly Weekly Report,* April 3, 1982, p. 779; *Governing Magazine,* August 1992, p. 6.

9   "Bingo Bourbon": obituary of John G. Fary, *Chicago Tribune,* June 8, 1984.

11   Divorce rate statistics: U.S. Department of Commerce, Bureau of the Census, *Statisitical Abstract of the United States* (Government Printing Office, 1958 and 1994), p. 72 (1958) and p. 104 (1994).

12   Lennox Corporation and Marshalltown, Iowa: *Governing Magazine,* July 1993, p. 9.

17   Hillary Rodham Clinton on being able to "walk down any street": quoted in profile by Michael Kelly, *New York Times Magazine,* May 23, 1993.

18   P. J. O'Rourke on authority: P. J. O'Rourke, *A Parliament of Whores* (Vintage, 1991), p. 233.

19   "All authority is equally illegitimate": Robert Paul Wolff, *In Defense of Anarchy* (Harper and Row, 1970), quoted in *Authority,* edited by Joseph Raz (New York University Press, 1990), p. 29.

20   "Rules and regulations": E. J. Dionne, *Why Americans Hate Politics* (Simon and Schuster, 1991), p. 31.

28   "As small townish as any village in the wheat field": Mike
      Royko, *Boss* (New American Library, 1971), p. 24.
28   "The urban equivalent of a village square": Horace Cayton
      and St. Clair Drake, *Black Metropolis,* rev. ed. (University of
      Chicago Press, 1993), p. 379.
30   "One of the rarest of the good things of life": Cayton and
      Drake, *Black Metropolis,* p. 664.
31   "Lifelong commitment to individualism": Paul Light, *Baby
      Boomers* (W. W. Norton, 1990), p. 131.

Chapter 2: The Uses of Sin

34   Murder of Leon Marcus: based on reporting in the *Chicago
      Daily News,* April 2, 1957, and on succeeding days. The
      Daily News is the primary source for the bulk of the detail
      about specific news events in Chicago in 1957.
38   "Spiritual pride of man": Reinhold Niebuhr, *The Nature
      and Destiny of Man* (Charles Scribner's Sons, 1949), p. 202.
39   "Defect in character": James Q. Wilson, *On Character*
      (American Enterprise Institute, 1991), p. 2.
39   "Gray sub-civilization": Nelson Algren, *Chicago: City on the
      Make* (University of Chicago Press, 1987), p. 95.
39   "Source of all creation": Isaac Rosenfeld, *Commentary,* June
      1957.
40   "October sort of city": Algren, *Chicago: City on the Make,*
      p. 72.
40   "Endless succession of factory town main streets": A. J.
      Liebling, *Second City,* reprinted in *Liebling at Home* (Wide-
      view Books, 1982), p. 166.
40   "When I walk down the street": Bill Gleason, *Daley of
      Chicago* (Simon and Schuster, 1970), p. 205.
40   "The sun will rise": Mike Royko, *Boss* (New American
      Library, 1971), p. 89.

41 "Our lady of the lake": Eugene Kennedy, *Himself: The Life and Times of Richard J. Daley* (Viking, 1978), p. 45.

41 "The old bosses": Richard J. Daley, quoted in *Time,* March 15, 1963.

42 "Something of a queer": John Hoellen, quoted in Milton Rakove, *We Don't Want Nobody Nobody Sent* (Indiana University Press, 1979), p. 299.

43 "Chicago ain't ready for reform" and "dog with the big nuts": Paddy Bauler, quoted in Len O'Connor, *Clout: Mayor Daley and His City* (Avon Books, 1976), p. 125.

44 "Put people under obligation to you": Jacob Arvey, quoted in Rakove, *We Don't Want Nobody Nobody Sent,* p. 6.

44 "It makes robots": Lynn Williams, quoted in Rakove, *We Don't Want Nobody Nobody Sent,* p. 247

45 "A City Hall uniform": Gleason, *Daley of Chicago,* p. 108.

46 "They cannot be controlled": Lynn Williams, quoted in Rakove, *We Don't Want Nobody Nobody Sent,* p. 248.

47 The Touhy and Sain insurance business: Ovid Demaris, *Captive City* (Lyle Stuart, 1969), p. 175.

47 "To be a success": Royko, *Boss,* p. 65.

47 Chicago Park District: As reported by the Chicago Association of Commerce and Industry, 1957.

48 "A tax on human effort": Charles Bowden and Lew Kreinberg, *Street Signs Chicago: Neighborhood and Other Illusions of Big City Life* (Chicago Review Press, 1981), p. 82.

50 "If he put a stop to it": Edward Banfield, *Political Influence* (Free Press, 1961), p. 257.

52 West Side bloc: Virgil Peterson, *Barbarians in Our Midst* (Little, Brown, 1952), p. 244.

53 "If one of his aides": Royko, *Boss,* p. 19.

54 "It was also fair speculation": Kennedy, *Himself: The Life and Times of Richard J. Daley,* p. 263.

55 "A feat rivaling the Manhattan project": Bill Furlong, *New York Times Magazine,* May 5, 1957.

Chapter 3: Midsummer in America

60   The account of events, fashions, and the mood of America in June 1957 is based on material from the following periodical sources: *Time, Life, Look, Newsweek, McCall's,* and *Coronet* magazines; the *New York Times, Chicago Daily News, Chicago Defender, Southwest News-Tribune* (Chicago), and *Elmhurst Press* newspapers; the *Encyclopedia Britannica Book of the Year, 1957,* and *Facts on File, 1957.*

64   Automobiles as jet planes: Thomas Hine, *Populuxe* (Knopf, 1986), p. 83.

80   "A show full of hatefulness": Humphrey Burton, *Leonard Bernstein: A Biography* (Doubleday, 1994), p. 268.

Chapter 4: Bungalow People

90   "6 rm brick": advertisement in *Southwest News-Herald,* September 1957.

90   Bungalow Belt: "We'll build a bungalow," article in *Chicago Magazine,* January 1985.

90   Bungalow interiors: much of the detail is based on material in Alice Halpin Collins, *Visitation Revisited* (privately published, 1982). I am grateful to Alderman Edward Burke and his staff for making this volume available to me.

103   The Bakery Workers and the AFL–CIO: John L. McClellan, *Crime Without Punishment* (Duell, Sloan and Pearce, 1962), p. 183.

104   Talman in 1957: *Talman: The First Fifty Years,* published by Talman Federal Savings, Chicago, 1971.

108   "Our era, despite its imperfections": *House Beautiful,* February 1957.

108   "Purring with contentment": *Life,* July 4, 1955.

Chapter 5: The Flock

112   Construction of church: *St. Nicholas of Tolentine: 50 Years in Chicago Lawn,* church pamphlet, 1966.

113   Architecture of church: pamphlet prepared for dedication, May 7, 1939, by Gerald A. Barry, church architect.

113   Life of St. Nicholas of Tolentine: pamphlet prepared for seventy-fifth parish jubilee, September 29, 1991.

113   "One homogeneous people": George Cardinal Mundelein, quoted in Charles Shanabruch, *Chicago's Catholics: The Evolution of an Identity* (University of Notre Dame Press, 1981), p. 222.

119   Size of Chicago archdiocese: *Life,* December 26, 1955.

119   Reforms of Raymond Hillenbrand: Steven M. Avella, *This Confident Church: Catholic Leadership and Life in Chicago, 1940–1965* (University of Notre Dame Press, 1992), p. 165.

119   "Liturgical reform seemed to be spreading": Avella, *This Confident Church,* p. 159.

119   Christian Family Movement: Avella, *This Confident Church,* p. 171.

132   "Sullen, suspicious cynics": John R. Powers, *The Last Catholic in America* (Saturday Review Press, 1973), p. 79.

132   Sister Raphael and St. Procopius: Robert Byrne, *Memories of a Non-Jewish Childhood* (Lyle Stuart, 1970), pp. 46, 47, 189.

133   Sister Mary Ignatius: Christopher Durang, *Sister Mary Ignatius Explains It All for You* (Dramatists' Play Service, 1982), pp. 46, 47.

133   "More kids come to hate the church": quoted in Peter Ochiogrosso, *Once a Catholic* (Houghton Mifflin, 1987), p. 54.

134   Father O'Reilly: Powers, *The Last Catholic in America,* p. 59.

Chapter 6: Frozen in Place

140   "A bunch of shacks": quoted in Dempsey Travis, *An Autobiography of Black Chicago* (Urban Research Press, 1981), p. 185.

141   "Triumphs and comforts of Bronzeville society": The source of much of the detail of daily life in Bronzeville in the 1950s is the city edition of the *Chicago Weekly Defender*.

144   "This sprawling city": Carl T. Rowan, *Saturday Evening Post,* October 19, 1957.

144   "This sick four-story hulk": Gwendolyn Brooks, "Lovers of the Poor," in *The Bean Eaters*, reprinted in *Blacks* (Third World Press, 1992), p. 351.

145   "A place to stay": quoted in Ray Quintanilla, "Memories of the Black Belt," *Chicago Reporter,* January 1994.

147   Creation of the "vertical ghetto" is discussed in detail in Arnold R. Hirsch, *Making the Second Ghetto* (Cambridge University Press, 1983), and Nicholas Lemann, *The Promised Land* (Knopf, 1991).

147   Career of Robert Abbott: James R. Grossman, *Land of Hope: Chicago, Black Southerners and the White Migration* (University of Chicago Press, 1989), p. 74.

152   Description of the Regal Theater: Dempsey Travis, *An Autobiography of Black Jazz* (Urban Research Press, 1983), p. 147.

154   "Foxy Cats club": Gwendolyn Brooks, *Maud Martha,* reprinted in *Blacks* (Third World Press, 1992), p. 222.

154   "The middle-class social club world": Horace Cayton and St. Clair Drake, *Black Metropolis,* rev. ed. (University of Chicago Press, 1993), p. 688.

Chapter 7: Pillars of Optimism

159   "The best part of my time and training": quotations and other details about Earl Dickerson are in the Dickerson Papers at the Chicago Historical Society.

162   "A church is highly organized": quoted in John Madigan, "The Durable Mr. Dawson," *Chicago Reporter,* August 9, 1956.

162   William L. Dawson and power: Dempsey Travis, *An Autobiography of Black Politics* (Urban Research Press, 1987), p. 163.

166 "It is also a cult": Horace Cayton and St. Clair Drake, *Black Metropolis,* rev. ed. (University of Chicago Press, 1993), p. 474.

170 "Betting is a human frailty": quoted in Madigan, "The Durable Mr. Dawson."

171 "In the world of sin": Cayton and Drake, *Black Metropolis,* p. 611.

Chapter 8: City of Faith

174 Size of churches: Horace Cayton and St. Clair Drake, *Black Metropolis,* rev. ed. (University of Chicago Press, 1993), p. 412.

174 "In their own churches": C. Eric Lincoln, *The Black Church Since Frazier* (Schocken Books, 1974), p. 113.

175 "I have known": Cayton and Drake, *Black Metropolis,* p. 672.

177 "A part of every organization": Cayton and Drake, *Black Metropolis,* p. 682.

179 "You in the taverns": Cayton and Drake, *Black Metropolis,* p. 646.

179 The intricacies of the Reverend Jackson's campaign to win and hold the NBC presidency are chronicled in the *Chicago Defender,* especially May and June 1953, and May and June 1957.

182 "Big white folk": Ralph Ellison, *Invisible Man* (New American Library, 1952), p. 127.

183 "All human beings": J. H. Jackson, *Unholy Shadows and Freedom's Holy Light* (Townsend Press, 1967), pp. 53, 54.

184 "The white man spends his money" and "Today's world is floating in corruption": C. Eric Lincoln, *The Black Muslims in America,* 3rd ed. (Eerdmans Publishing Co., 1994), pp. 84, 88.

184 "Nationwide conventions of the Black Muslims": Cayton and Drake, *Black Metropolis,* p. 799.

186   The 1957 election for president of the Chicago NAACP chapter is discussed in Dempsey Travis, *An Autobiography of Black Politics* (Urban Research Press, 1987), p. 261, and James Q. Wilson, *Negro Politics: The Search for Leadership* (Free Press, 1960), p. 63.

186   "I'm not interested in controlling the NAACP": Travis, *An Autobiography of Black Politics*, p. 270.

186   Frazier's views on the black middle class are expressed in E. Franklin Frazier, *Black Bourgeoisie* (Free Press, 1957), pp. 191, 204, 213.

188   Lorraine Hansberry, *A Raisin in the Sun* (Random House, 1959), p. 29.

189   Gwendolyn Brooks, *Kitchenette Building,* reprinted in *Blacks* (Third World Press, 1992), p. 20.

Chapter 9: Close Quarters

194   Details on early Elmhurst: Don Russell, *Elmhurst: Trails from Yesterday* (Elmhurst Bicentennial Commission, 1977).

200   Home of the Tewell family: most of the material on the homes in Brynhaven and Emery Manor and on the events in Elmhurst in 1957 is from the files of the *Elmhurst Press.*

205   "Spaciousness": *House Beautiful,* January, 1957.

206   "The modern house": Russell Lynes, *The Domesticated Americans* (Harper, 1963), p. 277.

207   "No-man's land" and "pigeon holes for sleeping": Bernard Rudofsky, *Behind the Picture Window* (Oxford University Press, 1955), p. 114.

207   "Warm waters and perfumed air": *House Beautiful,* 1957.

208   Lewis Mumford on private rooms: quoted in Max Lerner, *America as a Civilization* (Simon and Schuster, 1957), p. 632.

Chapter 10: The Joiners

210 "An age of group action" and "a collective as pervading": William H. Whyte Jr., *The Organization Man* (Simon and Schuster, Touchstone edition, 1956), pp. 78 and 5.

210 David Riesman, *The Lonely Crowd* (Yale University Press, 1951).

211 "You belong in Park Forest": Whyte, *The Organization Man,* p. 284.

211 "A new social institution: Whyte, *The Organization Man,* p. 280.

211 "Identical small boxes": Mary Mix Foley, *Architectural Forum,* 1957.

212 Mumford on "uniform, unidentifable houses": quoted in John Patrick Diggins, *The Proud Decades* (W. W. Norton, 1988), p. 183.

212 "Conceived in error" and "destruction of individuality": John Keats, *The Crack in the Picture Window* (Houghton Mifflin, 1957), pp. xii and 193.

213 "A neighborhood that could never be a community": Keats, *The Crack in the Picture Window,* p. 60.

222 "The contrary evils" and "why do we abuse the papists?": Julius Melton, *Presbyterian Worship in America* (John Knox Press, 1967), pp. 122 and 69.

223 Religion and popular culture: discussed in Douglas T. Miller and Marion Nowak, *The Fifties: The Way We Really Were* (Doubleday, 1977), p. 101.

224 "People turn to religion": Archbishop O'Boyle is quoted in Miller and Nowak, *The Fifties,* p. 101–2.

224 "A heaven scrubbed in detergent": Stanley Rowland, *The Nation,* July 28, 1956.

Chapter 11: The Taming of the Young

232   "This new and warmer way of life" and "had Ed been a father": *McCall's,* May 1954.

233   "Families function best": *Parents,* October 1956.

233   "Modern psychology backs up the common sense of parents": Sidonie Matsner Gruenberg, *New York Times Magazine,* September 19, 1954.

233   Benjamin Spock on "the long repressive reach of tradition": quoted in James Gilbert, *Another Chance: Postwar America: 1945–1968* (Temple University Press, 1986), p. 56.

233   "The roles of husband and wife": Russell Lynes, *A Surfeit of Honey* (Harper, 1957), p. 51.

233   "The family needs a head": *McCall's,* May 1957.

235   "One of the very best": papers of James B. Conant, Pusey Library, Harvard University.

235   "York was not just huge": details on life at York High School in the 1950s are taken largely from issues of the York student newspaper, the *York-Hi,* collected at the Elmhurst Historical Museum, Elmhurst, Illinois.

235   "Good social studies": papers of James B. Conant, Pusey Library, Harvard University.

235   "A comprehensive high school": James B. Conant, *The American High School* (McGraw-Hill, 1959).

239   "About one teacher in four": Edgar Z. Friedenberg, *Coming of Age in America* (Random House, 1965).

242   "Academic achievement counts for little": James B. Coleman, *The Adolescent Society* (Free Press, 1961), p. 260.

244   Controversy over going steady: Reported in *Life,* July 1957.

248   "The contrast of tight pressures": Max Lerner, *America as a Civilization* (Simon and Schuster, 1957), p. 545.

Chapter 13: The Next Generation

275   "Preceding the Great War": Mark Sullivan, *Our Times,* vol. 6 (Charles Scribner's Sons, 1926), p. 1.

275   Henry Ford on Greenfield Village: quoted in Roderick Nash, *The Nervous Generation* (Ivan R. Dee, 1990), p. 160.

276   Simon Straus on "premature senility": quoted in James Grant, *Money of the Mind* (Farrar, Straus & Giroux, 1992), p. 158.

276   "Acids of modernity": Walter Lippmann, *A Preface to Morals* (Macmillan, 1929), p. 51.

276   Joseph Wood Krutch, *The Modern Temper* (Harcourt Brace, 1929).

276   "The typical American in 1927 was nervous": Nash, *The Nervous Generation,* p. 136.

276   "Life seemed infinitely more impersonal": William W. Leuchtenburg, *The Perils of Prosperity* (University of Chicago Press, 1993), pp. 1–5.

278   William Wordsworth on the "vital and harmonious dependence": quoted in Paul Johnson, *The Birth of the Modern* (HarperCollins, 1991), p. 411.

279   "Contemplating our own society": Gertrude Himmelfarb, "A De-moralized Society," *Public Interest* (Fall 1994): 76, 80.

ACKNOWLEDGMENTS

For the past three years I have been engaging in an odd form of time travel, spending whole chunks of each day wandering on the planet of the 1950s, and then being jolted back home, sometimes when I really wanted to remain a little longer.

I am aware that this has been a little disconcerting for those at home and at work who expected me to be fully attentive to the present. They have been patient with my distractions and I am grateful to them for their patience.

I am equally grateful to those who indulged my desire to pursue this project in the first place. I am lucky enough to work for *Governing* magazine and for its parent, the Times Publishing Company of St. Petersburg, Florida—institutions that embody the loyalty and commitment of the 1950s in a decade when they are difficult to sustain. The preservation of those values is in large part the achievement of Andy Barnes, and I wish to thank him for that, as well as for supporting me in this venture and others in the past. Andy Corty was equally gracious in trusting me to spend a week each month on time travel and to return to the office safely. More than anyone, however, Peter Harkness, the editor and publisher of *Governing,* made this project possible, as he has so many ideas of mine, more than a few of them slightly wacky, over the last twenty years.

Wherever I went in Chicago, I found people who were willing to share with me their memories of the 1950s and their insights about living in a very different time. Dozens of residents and former residents of Elmhurst, Bronzeville, and St. Nick's parish spoke to me at length, and I learned something from each of them. A few of my debts, however, demand special acknowledgment.

Brian Bergheger, Nancy Wilson, and the staff of the Elmhurst Historical Museum opened their files to me, helped track down interviews, and let me use their office as a kind of clubhouse during some very cold winter days and evenings. I am very grateful to them.

Jim Vondrak, publisher of the *Southwest News-Herald,* did something similar for me in St. Nick's parish, suggesting sources I never would have found on my own and allowing me to read bound volumes of the paper going back four decades. Father Michael Goergen was generous in making available the facilities of St. Nick's church and in identifying parishioners to talk to. Jim Capraro gave me a superb tour of the Southwest Side, from Nabisco to the wooden Indian at Sixty-third and Pulaski. Father Andrew McDonagh read chapter 5 and did all he could to correct my errors. I know that he does not agree with some of my conclusions, which makes me value his courtesy even more.

U.S. Representative Bobby Rush was kind enough to run interference for me in my efforts to locate Bronzeville alumni who could help me understand life there in the 1950s. Obtaining copies of the city edition of the *Chicago Defender* from those years was a more difficult job than I imagined it would be. The reference staff of the Arlington County, Virginia, library, especially Sandra Florence, made diligent efforts in my behalf. I also appreciated the courtesies extended by the Firestone Library at Princeton University.

Paul Golob is the editor I have always needed and hope I deserve. One of these times I will run out of new ways to thank him. Rafe Sagalyn has been a continuing source of ideas and assistance.

My ultimate debt, as always, is to Suzanne, Lizzie, and Jennie. They make the 1990s worth returning to and living in.

PHOTO ACKNOWLEDGMENTS

Part I   State and Lake Streets, Chicago, 1959 *(UPI/Bettmann)*
Chapter 1 Ernie Banks *(AP/Wide World Photos)*
Chapter 2 Mayor Richard J. Daley *(AP/Wide World Photos)*
Chapter 3 1957 Dodge Royal *(Courtesy of Chrysler Corporation)*

Part II   St. Nicholas of Tolentine Church *(©Ralf-Finn Hestoft/SABA)*
Chapter 4 Octagon bungalow, St. Nick's Parish *(©Ralf-Finn Hestoft/SABA)*
Chapter 5 Elementary school class, 1953 *(Courtesy of St. Nicholas of Tolentine School)*

Part III   Forty-third Street and Prairie Avenue, 1954 *(Chicago Transit Authority photograph)*
Chapter 6 Bud Billiken Parade, 1948 *(Chicago Tribune photograph)*
Chapter 7 Congressman William L. Dawson *(Chicago Historical Society photograph ICHi-22461)*
Chapter 8 Statue of the Reverend J. H. Jackson *(©Ralf-Finn Hestoft/SABA)*

Part IV   Split-level house, Brynhaven, Elmhurst, Illinois *(©Ralf-Finn Hestoft/SABA)*
Chapter 9 Family watching television *(FPG International Corporation)*

Chapter 10   Elmhurst Presbyterian Church *(©Ralf-Finn Hestoft/ SABA)*

Chapter 11   Corridor, York Community High School, 1960 *(Courtesy of Elmhurst Historical Museum, Elmhurst, Illinois)*

Part V   State and Lake Streets, Chicago, 1995 *(©Ralf-Finn Hestoft/SABA)*

Chapter 12   Sixty-third Street and Kedzie Avenue, 1995 *(©Ralf-Finn Hestoft/SABA)*

Chapter 13   Children in suburbia, 1995 *(Suzanne Ehrenhalt)*

INDEX

ABOUT THE AUTHOR

Alan Ehrenhalt is executive editor of *Governing* magazine in Washington, D.C. Born in 1947 in Chicago, he received his bachelor's degree from Brandeis University and his master's degree from the Columbia University School of Journalism. He has been a reporter for the Associated Press, *Congressional Quarterly,* and the *Washington Star,* and for twelve years was political editor of *Congressional Quarterly.* He has also been a Nieman Fellow at Harvard University and a visiting scholar at the University of California, Berkeley. Ehrenhalt's first book, *The United States of Ambition,* was a finalist for the 1991 *Los Angeles Times* Book Prize and was a *New York Times* Notable Book of the Year. He lives in Arlington, Virginia, with his wife and two daughters.